Other translations by Hermann Pálsson

*

HRAFNKEL'S SAGA
THE CONFEDERATES

*

(*with Paul Edwards*)

GAUTREK'S SAGA
ARROW-ODD
THE BOOK OF SETTLEMENTS
HROLF GAUTREKSSON
EYRBYGGJA SAGA
EGIL'S SAGA
GÖNGU-HROLF'S SAGA

*

(*with Magnus Magnusson*)

NJAL'S SAGA
KING HARALD'S SAGA
THE VINLAND SAGAS
LAXDÆLA SAGA

*

(*with Denton Fox*)

GRETTIR'S SAGA

ORKNEYINGA SAG
The History of the Earls of Or

Orkneyinga Saga

THE HISTORY OF
THE EARLS OF ORKNEY

*Translated from the Icelandic
and introduced by*

HERMANN PÁLSSON
AND
PAUL EDWARDS

1978

THE HOGARTH PRESS

LONDON

Published by
The Hogarth Press Ltd
40 William IV Street
London WC2N 4DG

*

Clarke, Irwin & Co. Ltd
Toronto

First impression 1978
Second impression 1978

British Library Cataloguing in Publication
Data Orkneyinga Saga: The History of the
Earls of Orkney.
1. Sagas
I. Pálsson, Hermann II. Edwards,
Paul, b. 1926
839′.6′8   PT7281.06

ISBN 0-7012-0431-1

Printed in Great Britain by
REDWOOD BURN LIMITED
Trowbridge & Esher

For
GEORGE MACKAY BROWN

'[*May*] *he who wrote this record, he who has told it, and all who listen to it enjoy from that holy knight of God, Earl Magnus, blessings and the answer to their prayers for the remission of their sins and for everlasting joy.*'
ORKNEYINGA SAGA, Chapter 57

CONTENTS

ILLUSTRATIONS

The plates are published by kind permission of the Stofnun Árna Magnússonar, Reykjavík (1), and of the Department of the Environment, Edinburgh (all other plates).

The maps have been drawn by Denys Baker.

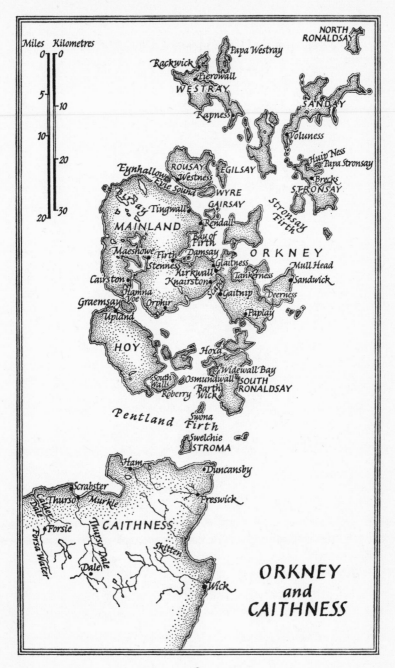

Miles Kilometres

NORTH
RONALDSAY

Papa Westray
Rackwick
Pierowall
WESTRAY
SANDAY
Rapness
Voluness
Huip Ness
EGILSAY Papa Stronsay
ROUSAY
Eynhallow Westness Brecks
Fuie Sound WYRE STRONSAY
GAIRSAY
Tingwall
Rendall Stronsay
MAINLAND Firth
Bay of
Firth
Maeshowe Damsay ORKNEY
Firth Mull Head
Stenness Glaitness
Kirkwall Tankerness Sandwick
Cairston Knairston Scapa
Hamna Gaitnip Deerness
Graemsay Voe Orphir
Upland Paplay
Hoxa
HOY
Widewall Bay
South Osmundwall SOUTH
Walls Barth RONALDSAY
Roberry Wick
Pentland Firth
Swona
Swelchie
STROMA
Ham
Duncansby
Scrabster
Thurso Murkle Freswick
Dale
Forsie CAITHNESS
Forsa Water Thurso Dale
Skitten
Dale
Wick

ORKNEY
and
CAITHNESS

THE FAROES–WEST NORWAY–
BRITISH ISLES

Miles 0   50   100   200   300
Kilometres 0   100   200   300   400   500

Sekk
Giske
Stad
SOGN
FAROES
HORDALAND
Henne
Isles
Florevaag
Aluen
Bergen
SHETLAND
Stole
Fair Isle
AGDER
Pentland Firth
ORKNEY
Sel
Isles
CAITH
SUTHER NESS Helmsdale
LAND
LEWIS Ausdale
Oykel Tarbat Ness
THE
HEBRIDES
ROSS Moray Firth
Banff
MORAY
Aberdeen
SCOTLAND
Loch
Watten
ATHOLL
TIREE
ARGYLL FIFE Isle of May
Firth of Forth
Edinburgh Berwick-on-Tweed
KINTYRE
GALLOWAY NORTHUMBER
LAND
ULSTER
Scarborough
Cleveland Stamford Bridge
Lough York Holderness
Larne ISLE Ravenseer
CONNACHT of MAN Grimsby R. Humber
Dublin ANGLESEY
IRELAND Menai
St.
WALES

Lundy
Isle

Scilly St. Mary's
Isles

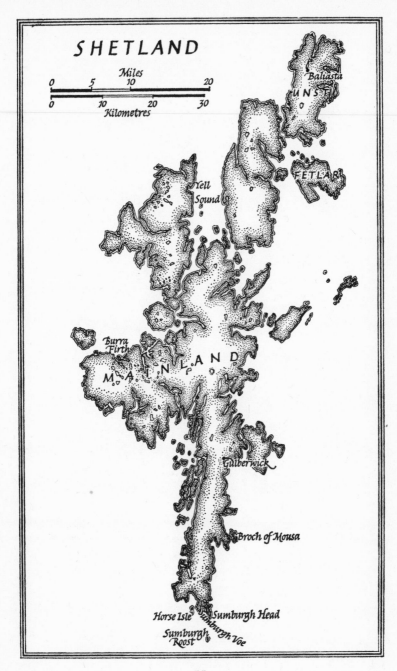

SHETLAND

Miles
0   5   10   20
0   10   20   30
Kilometres

Baliasta
UNST

FETLAR

Yell
Sound

Burra
Firth

MAINLAND

Gulberwick

Broch of Mousa

Horse Isle   Sumburgh Head
Sumburgh   Sumburgh Voe
Roost

INTRODUCTION

Orkneyinga Saga, or 'The History of the Earls of Orkney', to give it its alternative title, is a unique historical document without which much of our knowledge of the Northern Isles and Caithness would be irretrievably lost. The only medieval chronicle to have Orkney as the central place of action, it traces the lives of the Earls for over three hundred years, from the ninth century to the thirteenth, but its record impinges upon the history of other lands, in particular Norway and Scotland. *Orkneyinga Saga* has long been regarded as a work of great importance by scholars and others interested in the Viking Age, but for the people of Orkney it has a special significance, having become, since its first appearance in an English translation (1873), what might be called their secular scripture, inculcating in them a keener sense of their remote forebears and sharpening their awareness of a special identity. The saga creates vivid, though sometimes tantalisingly hazy, pictures of the islands at a time when they were still part of the Viking world, and both culturally and politically closer to Norway than Scotland, so that the narrative invites the people of Orkney and Shetland to recognise themselves as the inheritors and custodians of a dual culture, both Norse and Scottish.

A modern reader might be inclined to take such a work for granted and treat *Orkneyinga Saga* as if it had been generated spontaneously by the very events it describes. Indeed, the saga has a certain artless quality suggesting natural growth rather than the conception of a single author. But we cannot expect to grasp its significance fully without considering where, when, and for what purpose it was written. To begin with, *Orkneyinga Saga* was written not by an Orkneyman but by an Icelander, probably around 1200. The name of the author is unknown, but there seems little doubt that he must have been associated with the intellectual centre at Oddi in Southern Iceland, which had special connexions with Orkney during the last decades of the twelfth century and the beginning of the thirteenth. It was at Oddi that Icelandic historiography began, with the

13

writings (now lost) of Sæmund Sigfusson (1056-1133), whose grandson acted as foster-father to Snorri Sturluson (*c.* 1179-1241), the greatest author in medieval Iceland, and it is worth noting that *Orkneyinga Saga* was one of the sources used by Snorri in the compilation of the *Heimskringla*, or 'History of the Kings of Norway'. Two of Snorri's foster-brothers had certain dealings with Earl Harald Maddadarson of Orkney (d. 1206). Páll Jónsson (1155-1211) spent some time with Earl Harald on his way to study in England—later he became Bishop of Skalholt. More significant is that his brother Sæmund Jónsson (1154-1222) planned to marry Langlif, Earl Harald's daughter, though negotiations broke down when both the Earl and Sæmund were too proud to travel abroad for the wedding-feast. We find an important Orkneyman spending the years 1205-7 in Iceland, staying first with Snorri Sturluson, then with Sæmund. Also interesting in this connexion is that one of the clerics at Oddi, and probably Snorri's tutor, had a cousin who married Eirik Hakonarson of Orkney. Finally, like the Earls of Orkney, the men of Oddi traced their ancestry back to Earl Rognvald of More.

It seems reasonable to assume that the saga was written after 1192, when Earl Rognvald Kali, one of the author's favourite heroes, was proclaimed a saint. The marriage negotiations between Earl Harald and Sæmund took place some time during the years 1197-1206, and the saga could hardly have been written long after 1200. The original version ended with the death of Svein Asleifarson (Ch. 108), as can be seen from a Danish translation made about 1570. The present version took its shape at a later date and it has been suggested that the final chapters, and certain other additions, were made about 1234-5, when two distinguished Orkneymen were staying in Iceland, one a grandson of Svein Asleifarson and the other the son of the Lawman, Hrafn.

Another aid to the appreciation of the saga is some knowledge of its literary context. By the end of the twelfth century, Icelandic writers had compiled a number of works, not only on the history of their own country but on that of Norway. Some of the latter are now lost, but their aims and techniques appear to have been similar to those of *Orkneyinga Saga*, to give literary form to an oral tradition about national leaders, with the emphasis on personalities rather than politics. As a work of history, *Orkneyinga Saga* invites comparison with two major Icelandic chronicles of a slightly later date, the anonymous *Knytlinga Saga*, or 'History of the Kings of Denmark', written *c.* 1240-50, and Snorri's *Heimskringla*: or 'History of the Kings of Norway', compiled around 1230. The purpose of all three is to explore the history of a country through its rulers, and broadly speaking their structures are similar, beginning as they do with a section on the mythic origins of the ruling family, then progressing through legendary events to a historical period, which appears to start somewhere in the ninth century. As events approach the author's own time, they become more detailed and factual, while their fictive quality tends to diminish. All three works rely extensively on poetry quoted as source material, as well as on both an oral tradition and written material. The relationship between *Orkneyinga Saga* and *Heimskringla* is complicated by the fact that Snorri made use of the original version of *Orkneyinga Saga*, but then the reviser of the saga in turn made use of *Heimskringla*.

Orkneyinga Saga also shares certain features with fictive narratives about Icelandic heroes, such as *Njal's Saga*, *Eyrbyggja Saga*, *Grettir's Saga* and *Egil's Saga*. These, too, contain a considerable historical element, but though they follow an internal time scheme which is perfectly plausible, it is often difficult to date their events according to absolute chronology. Like these sagas, too, *Orkneyinga Saga* is characterised by a strong sense of the dramatic moment, and in short it could be said to combine the two essentials of good saga writing: a concern with social continuity, to satisfy men's curiosity about their past; and a talent for giving this memorable form by an inventive narrative skill.

Like a great deal of medieval history—the *Anglo-Saxon Chronicle* and Geoffrey of Monmouth's *History*, for example, as well as *Heimskringla*—*Orkneyinga Saga* deepens the sense of continuity by pushing back into a mythic or legendary past. It begins with figures clearly associated with the elements— Logi (flame), Kari (storm), Frosti (frost), Snær (snow), and Hler or Ægir, both names associated with the ancient Scandinavian sea-god. The opening episode has the marks of folk-legend, the search for an abducted princess, and in the figure of one of the searching brothers, Nor, Norway is given its eponymous founder. This early episode, however, is to be echoed in the historical narrative: for example, the trick of taking land by having a boat dragged over it, by means of which Gor makes his land-claim (Ch. 3), is used later in the saga by King Magnus Bare-Legs (Ch. 41); and the conflicts arising from the division of the kingdom between the brothers

Nor and Gor, and later on their sons, prefigure a recurrent theme of the narrative.

But from these early chapters, the saga moves rapidly to the historical figures of King Harald Fine-Hair and his supporter Earl Rognvald of More who, receiving Orkney from the King, hands it over to his brother, Sigurd the Powerful, first Earl of Orkney. Sigurd joins forces with Thorstein the Red, and Aud the Deep-Minded, one of the most important early settlers of Iceland, whose land-taking is described in another great medieval document from Iceland, the *Book of Settlements* (Chs. 100-110). The account of the death of Sigurd illustrates the pleasure taken by the author of the saga in a lively anecdote:

There was a fierce fight, but it wasn't long before Mælbrigte and his men were dead. Sigurd had their heads strapped to the victors' saddles to make a show of his triumph, and with that they began riding back home, flushed with their success. On the way, as Sigurd went to spur his horse, he struck his calf against a tooth sticking out of Mælbrigte's mouth and it gave him a scratch. The wound began to swell and ache, and it was this that led to the death of Sigurd the Powerful. He lies buried in a mound on the bank of the River Oykel. (Ch. 5)

The story of Earl Rognvald's sons which follows this episode (and which can also be found in the *Book of Settlements*, Ch. 309), is a good illustration of the way the author dramatises history:

Two Danish vikings, Thorir Tree-Beard and Kalf Scurvy, set up camp on the islands. When Earl Rognvald heard about it he flew into a rage and summoned Thorir and Hrollaug, his sons—Hrolf was away at the time on a viking expedition.[1] Rognvald asked which of them wanted the islands, and Thorir answered that it was up to the Earl himself to decide whether or not he should be the one to go.

'As I see it,' said the Earl, 'you'll be better here than anywhere else. Your path doesn't lie overseas.'

'Do you want me to go, then?' asked Hrollaug.

'You're not destined for the earldom,' replied Rognvald, 'your fate will take you to Iceland. You'll have many descendants there, and they'll be thought of as the noblest of men.'

After that the Earl's youngest son, Einar, came forward.

---

[1] In the account given in the *Book of Settlements*, Hrolf is present and also offers to go to Orkney. Rognvald replies that 'Hrolf's temperament was too violent for him to set up as ruler'.

'Do you want me to go to the islands?' he asked. 'I can promise you the greatest favour you could wish for, and that's never to have to see me again. There's little enough here to hold me, and I don't see myself as any more of a failure elsewhere.'

'Considering the kind of mother you have,' said the Earl, 'slave-born on each side of her family, you're not likely to make much of a ruler. But I agree: the sooner you leave and the later you return, the happier I'll be.'

Rognvald gave Einar a fully equipped ship of twenty benches and King Harald conferred on him the title of earl. (Ch. 6)

Here we have a formalised dialogue as each of the sons steps forward with his offer, though along with this goes a sense of character and of history. Earl Rognvald shows himself reluctant to hand over real power to those sons who have much initiative. Thorir is favoured because he leaves matters in his father's hands, and will succeed to the More earldom on Rognvald's death as he is unlikely to cause trouble while his father is alive. In the case of Einar—the real threat to his father (and, in the *Book of Settlements*, Hrolf too)—Rognvald's own aggressiveness leads to an underestimation, for the despised descendant of a slave-mother conquers all Orkney. Hrollaug is too much a man of peace for Rognvald, who underestimates him too, for he emerges as an individualist, a man who knows his own mind despite his unwarlike temper. And Hrolf's viking expeditions are to give him in due course a place in history as founder of Normandy and ancestor of William the Conqueror. So the passage places Iceland in a European context, marking out the peaceful settler, Hrollaug, from the power-seeking Viking princes and pirates, and thus making a distinction, to which we shall return, between contrasting impulses of the early Scandinavian world.

As in the *Sagas of the Icelanders*, the great men of Orkney are often simultaneously marauding sea-kings and hard working farmers, like Kveldulf, for example, in the opening chapter of *Egil's Saga*. Here is a sketch drawn by the saga of the life-style of one of its greatest figures, Svein Asleifarson:

This is how Svein used to live. Winter he would spend at home on Gairsay where he entertained some eighty men at his own expense. His drinking hall was so big there was nothing in Orkney to compare with it. In the spring he had more than enough to occupy him, with a great deal of seed to sow, which he saw to carefully himself. Then when that job was done, he would go off plundering in the Hebrides and in Ireland on what he called his

17

'spring-trip', then back home just after midsummer, where he stayed till the cornfields had been reaped and the grain was safely in. After that he went off raiding again till the first month of winter was ended. This he used to call his 'autumn-trip'. (Ch. 105).

Great halls such as these are the scenes of many a feast, killing, or burning throughout the narrative, and indeed, men who were both vikings and farmers would need such a hall, for, as in this example, they would have to have with them a number of men far exceeding the requirements of honest farming. Svein, later in the saga, is seen to have so much wealth and power that the Earl himself is none too happy about it:

After he had been home for a short while [Svein] invited Earl Harald to a feast, welcoming him with a magnificent banquet at which people had plenty to say about Svein's high style of life.

'I'd like you to stop your raiding, Svein,' said the Earl. 'It's always better to be safe back home, and you know that you're only able to keep yourself and your men on what you steal. Most troublemakers are fated to end up dead unless they stop of their own freewill.'

Svein looked at the Earl and there was a smile on his face.

'Fine and friendly words, my lord,' he said. 'I'll take your excellent advice, though there are people who might say you yourself are hardly the most peaceful of men.'

'I'm responsible for my own actions,' said the Earl, 'but I must say what I think.'

'I'm sure you've the very best of intentions, sir,' said Svein, 'so this is the way it's going to be: I'll give up raiding. I'm getting on in years and not up to all the hardships of war, but I'm going on one more trip in the autumn and I want it to be just as glorious as my spring-trip. When that's over, I'll give up raiding.'

'Hard to tell which comes first, old fellow,' said the Earl, 'death or glory.' (Ch. 106)

It is, indeed, to be Svein's last trip, for he dies fighting in Dublin. But a footnote to the great events in the drinking hall is provided by the last sentences of the chapter describing the death of Svein. 'The summer after his death,' we are told, '[his sons] set up partition walls in the great drinking hall he had built on Gairsay' (Ch. 178). With the viking-farmer Svein dead, it seems there is no longer any need for banquet-space, the world is changing, and soon a rare event is going to become commonplace: men are going to start to die in their beds.

Domestic passages, such as the one describing Svein as farmer, though characteristic of the *Sagas of the Icelanders*, are few and far between in *Orkneyinga Saga*, where the emphasis is on warfare, and the struggle for power, ranging it more with the *King's Sagas*. Apart from the account of the death and miracles of the holy Earl Magnus, which has much in common with hagiography, the saga might be called a catalogue of battles, killings and viking raids, but this would be misleading. The recurrent theme, linked as we have said to the opening sections on the legendary Nor and Gor and their sons, is the division of the earldom between two, sometimes three ambitious men, and the breaking up and re-assembling of power groups. The journeys to Norway to gain the approval and support of kings in a land itself divided, where brother fights brother, or the comings and goings of the frequently warring power groups on the mainland in Caithness and in the islands, the viking trips to the Hebrides, might superficially seem merely repetitive, but they create a narrative rhythm which could be considered one of the sustaining features of the story. These events are constantly illuminated by sharply observed and dramatised incidents, as we hope to have shown above, or as in this illustration of witchcraft going awry:

During the reign of the brothers Harald and Paul, a Christmas feast was arranged on Earl Harald's estate at Orphir and, as he was to provide for them both, he was busy with the preparations.

Their mother Helga and her sister Frakkok were staying there at the time and happened to be sitting in a small room getting on with their needlework, when Earl Harald came into the room. The sisters were sitting on the cross-dais, and a newly made linen garment, white as snow, was lying between them. The Earl picked it up and saw that in many places it was stitched with gold thread.

'Whose is this treasure?' he asked.

'It's meant for your brother Paul,' answered Frakkok.

'Why take such pains making clothes for him?' asked the Earl. 'You're not so particular when you make mine.'

The Earl had only just got up and was wearing nothing but a shirt and linen breeches, with a tunic thrown over his shoulders. He cast it off and began unfolding the linen garment, but his mother grabbed hold of it and told him there was no reason to be so envious just because his brother had some fine clothes. The Earl snatched it back and was about to put it on when the sisters pulled off their bonnets, tore their hair and said that if he put on the

19

garment his life would be at risk. Though they were both in tears he didn't let that stop him; but no sooner was the garment on his body than his flesh started to quiver and he began to suffer terrible pain. He had to go to bed and it wasn't long before he was dead. His death was deeply mourned by his friends. (Ch. 55)

One episode which might have been expected to reveal a different perspective from war and political chicanery is the voyage undertaken by Earl Rognvald to the Holy Land, which could be regarded as the central quest of the story. However, we should bear in mind that this is the period of the Crusades, and the Earl's ships are crewed by men who are as much vikings as pilgrims. They visit Narbonne in the early stages of the journey, and there are romance touches in the account. Queen Ermingerd enters with her maidens, and the girls play music to entertain their pilgrim-guests, but it doesn't take long for Rognvald to get his hands on her and his praises are hardly those of a courtly gentleman:

The Earl was sitting feasting one day when the Queen came into the hall escorted by a group of ladies and carrying a serving-bowl of gold. She was in her finest clothes, with her hair falling loose as is customary with virgins and a golden tiara upon her forehead. She served the Earl, while her companions began to entertain them with music. The Earl took her hand along with the bowl, and sat her on his knee, and for the rest of the day they had a great deal to say to one another. Then the Earl made a verse:

> *I'll swear, clever sweetheart,*
> *you're a slender delight*
> *to grasp and to cuddle,*
> *my golden-locked girl:*
> *Ravenous the hawk, crimson*
> *-clawed, flesh-crammed;*
> *but now, heavily hangs*
> *the silken hair.* (Ch. 86)

The poems, which constitute an important element of this section, and are, indeed, used as source material by the author, express the ambivalence of society in the North, Christian and pagan, violent yet deeply committed to magnanimity, a world where brother kills brother but the bonds of sworn friendship cannot be broken. Again and again, these poems yoke together images of affection and bloodshed, romantic love and earthy desire:

> *Most admired of maidens,*
> *gold-decked at our meeting,*
> *Ermingerd the exquisite*
> *once offered me her wine —*
> *now fiercely we bear*
> *fire up to the fortress,*
> *assault the stronghold*
> *with unsheathed sword-thrust.*
>
> *Once the wine-serving*
> *wench understood me,*
> *the touches of my tongue:*
> *I was content.*
> *I loved that good lady,*
> *but lime-bound stones*
> *crumble; now I cram*
> *the hawk with carrion.* (Ch. 87)

There are moments of something approaching the peace that passeth all understanding, of self-discovery on nearing Jerusalem for example:

> *A cross on this bard's*
> *breast, on his back*
> *a palm-branch: peacefully*
> *we pace the hillside.* (Ch. 88)

But this is uncharacteristic. The major set-piece of the journey is a battle in the Mediterranean with an Arab ship; the invocation to Christ is expressed in the spirit of the Crusaders:

> *First aboard the black*
> *boat, the unbending*
> *Red Audun, rampaging,*
> *that stern ravager.*
> *Christ helped us crimson*
> *the carrion, the dark*
> *-blue bodies piled*
> *black on the deck.* (Ch. 88)

But in a society in which a warrior-earl can end up as martyr, saint and miracle-worker, such contradictions are to be expected: and it should come as no great surprise that one of the toughest viking-captains on the expedition to the Holy Land should be the Bishop of Orkney.

The purpose of the saga is, partly at least, to explore such

21

social and psychological tensions as these in the history of the people of Orkney, and to help them understand themselves through a knowledge of their origins. Though based on fact, it is only partly governed by what actually happened: like other inspired chronicles, *Orkneyinga Saga* has its own coherence even when it departs from the historical fact. Another great work of history from this period, the Icelandic *Book of Settlements*, recording the settlement of Iceland during the years *c.* 870-930, sums up the essential purpose of such historical narratives as *Orkneyinga Saga*:

People often say that writing about the Settlements is merely irrelevant learning, but we think we can better meet the criticism of foreigners when they accuse us of being descended from slaves or scoundrels, if we know for certain the truth about our ancestry. And for those who want to know the ancient customs, and how to trace genealogies, it's better to start at the beginning rather than in the middle. Anyway, all civilized peoples want to know about the origins of their own society and the beginnings of their own race.[1]

The present translation follows the edition in *Íslenzk fornrit*, vol. 34, by Finnbogi Guðmundsson, 1965. The text is based on the vellum *Flateyjarbók* codex, written by two priests, *c.* 1390. The second part of chapter 8 and the start of chapter 12, however, derive from the late sixteenth-century Danish version mentioned earlier, and the anecdote of Earl Rognvald and the fisherman in chapter 85 comes from a copy written in the seventeenth century.

There are three previous translations: by Jón A. Hjaltalín and Gilbert Goudie, *The Orkneyinga Saga*, edited with an introduction by Joseph Anderson, Edinburgh 1873; by George W. Dasent, *The Orkneyingers' Saga* (Icelandic Sagas Vol. III), London 1894; and by A. B. Taylor, *The Orkneyinga Saga*, Edinburgh 1938. The last of these contains copious notes on historical, textual and cultural problems, and we are glad to acknowledge our debt to Dr Taylor's work, particularly in dealing with the difficult problem of identifying some of the obscure localities mentioned in the Saga. Dr Taylor's volume also has an excellent bibliography. For more recent publications on Orkney and Shetland dealing with the period of the

---

[1] *The Book of Settlements* (University of Manitoba Press, 1972). See the Translators' Introduction, p. 6.

Saga, we refer the reader to *The Northern Isles*, edited by F. J. Wainwright, Edinburgh 1962.

We should like to thank Mrs Bridget Mackenzie for allowing us to consult her translations of the verses, and Mrs Sheila Coppock for her careful scrutiny of the typescript. We are also grateful to Stefán Karlsson of the Stofnun Árna Magnússonar for choosing and providing us with a colour photograph of a page from the *Flateyjarbók*, featured on the cover. Finally, we should like to express our gratitude to the artist, Denys Baker, for his excellent maps, and to Hugo Brunner for his enthusiastic encouragement.

EDINBURGH   H. PÁLSSON
                                             P. EDWARDS

ORKNEYINGA
SAGA

1. THE ROAD TO NORWAY

There was a king called Fornjot who ruled over Finland and Kvenland, the countries stretching to the east of what we call the Gulf of Bothnia, which lies opposite the White Sea. Fornjot had three sons, Hler (whom we also call Ægir), a second called Logi and a third, Kari, the father of Frosti, who was in turn father of Snær the Old, the father of Thorri. He had two sons, Nor and Gor, and a daughter called Goi.

Being a great man for worship, Thorri would hold a sacrificial feast at midwinter every year. People called it *Thorri's Sacrifice* and from this the month got its name. One winter, at *Thorri's Sacrifice*, Goi disappeared and though a search was made for her she couldn't be found. When the month had passed, Thorri made preparations for another feast with the aim of finding out what had happened to her. This one came to be known as *Goi's Sacrifice*. But for all their efforts they were none the wiser.[1]

Three years later, Nor and Gor made a solemn vow to set out in search of Goi. Their arrangement was for Nor to scour the mainland and Gor all the islands and outlying skerries, making his way by ship. Each of them had a strong force of men.

Gor led his ships out of the Gulf and into the Aaland Sea, exploring all of the Svia Skerries and every island in the Baltic, then on to the Elfar Skerries and from there over to Denmark, searching every island. He called on his kinsmen, the descendants of Hler the Old of Læso Island, then got under way again, but there was still no trace of his sister.

His brother Nor waited until the moors were under snow so that he could travel on skis, then set out from Kvenland skirting the head of the Gulf, and so reached the land of the Lapps on the far side of Finnmark. The Lapps tried to bar the way and this led to a clash between them. But so great was the uncanny power and magic of Nor and his men that as soon as the Lapps heard their war-cry and saw them drawing their swords, they were scared out of their wits and ran away. From

---

[1] According to the Icelandic calendar, *Thorri* is the name of the month starting in the third week of January, and *Goa* is the following month. In pagan times, sacrifices were held at the beginning of *Thorri*.

there Nor and his men journeyed on westward to the Kjolen Mountains. For a long time they saw no sign of people, and for food they had to shoot birds and deer. When they came to the watershed where the rivers start to flow westwards, they took the same direction till they reached the sea. Ahead of them lay a great fjord, as big as a gulf, with large settlements and broad valleys stretching up from the sea. There they ran into a crowd of people who immediately started a fight, but the outcome was just as before; either the natives were killed, or they had to run, for Nor and his men went through them like tares through a field of wheat. After that he travelled right round the fjord, claimed the whole region as his property and made himself king over the territory east of the fjord.

Nor spent the summer there, and when it began to snow on the moors he set out and made his way up along the valley stretching inland from the south side of what is now called Trondheim Fjord. Some of his men he sent south along the coast through More, and for himself he claimed possession of the land wherever he travelled. After crossing the mountain south of the head of the valley, he pushed on down through the valleys on the far side till he reached a great lake which they called the Mjosen. Then he learned that his other party had been defeated by a King Sokni, so he and his companions journeyed west over the mountains to a district they called Valdres, and from there down to the sea, to a long narrow fjord now called Sognefjord, where they met up with Sokni. It was a hard fight since Sokni wasn't in the least put out by their magic, but Nor kept battling away, facing up to Sokni himself, and the outcome was that Sokni was killed along with a good many of his followers.

2. THE DIVISION OF NORWAY

Afterwards Nor travelled over to the fjord branching off Sognefjord to the north, now called Sokna Dale as Sokni had once ruled there. Nor stayed on a long time at a place called Norumfjord, and it's there that his brother Gor joined him, but neither of them had any word of their sister Goi. Gor had laid claim to all the islands on his way from the south and now the brothers divided the whole country between them. Nor was to have all the mainland and Gor the islands, wherever a ship with a fixed rudder could be sailed between them and the mainland.

When this was settled, Nor made his way to the Uplands to a region now called Heidemark, at that time ruled by King

28

Hrolf of Bjarg, son of the giant Svadi from the Dovre Mountain in the north. It was Hrolf who had abducted Goi Thorri's-daughter from Kvenland and right away he set out to confront Nor, challenging him to single combat. The fight went on for quite some time without either of them being wounded, so they came to terms, Nor getting Hrolf's sister for his wife and Hrolf keeping Goi.

From there Nor made his way back north to the country he had laid claim to and called it Norway. He ruled over it for the rest of his life as did his sons after him, except that they divided the kingdom between them. As time went by, the kingdoms dwindled in size as the number of rulers grew, which is how the country came to be split up into provinces.

3. THE SEA-KINGS

Gor ruled the islands, and that's why he came to be called a sea-king. So too were his sons Heiti and Beiti, a very aggressive pair. They made constant attacks on the territories of the sons of Nor and fought many a battle, sometimes one side winning, sometimes the other.

Beiti sailed for plunder up Trondheim Fjord. He used to anchor his ships at a place called Beitstad, or Beitstadfjord. He had one of his ships hauled over from Beitstad north across Namdalseid to Namsen on the far side, with Gor sitting aft, his hand on the tiller. So he laid claim to all the land lying to port, a sizeable area with many settlements.

Heiti, the son of Gor, was the father of the sea-king Sveidi, father of Halfdan the Old, father of Earl Ivar of the Uplands, father of Eystein the Clatterer, father of the wise counsellor, Earl Rognvald the Powerful.

4. TO SHETLAND AND ORKNEY

Earl Rognvald campaigned with King Harald Fine-Hair who gave him charge of North More, South More and Romsdale. Earl Rognvald married Ragnhild, the daughter of Hrolf Nose, and it was their son Hrolf who conquered Normandy. This Hrolf was so big that no horse could carry him, which is why he was given the name Göngu-Hrolf.[1] The earls of Rouen and the kings of England are descended from him.

---

[1] Literally, 'Hrolf the Walker'. He should not be confused with his namesake the hero of *Göngu-Hrolf's Saga*, to be published by Southside in 1977.

Rognvald and Ragnhild had two other sons, called Ivar and Thorir the Silent, and Rognvald also had natural sons whose names were Hallad, Hrollaug, and the youngest, Einar.

One summer Harald Fine-Hair sailed west over the North Sea in order to teach a lesson to certain vikings whose plunderings he could no longer tolerate. These vikings used to raid in Norway over summer and had Shetland and Orkney as their winter base. Harald conquered Shetland, Orkney and the Hebrides,then sailed all the way to the Isle of Man where he laid its settlements in ruins. During his campaign he fought a number of battles, winning himself territories further west than any King of Norway has done since. In one of these battles Earl Rognvald's son Ivar was killed. On his way back to Norway, King Harald gave Earl Rognvald Shetland and Orkney in compensation for his son, but Rognvald gave all the islands to his brother Sigurd, the forecastleman on King Harald's ship. When the King sailed back east he gave Sigurd the title of earl and Sigurd stayed on in the islands.

5. A POISONED TOOTH

Earl Sigurd became a great ruler. He joined forces with Thorstein the Red, the son of Olaf the White and Aud the Deep-Minded, and together they conquered the whole of Caithness and a large part of Argyll, Moray and Ross. Earl Sigurd had a stronghold built in the south of Moray. A meeting was arranged at a certain place between him and Mælbrigte, Earl of the Scots, to settle their differences. Each of them was to have forty men, but on the appointed day Sigurd decided the Scots weren't to be trusted so he had eighty men mounted on forty horses.

When Earl Mælbrigte realised this, he spoke to his men.

'Now,' he said, 'Sigurd has made fools of us. I can see two men's legs on both flanks of each horse, so there must be twice as many men as there are horses. Still, we must show our courage. Each of us must try to kill at least one man before we die ourselves.'

But as the Scots prepared themselves to face the enemy, Sigurd saw what they had in mind.

'Now,' he said, 'I want half of our men to dismount and outflank them when we come to blows, while the rest of us ride at them as hard as we can and break their ranks.'

And that is what happened. There was a fierce fight but it wasn't long before Mælbrigte and his men were dead. Sigurd had their heads strapped to the victors' saddles to make a show of his triumph, and with that they began riding back home, flushed with their success. On the way, as Sigurd went to spur his horse, he struck his calf against a tooth sticking out of Mælbrigte's mouth and it gave him a scratch. The wound began to swell and ache, and it was this that led to the death of Sigurd the Powerful. He lies buried in a mound on the bank of the River Oykel.

Sigurd had a son called Guthorm who ruled the earldom for a year but died childless. When Earl Rognvald of More heard about these deaths, he sent his son Hallad west to the islands and King Harald gave him the title of earl.

Earl Hallad came to Orkney and took up residence on Mainland. Vikings would raid the islands as well as Caithness, looting and killing, but when the farmers complained of their losses to Earl Hallad, it seemed to him beyond his power to right matters for them: so, tiring of his rule, he gave up the earldom and went back to Norway as a common landholder. This excursion of his made him a laughing-stock.

6. FORECASTS

Two Danish vikings, Thorir Tree-Beard and Kalf Scurvy, set up camp on the islands. When Earl Rognvald heard about it he flew into a rage and summoned Thorir and Hrollaug, his sons—Hrolf was away at the time on a viking expedition. Rognvald asked which of them wanted the islands, and Thorir answered that it was up to the Earl himself to decide whether or not he should be the one to go.

'As I see it,' said the Earl, 'you'll be better here than anywhere else. Your path doesn't lie overseas.'

'Do you want me to go, then?' asked Hrollaug.

'You're not destined for the earldom,' replied Rognvald, 'your fate will take you to Iceland. You'll have plenty of descendants there, and they'll be thought of as the noblest of men.'

After that the Earl's youngest son, Einar, came forward.

'Do you want me to go to the islands?' he asked. 'I can promise you the greatest favour you could wish for, and that's never to have to see me again. There's little enough here to hold me, and I don't see myself as any more of a failure elsewhere.'

'Considering the kind of mother you have,' said the Earl, 'slave-born on each side of her family, you're not likely to

make much of a ruler. But I agree; the sooner you leave and
the later you return, the happier I'll be.'

Rognvald gave Einar a fully equipped ship of twenty
benches and King Harald conferred on him the title of earl.

7. VIKINGS AND PEAT

Einar sailed west to Shetland to gather forces, then south to
Orkney to face Kalf and his vikings, killing both Kalf and
Thorir in battle. Someone composed this couplet:

> *Turf-Einar gave Tree-Beard*
> *To the trolls, killed Kalf Scurvy.*

After that he took over the island territories and became a
great leader. He was the first man to dig peat for fuel, firewood
being very scarce on the islands, at Tarbat Ness in Scotland.

Einar was tall and ugly, and though he was one-eyed he was
still the most keen-sighted of men.

8. TROUBLEMAKERS FROM NORWAY

When they grew up the sons of Harald Fine-Hair turned out
to be very arrogant and caused a lot of trouble in Norway,
bullying the King's earls, killing some of them and driving
others from their estates. Halfdan Long-Leg and Gudrod
Gleam, King Harald's sons by Snæfrid, attacked Earl
Rognvald of More, killed him, and assumed his authority.
King Harald flew into a rage when he heard about this and
set out after his sons. Halfdan went aboard ship and escaped
west across the sea but Gudrod gave himself up to his father.
In compensation for the death of Rognvald, King Harald
gave his daughter Alof the Fecund as wife to Thorir, along
with Thorir's own patrimony and the title of earl.

Halfdan Long-Leg arrived in Orkney and when the news
got around that one of King Harald's sons had turned up it
frightened everyone. Some of the people offered him allegiance,
but Earl Einar fled the islands over to Scotland. Halfdan
conquered the islands and set himself up as king over them.
Later in the year, however, Einar came back to fight him
and though the battle was fierce Einar came out as victor.
Around evening time when it was growing dark Halfdan
jumped overboard, and Einar composed this verse:

1. Part of a page from *Flateyjarbók* (See Ch. 20, pp. 49-51)

2. St Magnus' Church, Egilsay: 'It was clear to Magnus that he could expect treachery. He went ashore with his men up to the church to pray, and there he spent the night.' (Ch.48)

3. Christ Church Cathedral on the Brough of Birsay: 'The story goes that in general the men most deeply involved in the betrayal of the holy Earl Magnus died cruel and violent deaths. This took place when William was Bishop of Orkney, the first resident bishop in the islands, and the episcopal seat was at Christ Church, Birsay.' (Ch. 52)

> *Not from Hrolf's hand*
> *nor Hrollaug's, the hurled shaft,*
> *no death-dart. Our*
> *duty is to the dead,*
> *our father: here the fight*
> *grows fierce, while at More*
> *what says the ale-swilling earl?*
> *Nought of the sword-swing.*

In the morning, as soon as it was light, they set out and scoured the islands to see whether anyone had got away.

'I don't know what it is bobbing up and down over there,' said Earl Einar. 'It's either a bird or a man. Let's go and find out.'

And that's where they found Halfdan Long-Leg. Einar had his ribs cut from the spine with a sword and the lungs pulled out through the slits in his back. He dedicated the victim to Odin as a victory offering, then made this verse:

> *While sturdy spade-beards*
> *were stalking sheep,*
> *in Orkney I was, busy*
> *butchering a king's boy;*
> *true, all I'm told,*
> *how the trusty lord threatens*
> *me, who sheared a slice*
> *from his family shield.*

Then he made another:

> *Happy am I, keen*
> *heroes have spear-hacked,*
> *bloodied the king's boy:*
> *brave the bold act*
> *—but hard to hide*
> *what a howling I've caused:*
> *the corbie croaks*
> *over carrion in Orkney.*

Einar had a burial mound built for Halfdan, then he made this verse:

> *The folk-lord is fallen,*
> *the fee paid for Rognvald;*
> *sweetly the Norns shaped*
> *for me my quarter-share.*

33

Cast the stone, keen
lads, on Long-Leg's cairn
as we celebrate here
the settling of the scot.

When the news reached Norway, Halfdan's brothers were so angry they threatened to go to Orkney to avenge him, but King Harald made sure that nothing came of it.

This is what Einar said when he heard about their threats:

Of no mean mettle,
men come from many
a country, keen to do
combat with me, to kill:
but, till they fell me, few
know what is fated, know
who will tumble, torn
by the eagle's talon.

A little later King Harald travelled west over the sea to Orkney and Einar fled to Caithness. Next, mediators set about the task of reconciling them. King Harald imposed a tax on the islands amounting to sixty gold marks. Einar offered to pay the whole sum out of his own pocket on condition that he should hold all the estates in fee, and to these terms the farmers agreed since the wealthier ones hoped to redeem their estates later, while the poorer farmers were unable to pay the tribute anyway. So Einar paid out the whole sum and for a long time afterwards the earls held in fee all the estates, until Earl Sigurd gave them back to the farmers of Orkney.

King Harald went back to Norway, but Earl Einar ruled over Orkney for many years and died in his bed. Einar had three sons, one called Arnkel, the next Erlend, and the third Thorfinn Skull-Splitter.

After King Harald died, Eirik Blood-Axe ruled over Norway for a couple of years, then Hakon, King Athelstan's foster-son, took over power and Eirik fled the country. He sailed west across the North Sea, waging war in Scotland and in the north of England. When King Athelstan heard about this he sent messengers to Eirik with an offer of land, saying that he had been a close friend of King Harald and wanted Harald's son to benefit from it. He added that he hoped to make peace between his foster-son Hakon and Eirik. King Eirik accepted the offer and was given charge of Northumbria, which makes up one-fifth of England, but as he had little land and a large following he ran short of money, which is why he spent the summers plundering, while staying in his kingdom over winter.

That is how matters stood for the rest of Athelstan's life. He died after reigning fourteen years and was succeeded by his brother Edmund, who was less friendly towards the Norwegians, not liking King Eirik's rule over Northumbria.

One spring, King Eirik sailed north beyond Scotland all the way to Orkney, where he was joined by Earls Arnkel and Erlend, the sons of Turf-Einar. From there they sailed to the Hebrides, adding considerably to their forces. Next he went looting in Ireland and then did the same in Strathclyde. Finally he went south to England and began plundering there just as he'd been doing elsewhere.

King Edmund had put a king called Olaf in charge of defences. Eirik had a sizeable force which he marched inland some distance from the ships, but King Olaf had gathered a massive army and set out after him. There was a fierce battle and during the forenoon the English were killed in large numbers, but for every man who died three came to take his place. Late in the afternoon the Norwegian losses were too much for them and the outcome was that King Eirik and six other kings, one called Guthorm, were killed there. Earls Arnkel and Erlend died too.

When Gunnhild and her sons heard that King Eirik had been killed plundering in England they realised there was little chance of peace there, so they got themselves ready for a hasty departure and sailed north to Orkney, where Earl Thorfinn Skull-Splitter was ruling at the time. Gunnhild's sons took over power in the islands and used them as their base in winter, spending the summers on viking expeditions.

During their stay in Orkney, Gunnhild and her sons heard that there was war between King Harald Gormsson of Denmark and King Hakon, Athelstan's foster-son, and having expectations of help from King Harald they set out to visit him. Before they left Orkney they gave Ragnhild, daughter of King Eirik and Gunnhild, in marriage to Arnfinn, son of Earl Thorfinn.

Earl Thorfinn took control of the islands. A strong ruler and warrior, he died in his bed and was laid in a burial mound at Hoxa in North Ronaldsay. People thought him a very great man.

9. INTRIGUES

Earl Thorfinn had five sons, one called Arnfinn, the next Havard the Fecund, the third Hlodvir, the fourth Ljot, and the fifth Skuli. Ragnhild Eirik's-Daughter plotted the death of her husband Arnfinn at Murkle in Caithness, then married his brother Havard the Fecund who succeeded to the earldom. Under his rule the islands enjoyed peace and prosperity.

Earl Havard had a nephew called Einar Buttered-Bread, a respected chieftain with a good following. He used to go plundering in the summer. Havard invited him to a feast and in the course of it Einar and Ragnhild talked a lot together. She kept telling him what a fine leader he was and how much better fitted for the earldom than his uncle Havard. It would be a luckily-matched woman, she said, who married him. Einar pleaded with her not to say such things, a respectable married woman and the wife of the greatest man in Orkney.

'My married life with Havard won't last much longer,' she said, 'and to tell you the truth, though you may not want the honour for yourself, there are men in Orkney who wouldn't be so high-minded about it.'

So she prodded him on, and Einar, swayed too by his greed, let her influence him. Eventually he was persuaded to betray the Earl his uncle. Ragnhild and Einar made a bargain that he was to kill the Earl and then she would marry him.

Not long after, Einar got ready for a journey, but before he set out a seer in his company gave him a warning.

'Don't do your work today,' he said, 'leave it till tomorrow. If you won't, there are going to be killings in your family for years to come.'

But Einar ignored his words.

At that time, Earl Havard was staying at Stenness on Mainland. That's where he and Einar came face to face and where he was killed after a short, sharp battle. The place is called Havard's Field nowadays.

When people heard about it they spoke bitterly of Einar's contemptible part in the affair and Ragnhild refused to have anything to do with him. She said it was an out-and-out lie that she'd made him any promises, and sent for Einar Hard-Mouth, the son of another of Havard's sisters. When they met, Ragnhild told him it was a disgrace that the Earl's kinsmen had taken no revenge and that she would do all she could to make sure vengeance was carried out.

'It's plain to see,' she said, 'the man who avenges the Earl will earn the respect of all decent people and be the one to get the earldom too.'

'Common talk has it, my lady, that you don't always say quite what you're thinking,' said Einar. 'Anyone who carries this off will want more than the earldom: he'll expect other things from you just as important.'

So their conversation came to an end. After that, Einar Hard-Mouth led an attack on Einar Buttered-Bread and killed him, but then Ragnhild sent for Ljot, the brother of Arnfinn and Havard, and it was him she married. Ljot took over the earldom and turned out to be an excellent leader.

So, though Einar Hard-Mouth had killed his own cousin, he was still no closer to the earldom. Far from pleased with the way things had gone, he decided to gather troops and take the islands by force. However, he found it difficult to muster enough of them, as the men of Orkney preferred to serve the sons of Thorfinn Skull-Splitter. Shortly after, the Earl had Einar Hard-Mouth put to death.

10. CONTENTION IN CAITHNESS

Skuli, Ljot's brother, travelled across to Scotland where he was given the title of earl by the King of Scots. Then he went north to Caithness to gather an army, and from there he sailed back to Orkney to claim the earldom from his brother. Ljot gathered an army, too, and set out with a large force to confront Skuli. When they met, Skuli insisted on making a fight of it, but after a fierce battle Ljot won the victory and Skuli fled, first over to Caithness and then south to Scotland. Ljot went after him and spent some time in Caithness adding to his army.

Later, Skuli rode back north with a large following supplied by the King of Scots and Earl Macbeth, and the brothers met in the Dales of Caithness. The battle was hard-fought, with the Scots attacking fiercely in the early stages, but when Ljot urged his men to fight and stand firm the Scots failed to gain ground. Ljot kept shouting encouragement to his men and he himself fought like a hero. After a while the Scottish ranks began to crumble and soon they were on the run. Skuli battled on, but in the end he was killed.

Earl Ljot took over in Caithness and this led to trouble with the Scots, who were angry over their defeat. When Earl Ljot was in Caithness, Earl Macbeth came north from Scotland with a large army and they met at Skitten in Caithness. Ljot was outnumbered but fought so well that the Scots had to fall back. The battle was a short one: all the Scots who survived took to flight, most of them wounded. After this victory, Ljot went back to the islands. Many of his men were suffering from wounds and Ljot himself had one that led to his death. People thought it a great loss.

11. THE MAGIC BANNER

After Ljot's death, Hlodvir took charge of the earldom and ruled well. He married Eithne, the daughter of King Kjarval of Ireland and their son was Sigurd the Stout. Hlodvir died in his bed and was laid to rest in a burial mound at Ham in Caithness.

After Hlodvir, his son Sigurd took over the earldom. He was another great chieftain and ruled over several dominions. He was powerful enough to defend Caithness against the Scots and used to go on viking expeditions every summer as well, plundering in the Hebrides, Scotland and Ireland.

One summer it happened that a Scottish earl called Finnleik challenged Sigurd to fight him on a particular day at Skitten. Sigurd's mother was a sorceress so he went to consult her, telling her that the odds against him were heavy, at least seven to one.

'Had I thought you might live for ever,' she said, 'I'd have reared you in my wool-basket. But lifetimes are shaped by what will be, not by where you are. Now, take this banner. I've made it for you with all the skill I have, and my belief is this: that it will bring victory to the man it's carried before, but death to the one who carries it.'

It was a finely made banner, very cleverly embroidered with the figure of a raven, and when the banner fluttered in the breeze, the raven seemed to be flying ahead.

Earl Sigurd lost his temper at his mother's words. He got the support of the Orkney farmers by giving them back their land-rights, then set out for Skitten to confront Earl Finnleik. The two sides formed up, but the moment they clashed Sigurd's standard-bearer was struck dead. The Earl told another man to pick up the banner but before long he'd been killed too. The Earl lost three standard bearers, but he won the battle and the farmers of Orkney got back their land-rights.

12. DEATH IN IRELAND

After his return from Wendland, Olaf Tryggvason spent four years looting in the British Isles. Then he was baptised in the Scillies and from there sailed to England where he married Gyda, the sister of King Kvaran of Ireland. Next he spent a while in Dublin till Earl Hakon sent Thorir Klakka out west to lure him away from there.

Olaf sailed east with five ships and didn't break his journey until he reached Orkney. At Osmundwall he ran into Earl Sigurd, who had three ships and was setting out on a viking expedition. Olaf sent a messenger to him, asking Sigurd to come over to his ship as he wanted a word with him.

'I want you and all your subjects to be baptised,' he said when they met. 'If you refuse, I'll have you killed on the spot, and I swear that I'll ravage every island with fire and steel.'

The Earl could see what kind of situation he was in and surrendered himself into Olaf's hands. He was baptised and Olaf took his son, called Hvelp or Hundi, as a hostage and had him baptised too under the name of Hlodvir. After that, all Orkney embraced the faith. Olaf sailed east to Norway taking Hlodvir with him, but Hlodvir didn't live long and after his death Sigurd refused to pay homage to King Olaf.

Earl Sigurd married the daughter of Malcolm, King of Scots, and their son was Earl Thorfinn. Earl Sigurd had three other sons, called Sumarlidi, Brusi and Einar Wry-Mouth.

Five years after the Battle of Svoldur, Earl Sigurd went to Ireland in support of King Sigtrygg Silk-Beard, leaving his elder sons in charge of the earldom.[1] Thorfinn he sent over to Scotland to be fostered by the King, the boy's maternal grandfather. Earl Sigurd arrived in Ireland, joined up with King Sigtrygg and set out to fight King Brian of Ireland. The battle took place on Good Friday. No one would carry the raven banner, so the Earl had to do it himself and he was killed. King Sigtrygg ran away, and although King Brian won the victory, he lost his life.

13. EARL SIGURD'S SONS

After the death of Earl Sigurd three of his sons, Sumarlidi, Brusi and Einar, took over the earldom and divided it between

[1] The dating is incorrect. The Battle of Svoldur was fought in A.D. 1000, and Earl Sigurd was killed in the Battle of Clontarf near Dublin, on Good Friday, April 23, 1014.

them, for Thorfinn was only five years old when his father was killed, living with his grandfather, King Malcolm of Scotland. The King of Scots gave Thorfinn Caithness and Sutherland, granted him the title of earl, and appointed counsellors to govern with him.

Earl Thorfinn developed early, growing into a tall, strong, black-haired man. As he grew older, everyone could see that he was going to turn out greedy. His brothers Einar and Brusi were very different from each other in character. Einar was ruthless and grasping, a hard and successful fighting man, while Brusi was gentle, restrained, unassuming and a fine speaker. In character, Sumarlidi was more like Brusi than Einar. He was the eldest of the brothers but had the shortest life, dying in his bed.

After Sumarlidi's death, Earl Thorfinn claimed his brother's share of Orkney, but Einar argued that Caithness and Sutherland, which were in Thorfinn's hands, had been part of his father's earldom. He insisted that these territories constituted over a third of the earldom and refused to give Thorfinn more than the share he already had.

Brusi, on the other hand, was willing to let Thorfinn have a larger share.

'I've no wish to take more of the earldom than the third that belongs to me by right,' he said.

After that, Einar took over two-thirds of Orkney. He was a strong ruler and his following was a large one. The levies he used to impose were severe and in summer he would go raiding even though the loot he got wasn't all that plentiful. The farmers grew tired of this sort of thing, but when it came to squeezing payments out of them, Earl Einar made no compromises and stood for no arguments. He was a great bully, and all the dues and duties imposed on the farmers led to a serious famine in his part of the earldom, but on the other islands, where Brusi was in charge, the farmers enjoyed peace and prosperity. As a result he was well-liked by everyone.

14. OPPOSITION

There was a wealthy man called Amundi farming at Sandwick on Mainland. He had a son called Thorkel, one of the most promising youngsters in Orkney at the time. Amundi was a shrewd man and among the best respected people in the islands.

One spring, after Earl Eidar had imposed his usual harsh levy, the farmers started grumbling about it and brought their complaints to Amundi, asking him to have a word with the Earl on their behalf.

Amundi said the Earl wasn't a good listener.

'Nothing will be gained by it,' he said, 'and, considering the tempers on both sides, there's yet another risk. If we were to fall out with the Earl, it would make matters even worse. I'm having nothing to do with it.'

After that the farmers talked matters over with Thorkel. He was far from keen to plead their cause, but people kept nagging on at him till he gave them his promise. Amundi thought it had been rash of him to do so.

At a meeting the Earl held with the farmers, Thorkel spoke up for them, describing their hardships and pleading with the Earl to be more easy-going with his people. The Earl made a friendly reply and said he would take notice of what had been said.

'I'd intended to have six ships on my expedition,' he said, 'but now I've made up my mind to take only three. But as for you, Thorkel, don't make any more requests like that.'

The farmers thanked Thorkel warmly for his help.

The Earl set out on his viking expedition and returned in the autumn. Next spring he imposed a levy and summoned all the farmers to an assembly. Thorkel was there to plead with him again for leniency to the farmers, but got the angry response that his words would only make things worse for everyone. The Earl was in such a rage, he swore that only one of them would see the assembly next spring, and with that the meeting broke up.

Amundi heard what had happened between Thorkel and the Earl and advised his son to go away, so Thorkel went over to Earl Thorfinn in Caithness and stayed there for some time. He fostered Thorfinn while the Earl was young, and for that he was nicknamed Thorkel the Fosterer. He was a fine man.

Many people of importance left Orkney because of Earl Einar's harsh rule, most of them joining Earl Thorfinn, though some of them went to Norway and other countries.

15. RECONCILIATION

When Earl Thorfinn came of age, he sent word to his brother Einar claiming one-third of the islands as his share of the earldom. Earl Einar wasn't keen to trim his power quite so drastically, and when this was reported to Earl Thorfinn he began mustering forces in Caithness. Earl Einar heard about it and set out against Thorfinn looking for a fight. Earl Brusi gathered a force too and went to see the earls with the idea of making peace between them. They were reconciled on these conditions, that Earl Thorfinn was to have his rightful third of the Orkney earldom, while Earls Einar and Brusi would unite their shares under joint rule. Einar was to be head of state and take charge of the defences. On the death of either brother the survivor was to inherit his dominion, but the bargain was uneven since Brusi had a son, Rognvald, while Einar had none.

Earl Thorfinn appointed stewards to take charge of his part of the Orkney earldom, but he himself lived much of the time in Caithness.

Earl Einar spent most summers plundering in Ireland, Scotland and Wales. One summer in Ireland he fought against King Konofogor of Ireland at Lough Larne and suffered a crushing defeat with heavy loss of life. Next summer Eyvind Aurochs-Horn put out from Ireland east towards Norway but ran into a fierce gale which forced him to take shelter at Osmundwall where for a time he was stormbound. Einar heard about it, set out with a strong force, captured Eyvind and had him put to death, though he spared the lives of most of his men. In the autumn these men went back to Norway and told King Olaf how Eyvind had been killed. The King hadn't much to say about it, though it was plain he thought Eyvind's death a great loss and took the whole episode as a personal affront. As a rule the King said little about the more serious offences against him.

Earl Thorfinn sent his foster-father Thorkel over to the islands to gather tributes. Earl Einar held Thorkel largely responsible for the uprising at the time Thorfinn claimed the islands and Thorkel made a hurried return to Caithness to tell Earl Thorfinn that Einar would have killed him, had friends and kinsmen not given warning.

'So now,' said Thorkel, 'I've a choice. Either I can face up to the Earl and settle the matter once and for all or go so far away that he won't be able to lay hands on me.'

Earl Thorfinn urged him strongly to go east to Norway and see King Olaf.

'You'll win the respect of the best people wherever you go,' he said, 'and I've learned enough about your mettle, and Earl Einar's, to know that neither of you will hold back for long.'

So Thorkel got ready to go and see King Olaf. In the autumn he sailed across to Norway and spent the winter with the King on the friendliest of terms. The King often consulted Thorkel and thought him a shrewd and enterprising man, as indeed he was. From the way Thorkel spoke, the King could tell that his attitude to the Earls wasn't unbiased, being friendly towards Thorfinn but bitter when talking about Einar. Early in the spring King Olaf sent a ship west to Earl Thorfinn with a request for the Earl to come and see him and, since the message included an offer of friendship, the Earl decided to go.

16. MURDER OF AN EARL

Earl Thorfinn sailed east to Norway and King Olaf gave him a cheerful welcome. Thorfinn stayed there for a good part of the summer and when he was ready to go back home King Olaf gave him a fine, big, fully-equipped longship. So the Earl gave Thorkel his foster-father the ship in which he himself had sailed to Norway earlier that summer and they returned home together. The King and Earl Thorfinn parted on the best of terms and by the autumn Thorfinn was back in Orkney.

When Earl Einar heard this, he gathered forces and took to his ships. Again Earl Brusi went to see his brothers on a peace mission and again they came to terms, sealing their agreement with oaths. Thorkel the Fosterer was to be reconciled with Earl Einar and become his friend. The stipulation was that each should hold feasts for the other, the first turn being Thorkel's, who invited Earl Einar to Sandwick. He came to the feast but despite the lavish hospitality he was in a sour temper. The banquet was held in a great hall with a door at either end.

On the last day of the feast Einar got ready to leave. Thorkel was supposed to travel with him to the other feast, but when he sent his men to spy out the route to be travelled later in the day, they reported armed men in ambush at three different spots.

'To tell you the truth,' they said, 'it looks to us like treachery.'

Once Thorkel had learned all this, he delayed his departure and called his men together. Earl Einar told him to get ready as it was time to set off, but Thorkel said he still had a lot to see to, and kept going out of the hall, then coming back in again. A fire was burning on the floor. Thorkel came in through one of the doors accompanied by an Icelander called Hallvard from the East Fjords, who closed the door behind them.

Thorkel made his way up through the hall, walking between
the fire and the bench where the Earl was sitting.

'Aren't you ready yet?' asked the Earl.

'Yes, I'm ready now,' said Thorkel striking him on the head,
and the Earl slumped forward onto the floor.

'I've never seen such a useless lot,' said Hallvard. 'Can't
you pull the Earl out of the fire?'

He hooked his curved axe round the back of the Earl's
neck and heaved him up onto the wooden platform, then he
and Thorkel ran out through the other door where Thorkel's
men were waiting, fully armed. The Earl's companions picked
him up and saw that he was dead, but none of them raised a
finger to avenge him, for which there were several reasons:
everything had happened very suddenly, no one having
expected anything of the sort from Thorkel; most of the men
in the hall were unarmed and Thorkel had plenty of reliable
friends with him; and in the end, it was Thorkel's destiny that
he should be the one to come out alive.

Thorkel went back to his ship and the Earl's men to theirs.
That day, with winter coming on, Thorkel set out and sailed
east over the sea, reaching Norway safe and sound. He went at
once to see King Olaf and was given a friendly reception, the
King being quite pleased with what Thorkel had done, and
there Thorkel stayed over winter.

17. NEW LINKS WITH NORWAY

After the killing of Earl Einar, Brusi took over his part of the
earldom. Most people knew the terms of the agreement
between Einar and Brusi, but Earl Thorfinn thought it only
right that he and Brusi should share the islands equally
between them. Still, the following winter Brusi ruled over
two-thirds of the earldom.

In the spring Thorfinn demanded half of the islands but
Brusi rejected his claim. They had meetings to talk matters
over and mutual friends tried to reconcile them, but still
Thorfinn insisted that half of the islands were his. He went so
far as to say that a third of the islands was quite enough for a
man of Brusi's mettle.

'I was satisfied with the third I'd inherited from my father,'
said Brusi, 'and nobody challenged my right to it. Now, I've
inherited another third rightfully from my brother Einar and,
though I can't make an issue of it, brother, all the same, rather

than just hand over my lands I'll find something that I can do.'

And with that the meeting broke up.

When Brusi realised that he could not hold his own against Thorfinn, who had greater power and also the support of his grandfather, the King of Scots, he decided to go abroad and sail east to see King Olaf, taking with him his two-year-old son Rognvald. He went to see King Olaf who gave him a friendly welcome. The Earl stated his business and told the King exactly how matters stood between him and his brother. He asked the King to help him hold on to his earldom and promised in return his fully committed friendship. The King's reply was to point out that Harald Fine-Hair had taken possession of the odal rights in Orkney.

'Ever since then the Earls of Orkney have held them as fiefs, never as personal property,' he said. 'It's borne out by the fact that when Eirik Blood-Axe and his sons were in Orkney the Earls paid them homage, and when my kinsman Olaf Tryggvason was there, Earl Sigurd your father became his man. Now that I've inherited everything from Olaf, these are the terms I'll offer you: I'll let you have the islands in fee as long as you become my man. Once you get my support, we'll see which is the stronger, my aid to you or the King of Scots' support for your brother Thorfinn. But if you turn my offer down, then all the property and odal rights my forebears have held in the isles I mean to take over myself.'

The Earl thought about this and talked it over with his friends, asking their advice on whether or not he should make a settlement and become King Olaf's man.

'Now that the King has made me a straight offer, it raises doubts about what might happen on parting if I were to say no. He's convinced the islands are his and, now that we've placed ourselves in his hands by coming here, it would be easy for an ambitious man like him to do whatever he wants with us.'

Though the Earl realised neither choice was perfect, he decided to surrender himself and his earldom to the King. With that, King Olaf appropriated the authority and over-lordship of the Earl's heritable lands, and the Earl swore an oath of fealty to become the King's man.

18. EARL THORFINN AND KING OLAF

Earl Thorfinn was told that his brother Brusi had gone east looking for support from King Olaf, but he was confident

about his own chances since he himself had already been to
visit the King and had gained his friendship and he knew, too,
that there were plenty of people who would rally to his side.
Yet he decided to get ready as quickly as possible and sail to
Norway, intending to come so close on the heels of his brother
that Brusi would have no time to complete his business before
he himself saw the King. However, things turned out
differently from what he'd hoped, for by the time he reached
King Olaf the agreement between Brusi and the King had
already been sealed and settled. It was only after he met
King Olaf that Thorfinn realised Brusi had surrendered his
earldom. When Earl Thorfinn and King Olaf met, the King
laid the same claim to the lands in Orkney as he had in the
case of Earl Brusi and made a similar demand that Thorfinn
should surrender to him the third he had previously held. The
Earl answered the King politely, saying how highly he valued
his friendship.

'Were you ever to need my help against other rulers, my
lord,' he said, 'it would be yours for the asking. But it's not
possible for me to pay homage to you. I'm already the Earl of
the King of Scots and subject to him.'

The King sensed the evasiveness of the Earl's answer to his
demand.

'If you refuse to become my liegeman, Earl Thorfinn,' he
said, 'there's another possibility. I can put any man I like
in charge of Orkney. I want you to swear oaths never to lay
claim to these lands and to leave in peace whomsoever I decide
to appoint. If you won't agree to this, then I take it that the
man I appoint must expect trouble from you and, in that case,
don't be surprised if the valley confronts the mountain.'[1]

Thorfinn asked the King for a chance to think things over,
and that Olaf gave him, allowing the Earl time and opportunity to talk the matter over with his friends. Then the Earl
asked the King to give him till next summer, as he wanted
to go home first.

'All my advisers are there,' he said, 'and I'm only a
youngster.'

But the King told him to make up his mind on the spot,
one way or the other.

Thorkel the Fosterer was with the King at the time. He
sent men privately to Earl Thorfinn to warn him that, now

[1] This alludes to *Isaiah* xl, 4: 'Let every valley be filled in, every
mountain and hill be laid low, let every cliff become a plain, and the
ridges a valley.'

he was in the King's power, then no matter what plans he had in mind, he should not be so rash as to part from King Olaf without having made a settlement. The Earl realised that he had no choice but to let the King have his way. All the same, he was reluctant to give up all hope of keeping his ancestral lands, nor did he care to be forced without a fight to swear oaths granting those lands to men with no birthright to them. But, since he had doubts as to whether he would otherwise be given leave to go, he made up his mind on the spot to put himself in the King's hands and become his liegeman just as his brother Brusi had done. The King could see how much more ambitious Thorfinn was than Brusi and trusted him less, for he realised that Earl Thorfinn could rely on the support of the King of Scots should he want to break the agreement. King Olaf was shrewd enough to see that Brusi had acted reluctantly throughout the negotiations and had promised no more than he intended to honour. Thorfinn on his part seemed happy about everything once he had made up his mind what to do. He had accepted every condition quite cheerfully, without trying to find a way round the King's original demands. But the King suspected that Thorfinn had no intention of keeping to the letter of the agreement.

19. KING OLAF'S VERDICT

As soon as King Olaf had thought the whole matter over, he had the trumpet sounded to call everyone to a meeting and asked both Earls to attend. This was the speech he made:

'I'm going to state publicly the terms of the agreement with the Earls of Orkney. They've conceded that Orkney and Shetland come under my overlordship and they've sworn their allegiance to me, so now I plan to give Earl Brusi one-third of the islands in fee, and Thorfinn another third, the territories that they've been in control of. But the third part, that belonging to Earl Einar, I claim for myself, since he killed my retainer and close companion Eyvind Aurochs-Horn and I mean to dispose of that part of the earldom in any way I see fit. My next condition is that you two brothers, my earls, make a settlement with Thorkel Amundason over the killing of your brother Einar. If you agree, then I want to dictate the exact terms of the settlement.'

On this occasion, as before, the brothers agreed to all the King's demands. Then Thorkel came forward and formally accepted the King's verdict, whereupon the meeting broke up.

The King awarded compensation for the killing of Einar, the sum to be the same as for three landed-men, though because of Einar's own offences one-third of the sum was to be remitted.

Earl Thorfinn asked the King for leave to return home and as soon as it was granted he began to make rapid preparations for the voyage. One day the Earl was drinking on board, ready to sail, when Thorkel Amundason suddenly appeared before him, placed his head upon the Earl's knee and said that he could do whatever he liked with him. Thorfinn asked him why he was doing this.

'Get up,' he said, 'we've already been reconciled by the King's command.'

Thorkel did as he was told.

'As far as they concern Brusi, I'll abide by the terms of the settlement fixed by the King,' he said, 'but as for you, I want you alone to settle the matter. The King may have granted me ownership of my estates in Orkney and the right to live there, but I know your nature well enough to realise that I couldn't go to the islands until I had your trust. I'll even promise not to return to the islands despite what the King has stipulated.'

The Earl sat in silence, then slowly he began to speak.

'If you want me to settle the differences between us, Thorkel,' he said, 'rather than accept the King's verdict, then the first part of our agreement must be that you come with me to Orkney, stay with me, and never leave me without my permission. You'll be duty bound to defend my realm and do whatever I wish to be done, for as long as we both live.'

'As you wish, sir,' said Thorkel, 'that and anything else in my power.'

At that he stepped forward and gave a solemn undertaking to do whatever the Earl asked of him. The Earl said he would fix the compensation later and had Thorkel confirm his agreement with oaths. After that Thorkel made preparations to sail with him and as soon as they were ready they put out to sea. The Earl and King Olaf never met again.

Earl Brusi stayed behind and got himself ready in a more leisurely fashion. Before Brusi sailed, King Olaf summoned him to a meeting.

'It seems a good idea, Earl Brusi, for me to appoint you my personal agent there in the west,' he said. 'Within the earldom, I want you to have charge of the two-thirds you've been governing, and to be a man of no less importance and power, now you're my liegeman, than you were before. But to make sure I can rely on you I want your son Rognvald

here with me. I'm sure that with my trust and two-thirds of
the earldom, you can hold your own comfortably against Earl
Thorfinn.'

Brusi accepted the two-thirds gladly. He stayed on for a
while, then put out to sea, reaching Orkney in the autumn.

Rognvald Brusason stayed behind with King Olaf. Rognvald
was one of the handsomest of men, with a fine head of golden
hair, smooth as silk. At an early age he grew to be tall and
strong, earning a great reputation for his shrewdness and
courtesy, and he stayed on with King Olaf for a long time.
Ottar the Black refers to it in a poem he made about King
Olaf:

> *Great rulers have good reason*
> *to regard you; trust*
> *you show in their strength:*
> *Shetlanders will serve you.*
> *Before your coming*
> *no commander so courageous*
> *in all the eastlands, you*
> *overlord of Orkney.*

When the brothers came west to Orkney, Brusi took charge
of two-thirds and Thorfinn of one. Thorfinn spent most of the
time in Caithness and Scotland, leaving his stewards to look
after the islands, where Brusi had sole charge of the defences.
At that time the islands were under constant threat of war,
as Norwegians and Danes, sailing to the west and returning by
way of Orkney, often came ashore there to plunder the head-
lands. Brusi criticised Thorfinn for making no contribution to
the defences of Orkney and Shetland despite all the taxes and
tributes he collected from his own territory. So Thorfinn made
an offer. Brusi could have one-third of the earldom and
Thorfinn would have the other two-thirds and be in sole
charge of the defences himself. Although this arrangement
didn't come into effect straight away, the outcome was that
Thorfinn got two-thirds of the islands and Brusi one. This
happened at the time Canute was ruler of Norway and Olaf
a fugitive abroad.

20. KARL HUNDASON

Earl Thorfinn grew to be a great chieftain. He was unusually
tall and strong, an ugly-looking man with a black head of hair,
sharp features, a big nose and bushy eyebrows, a forceful man,

greedy for fame and fortune. He did well in battle, for he was both a good tactician and full of courage. When his grand-father Malcolm, King of Scots, gave him the title of earl and authority over Caithness he was five years old, as we've already said. At fifteen he began to lead raiding expeditions abroad against the lands of other chieftains, and these are the words Arnor the Earl's-Poet wrote about him:

> *In helm-storm the high*
> *heart made swords sweat,*
> *crimsoned ere fifteen years*
> *the claws of corbies.*
> *No stripling under sky-vault*
> *more steadfast, sure*
> *in conquest for his country,*
> *than this kinsman of Einar.*

Earl Thorfinn got ample support from his grandfather the King of Scots. This source of power being so close at hand strengthened his position in Orkney a great deal. The King of Scots died some time after the reconciliation of Thorfinn and his brother Brusi, and the next man to take over power in Scotland was Karl Hundason. He claimed Caithness, just as the earlier Kings of Scotland had done, and expected the same payment of tributes as from elsewhere: but Earl Thorfinn, who held Caithness, thought it no more than his proper inheritance from his grandfather and refused to pay any tribute for it. This led to bitter feelings between him and Karl Hundason and each of them kept attacking the other's terri-tory. King Karl wanted to instal a man called Mutatan or Muddan as chieftain in Caithness. The man was the King's nephew and got the title of earl, after which he rode north to Caithness, gathering troops in Sutherland.

News of this reached Earl Thorfinn. He mustered an army in Caithness, then Thorkel the Fosterer came to join him with a large band of men. After that Thorfinn set out with superior numbers to confront Muddan, but as soon as the Scots realised they were outnumbered they decided not to fight and rode back to Scotland. Earl Thorfinn chased after them, conquering Sutherland and Ross, and plundering throughout Scotland before he went back to Caithness. Thorkel returned to the islands and the troops from the south went home.

Earl Thorfinn stayed on in Caithness at Duncansby, keeping

five well-manned longships with him so that he had a considerable force. Muddan went to see King Karl at Berwick and told him how badly things had turned out. When he heard how his territories had been looted, King Karl flew in a rage and without wasting any time he took to his longships, eleven of them, with a large number of men aboard. He sailed north of Scotland, but sent Muddan back to Caithness with a substantial army, to ride deep inland. The way things were arranged, Muddan was going to attack from the south, so Thorfinn would be caught in a trap.

Now as for Karl, he sailed on and landed in Caithness at a place not far from where Thorfinn was. Earl Thorfinn decided to board ship and sail across the Pentland Firth to Orkney. They were so close to each other that Karl and his men were able to make out the sails of Thorfinn's ship as he was crossing the Firth, so they kept on after him. Thorfinn's troops hadn't seen the enemy ships and held course eastwards to the islands, heading for Sandwick. Thorfinn cast anchor off Deerness and right away sent word to Thorkel to collect fighting men. Brusi was in charge of the isles to the north and that's where he was staying at the time. As we've said, Thorfinn was waiting off Deerness, and it was late in the evening when he got there, so next morning at dawn, when Karl's eleven ships rowed up, he was taken by surprise. There were only two choices open to him, either to swim ashore and surrender all his ships and goods to the enemy or else make a stand and let fate decide. So he called his men together and told them to get their weapons ready. He wasn't going to run, he said, and ordered them to row straight at the enemy. The two sides grappled their ships together, with Thorfinn urging on his men, telling them to keep their courage up and fight hard because the Scots would never stand up to pressure. It was a long hard battle and for some time no one could tell how it would turn out. Arnor speaks of this battle in his poem on Thorfinn:

> *Made clear then to King Karl*
> *the close of his iron-fate,*
> *east of Deerness, defied*
> *and defeated by warrior-kin.*
> *Confronting the foe, Thorfinn's*
> *fleet of five ships*
> *steered, steadfast in anger*
> *against Karl's sea-goers.*

Ships grappled
together; gore, as foes fell,
bathed stiff iron, black
with Scots' blood;
singing the bows spilt
blood, steel bit; bright
though the quick points quaked,
no quenching Thorfinn.

So Earl Thorfinn gave fierce encouragement to his men, edging his ship close up to Karl's. As the fighting grew savage, before the mast of the King's ship, the Scots began to offer little resistance and Earl Thorfinn thrust his way from the forecastle to the stern. When he saw the ranks thinning out, he shouted for his followers to come and join him aboard. King Karl saw what was happening and ordered his own men to cut the ropes and sail off, but just at that moment Thorfinn and his crew managed to grapple the King's ship with their own hooks and Thorfinn called on them to carry his banner aboard. He followed close behind with a large band of men. Karl jumped overboard with the rest of the survivors from his ship, but most of the crew had already been killed. Karl managed to scramble onto another ship and ordered the crew to start pulling away: so the Scots were routed, with Thorfinn and his men chasing after them. In the words of Arnor:

Long the loud war
-thunder, the spear-lunge;
though few, my lord's force
made his foes fly
while, over the wounded (once
sword-washers), the war-bird
screamed: south of Sandwick
shone the lord's battle-sun.

Karl retreated south to the Moray Firth, where he went ashore and began to gather fresh forces.

After the battle Thorfinn travelled back home and Thorkel the Fosterer came to join him there. Their combined army was a large one. They sailed south to the Moray Firth after Karl and his men and once they reached Scotland they began plundering. Then they learned that Muddan was north at Thurso in Caithness with a strong force of men. He had sent for troops from Ireland, where he had a good many friends and kinsmen, but he was still waiting for the reinforcements to arrive.

Thorfinn and his men decided that Thorkel the Fosterer should go north to Caithness with some of their troops while Thorfinn lay at anchor off Scotland and carried on plundering there. Thorkel was able to travel in secrecy for all the people of Caithness were faithful and loyal to him. As a result, there was no news of his movements until one night he turned up in Thurso, seized the house Muddan was in, and set fire to it. Muddan was asleep in an upstairs-room and as he jumped off the balcony Thorkel took a swing at his neck, slicing off his head. After that some of Muddan's men surrendered while others ran off and escaped. A good many were killed there, though plenty were given quarter.

Thorkel stayed there a short while, then went back to the Moray Firth, taking with him all the troops from Caithness, Sutherland and Ross. He joined up with Earl Thorfinn south in Moray and told him all about his excursion. The Earl thanked him warmly for what he had done and they spent some time there, raiding and plundering.

Now we come back to King Karl. After the battle with Earl Thorfinn he travelled south to Scotland for fresh troops, both in the east and the west as far south as Kintyre. The forces Muddan had sent for from Ireland came and joined up with him. The whole of this army he led against Earl Thorfinn. They faced each other at Tarbet Ness on the south side of the Moray Firth. The Scots had the larger force of men and, as the battle raged, Thorfinn marched before his ranks, a golden helmet on his head, a sword at his waist, wielding a great spear in both hands. People agree that he went ahead of all his troops. To begin with he led an attack on the Irish column. Thorfinn and his men were so relentless, the Irish fell back at once and never recovered the ground they lost. Next, Karl had his banner carried forward against Thorfinn, but the hard fight which followed ended with Karl on the run. Some people say he was killed there, but this is how Arnor the Earl's-Poet describes the affair:

Well the red weapons
fed wolves at Tarbet Ness,
young the commander who
created that Monday-combat.
Slim blades sang there
south on Oykel's bank;

fresh for the fray, he
outfaced the Scots' king.

High in hand, his
spear held against Irishmen,
he pressed home his point,
Shetland's prince, in battle.
Raised high as shield,
-rim was his reputation,
Hlodvir's kin; keen warriors
he captured in combat.

Earl Thorfinn chased them deep into Scotland, then marched through much of the country, conquering all the way south as far as Fife, and laid the region under his rule. Wherever he went, people surrendered to him. In Fife, he decided to send Thorkel the Fosterer back north with some of the troops. When the Scots heard that the Earl had divided his army, some of those who had sworn him allegiance rebelled against him. As soon as the Earl heard of the treachery he called his troops together and set out to face the rebels. The Scots were slow to attack once they realised that the Earl was ready for them, so he set about them quickly and, lacking the courage to defend themselves, the Scots ran, scattering in all directions into the brakes and forests. When the earl had routed the Scots he called his troops together and told them he planned to raze the whole of the district where they happened to be at the time and so pay back the Scots for their treachery and their enmity. At that the Earl's men went from village to village, burning everywhere so that not a single cottage was left standing. They killed all the adult men they could find, and the women and old people ran off into the brakes and forests. The Earl's troops took a great many captives and herded them off like cattle: in the words of Arnor the Earl's-Poet.

Shattered were the Scots'
settlements that fear-day.
Thatch smoked, fire
flared over fields.
The true prince took
payment for treachery,
thrice in one short
summer he struck them.

Next Earl Thorfinn made his way north through Scotland back to his ships, conquering wherever he went. He travelled north as far as Caithness and spent winter there. After that he used to lead expeditions to plunder in the west every summer, but over winter he would take things easy. He made something of a name for himself in Orkney by feasting his men, and others too, people of great reputation, on meat and drink throughout the winter, in the same way that kings and earls in other lands would entertain their followers around Christmas, so there was no need for anyone to search for taverns. In the words of Arnor the Earls'-Poet,

> *Through serpent-sleep*
> *of winter, the splendid son*
> *of Rognvald drank his*
> *draughts, glory-drenched.*

It was around this time that Earl Brusi died and then Earl Thorfinn took over the whole of Orkney.

21. ROGNVALD IN RUSSIA

Now we come back to Rognvald Brusason. He took part in the Battle of Stiklestad in which King Olaf the Saint was killed, but Rognvald got away along with other fugitives. He rescued from the battle King Olaf's brother, Harald Sigurdarson, who was badly wounded. Rognvald left him with a peasant to recover from his wounds and travelled east over the Kjolen Mountains to Jamtland, and on from there to Sweden where he met King Onund. Harald stayed with the peasant until his wounds were healed, then with the peasant's son as guide he made his way east to Jamtland and from there to Sweden, travelling secretly. Harald made this verse while they were riding through a thicket:

> *From copse to copse I crawl*
> *and creep now, worthless:*
> *who knows how highly*
> *I'll be heralded one day.*

In Sweden Harald went to see Rognvald Brusason. Then they travelled east together to Russia along with many of the troops who had been with King Olaf. They kept on the move until they reached Novgorod, where King Jaroslav gave them a kindly welcome on account of the holy King Olaf. All the Norwegians joined up with Earl Eilif, the son of Earl Rognvald

Ulfsson, to take over the defences of Russia, and it was there
that Rognvald Brusason stayed when King Harald Sigurdarson
went to Byzantium, defending the country for several years
during the summer but staying in Novgorod over winter.
King Jaroslav thought very highly of him, as did everyone
else. As we said earlier, Rognvald was taller and stronger than
other men, outstandingly handsome and so talented there
wasn't a man to match him. According to Arnor the Earl's-
Poet, Rognvald fought ten pitched battles around Novgorod:

> Grown of age, Fate-guided
> to Russia, greedy for war,
> ten times for him
> teemed the arrow-storm.

When Einar Belly-Shaker and Kalf Arnason went east to
Russia looking for Magnus Olafsson, they came upon Rognvald
in Ladoga Town. Just as Rognvald was about to set on Kalf,
Einar explained why they had come, that Kalf repented of
his crime of killing King Olaf the Saint and wanted to make
amends to his son Magnus. He added that Kalf wanted Magnus
to be King of Norway and would offer his support against the
Canute faction, whereupon Rognvald calmed down. Einar
suggested that Rognvald come with them to Novgorod and
argue their case before King Jaroslav. Rognvald agreed, so
they hired horses at Ladoga and made their way to see King
Jaroslav at Novgorod. They explained to him that they were
not going to put up any more with the arrogant behaviour of
Canute's followers, particularly Ælfgifu, and were ready to do
anything rather than serve them any longer. Then they asked
King Jaroslav to let King Olaf's son Magnus rule them. Their
request was supported by Rognvald, Queen Ingigerd and
many others, but the King wasn't very keen to hand Magnus
over to the Norwegians, in view of the way they had treated
Magnus' father, the holy King Olaf. All the same, after the
eleven greatest men among the Norwegians had sworn King
Jaroslav oaths that they were acting in good faith, that is
what was agreed. Rognvald was supposed to be the twelfth to
swear the oath, but Jaroslav had so much confidence in him
that he was exempted from taking it. Kalf swore Magnus an
oath that he would stay by his side at home and abroad
and do whatever Magnus wanted to strengthen his kingdom
and its independence.

After that the Norwegians made Magnus their king and

swore him their allegiance. Kalf and Magnus stayed in
Novgorod till after Christmas, then travelled to Ladoga and
got some ships there. In the spring as soon as the ice melted
they set out on their voyage. Rognvald Brusason travelled
west with King Magnus, first of all to Sweden as reported in
King Magnus' Saga, then to Jamtland, and from there west
across the Kjolen Mountains to Verdale. When Magnus arrived
in Trondheim Province, everyone there swore him allegiance.
He went to Trondheim and at the Eyrar Assembly he was
formally declared king over the whole country. After that his
relations with King Svein followed the course described in the
Lives of the Kings of Norway.

When Rognvald Brusason arrived in Norway he was told
that his father had died and that Earl Thorfinn had taken
over all the islands. Rognvald wanted badly to visit his
inherited lands and asked King Magnus for leave to go there.
The King could see how important this was to Rognvald and
he promised him his full support. He gave Rognvald the title
of earl and three fully-equipped longships and added to this
the third of Orkney in fee, which King Olaf had owned and
had granted to Rognvald's father Brusi. King Magnus
promised his true friendship to Rognvald and said that he
would have his support whenever he needed it: and so they
parted, the very best of friends.

22. ROGNVALD AND THORFINN

Earl Rognvald Brusason sailed west to Orkney, went at once
to the estates his father had owned and sent a message to his
uncle Earl Thorfinn claiming the third of the islands that had
belonged to his father. Moreover, he added, King Magnus had
granted him in fee the third of Orkney that had belonged to
King Olaf, so that he was making claim not just to one-third,
but two, and wanted his uncle Earl Thorfinn to recognise this.
Now, at that time Thorfinn was having a great deal of trouble
with the Hebrideans and the Irish and needed reinforcements
badly, so in his reply he told the messengers that Rognvald
ought certainly to take control of that third of the islands
which was his by right.

'But,' he said, 'the other third, the part King Magnus claims,
is a different matter. The reason we agreed to King Olaf's
claim of ownership was because we were entirely in his hands,
not because we thought he had any right to it. The best way
to preserve peace between my nephew Rognvald and myself

will be to keep quiet about that part of the islands, for the argument about it has been going on far too long. However, if my kinsman Rognvald will be loyal and support me, as our relationship demands, I think that part of the earldom would be in good hands if he were to have control over it, as a pleasure to himself and a source of strength to us both. His help is worth more to me than any taxes I collect there.'

The messengers went back and told Earl Rognvald that Thorfinn had agreed to let him have two-thirds of the islands on condition that he would give Thorfinn his support and acknowledge their bonds of kinship, as was proper for them both. Rognvald said that he thought his claim had been for no more than belonged to him, but since Thorfinn had given up rule over the islands so readily, he would certainly grant him all the help and honest friendship that their kinship demanded.

Rognvald now had firm possession of two-thirds of the islands and throughout winter that was the way things stood. But early in the spring Earl Thorfinn sent word to his nephew Rognvald asking him to join a raiding expedition, along with as many men as he could muster. Once Rognvald got the message he wasted no time, but gathered a strong force and all the ships he could find. As soon as they were prepared, he set off to join Earl Thorfinn, who also had his troops equipped and ready. He gave his nephew a friendly welcome and they went into partnership.

During the summer Thorfinn and Rognvald raided in the Hebrides, in Ireland, and over a wide area in the west of Scotland. Everywhere they went, Thorfinn laid the land under his rule. That summer they fought a fierce battle at a place called Loch Vatten, in which a great many men were killed. The battle was a short one, and the Earl and his nephew won a brilliant victory. Arnor the Earl's-Poet refers to it:

> *At Loch Vatten my leader*
> *left marks of lordhood;*
> *great perils I passed through*
> *with that warrior-prover.*
> *Sharply from the ships*
> *was borne the shieldwall,*
> *over the wounded, agape,*
> *walked the grey wolf.*

After the battle they came back to Orkney and spent a quiet winter there. This was how things were for eight years, with Earl Rognvald ruling over two-thirds of the islands in a way Earl Thorfinn could not fault. Every summer they went on raiding expeditions, sometimes together, sometimes separately. In the words of Arnor:

> *The warrior laid waste*
> *now the Welsh, now the Irish,*
> *now feasted the Scots*
> *with fire and flame.*

Whenever the kinsmen met they got on well together, though when troublemakers tried to stir matters up between them it often led to bad feeling. Earl Thorfinn resided most of the time in Caithness while Earl Rognvald remained in the islands.

23. RAIDERS IN ENGLAND

One summer Earl Thorfinn went raiding in the Hebrides and in various parts of Scotland. He himself lay at anchor off Galloway where Scotland borders on England, but he sent some of his troops south to raid the English coast, as the people had driven all their livestock out of his reach. When the English realised that the vikings had arrived, they gathered together, made a counter-attack, recovered all that had been stolen and killed every able-bodied man among them except for a few they sent back to tell Thorfinn this was how they discouraged the vikings from their raids and looting. The message was put in distinctly abusive terms.

The messengers went to Earl Thorfinn and told him how badly things had turned out. The Earl was none too happy about his men being killed but said there was nothing to be done about it, though he added that, if the English were to be paid back for their mockery and abuse, he was the man to do it and, though they had to part for the time being, as long as he was still alive the following summer they would surely be meeting again.

24. REVENGE ON THE ENGLISH

At the time, Hardicanute ruled both England and Denmark. After the defeat, Earl Thorfinn sailed to Orkney and spent the winter there, but early in the spring he raised a levy throughout his earldom. He also sent word to his nephew Rognvald, asking him for help, and Rognvald agreed to give it, mustering forces in every part of his own earldom, while Thorfinn gathered troops in the rest of Orkney and in Caithness. Large numbers of Scots and Irish flocked to join him as well as a good many from all over the Hebrides and, as he had threatened, he led these troops against the English. Hardicanute was in Denmark at the time. As soon as the Earls landed in England they began pillaging and looting. The commanders in charge of England's defences marched their troops against them and there was a hard, fierce battle, but the Earls of Orkney won the day. After that they ravaged far and wide throughout England, killing, looting and burning wherever they went, as Arnor says:

> The English will ever
> remember this edge-storm;
> no greater ring-giver
> ever roamed with war-guard.
> Keenly the slender swords
> cut down Old Rognvald's kin;
> south of Man, staunch
> the step of the warriors.

> Against England the Earl
> urged his banner;
> oft his war-band
> blooded the hawk-beak:
> fire shrank the halls
> as the folk ran, flame
> ravaged, smoke reared
> reeking skyward.

> Through forts the famed one
> went fearless to the fight-throng,
> many a horn howling, but
> high his banner.
> Nothing weakened the warriors
> of the wolf-lord; war
> dawned then, steel dazzled,
> wolves dined on the dead.

Earl Thorfinn fought two pitched battles in England, along with many more sorties and killings. After spending most of the summer there, he went back to Orkney in the autumn and stayed there over winter.

25. THE EARLS FALL OUT

It was about this time that Kalf Arnason had to flee abroad to escape from King Magnus. He sailed west over the sea to Earl Thorfinn, who was married to his niece Ingibjorg the Earls'-Mother, daughter of Earl Finn Arnason. Kalf and Earl Thorfinn were very close.

Kalf had a large following which placed a heavy burden on the Earl's finances. Plenty of people told him that he shouldn't let Rognvald have two-thirds of the islands, considering his heavy outlay. Soon after that he sent messengers to the islands, claiming from Rognvald the third which had once belonged to Earl Einar Wry-Mouth. When Rognvald heard this he talked things over with his friends, then called in Earl Thorfinn's envoys and told them that the third they were claiming had been given him in fee by King Magnus, who regarded it as a part of his own patrimony. It was up to King Magnus, he said, to decide which parts of the islands each of the Earls should have and he was not going to surrender his portion while King Magnus wanted him to keep it.

With that the envoys went home and gave Earl Thorfinn the message, adding that in their opinion he was never going to win his claim without a fight. When he heard this, Thorfinn flew into a rage and said it was absurd that his brother's inheritance should belong to King Magnus. The only reason they had agreed to that, he said, was because they'd been in King Olaf's clutches at the time, and it was no proper way to share out the inheritance.

'If I'm to lose my brother's inheritance unless I fight for it,' he said, 'then it's a poor way for Rognvald to repay the favour I did him, letting him rule the land all this time.'

He was in such a fury that soon afterwards he sent men to the Hebrides and south to Scotland to gather forces. He would lead his troops against Earl Rognvald, he declared, and lay claim without mercy to whatever he could not win peacefully.

When Earl Rognvald was told about this, he called his friends together and complained that his uncle Earl Thorfinn meant to lead an army against him and start a war. He asked them what support they would give him and told them that he was not going to give up his possessions without a fight. When he asked for their advice there was a wide difference of opinion. Some agreed with Earl Rognvald and said he had good reasons for not wanting to divide his earldom. But others argued that it would only be fair for Thorfinn to

control what had once belonged to Earl Einar, even though
Rognvald had been ruling it for some time. They added that
it would be unwise of Rognvald to fight Thorfinn, since he
could only collect his forces in two thirds of Orkney, whereas
Thorfinn had not only the remaining third, but Caithness,
most of Scotland, and all the Hebrides as well. Other people
wanted to arrange a settlement, suggesting that in order to
bring the two earls to terms Rognvald should offer Thorfinn
half of the islands.

Rognvald saw that everyone had his own ideas about it,
though none of them wanted him to risk making war. All the
same, he declared his own intention. Rather than agree to
the division of the earldom, he would give it up and go to his
foster-brother, King Magnus, to find out how far the King
would support him in getting it back.

After that he got ready for the voyage and sailed east
non-stop until he came to King Magnus. Without delay he
explained how matters stood. The King gave him a friendly
welcome and invited him to stay as long as he wanted,
offering him as much land in fee as he needed to support
himself and his men in comfort. Earl Rognvald told the King
he would like his help in getting back the earldom and King
Magnus agreed gladly to do whatever he wished.

Earl Rognvald stayed in Norway for only a short time, then
made his way back to Orkney with a large well-equipped
army supplied by King Magnus. He also brought a message to
Kalf Arnason that he could have back his estates in Norway
and the right to live there, provided he backed Earl Rognvald
against Earl Thorfinn.

26. A SEA BATTLE

Earl Rognvald put out from Norway and sailed west towards
Orkney. He landed first in Shetland, gathered forces there,
then sailed south to Orkney where he called together his
friends and recruited more men. Earl Thorfinn, who was in
Caithness, soon got word of Rognvald's return and gathered
troops in Scotland and the Hebrides. Earl Rognvald passed
on King Magnus' message to Kalf Arnason, who seemed satisfied with the conditions laid down by the King.

Earl Rognvald collected together his forces in Orkney,
planning to sail to Caithness, and when he reached the
Pentland Firth he had thirty large ships. Then he came face
to face with Thorfinn, who had sixty ships, most of them quite

small. They met off Roberry and at once the fighting started. Kalf Arnason came up with six large ships but kept out of the battle. Each of the Earls encouraged his men as the fighting grew fierce, but soon Thorfinn began to suffer heavy losses, mostly because the ships in the two fleets differed so much in size. He himself had a big ship, well fitted-out, and he used it vigorously in attack, but once his smaller ships had been put out of action, his own was flanked by the enemy and his crew placed in a dangerous situation, many of them being killed and others badly wounded. Earl Rognvald kept urging his men to board Thorfinn's ship, but, realising the danger he was in, Thorfinn ordered his crew to cut the grappling ropes and row ashore. There he had seventy bodies carried off the ship and he ordered ashore those too badly wounded to fight. He asked Arnor the Earl's-Poet, who was a member of his crew, to leave as well, for he was very fond of him, and Arnor went, making this verse:

> *Straight and sure,*
> *true service to one's lord—*
> *unwilling, this one,*
> *to war with Brusi's son:*
> *awkward our choice*
> *when Earls are eager*
> *to fight—friendship*
> *is far from easy.*

Earl Thorfinn crewed his ship with the best men he had left, then went to Kalf and asked for his help, saying that ever since Kalf had been forced to leave Norway he had lost all chance of buying back the friendship of King Magnus.

'Even when you were on the friendliest of terms with him,' said Thorfinn, 'you couldn't protect yourself. You must see, if Rognvald gets the better of me and joins up with King Magnus as a power on this side of the North Sea, you'll hardly be welcome here; but if the victory's mine, you'll never go short of anything that I can provide. The two of us together needn't be afraid of anyone here in the west, as long as we're of one mind. And you won't want people to think that while I was fighting for both our freedoms, you were skulking here like a cat in a cave. The family bonds holding us together demand that each of us give the other all the aid he can, particularly now that we're up against outsiders too.'

After Kalf had listened to the Earl's arguments he called his

men together and told them to fight for Thorfinn. Here is
what Bjarni the Gold-Brow-Poet said:

> *I heard how you closed,*
> *Kalf, with Finn's kinsman,*
> *sailed your ships-of-war*
> *straight at his fleet;*
> *keen to kill, you*
> *crashed upon Brusi's kin;*
> *helpful, your hate,*
> *when you upheld Thorfinn.*

Earl Thorfinn and Kalf told their men to put their backs
into the rowing, but by the time they reached the scene of
action a great many of Thorfinn's troops were dead, and the
rest were about to run for their lives. Thorfinn sailed his ship
right up to Rognvald's in the thick of the fighting. Here are
the words of Arnor:

> *I saw both my benefactors*
> *battering the other's men*
> *—fierce was my grief—*
> *fighting on the Firth.*
> *The sea bled, streamed dark*
> *on the plank-nails, sobbing*
> *with blood on the bulwark*
> *-shields of the boat.*

Kalf attacked the smaller ships of Rognvald's fleet and it
did not take him long to clear their decks, since his own stood
so much higher. When the troops levied in Norway saw the
ships next to them being put out of action, they loosed their
ships from the ropes that had been holding them together
and took to flight, leaving only a few in support of Rognvald's
ship. That was the turning point of the battle, for as Arnor the
Earl's-Poet says:

> *He could have conquered,*
> *and claimed that old country,*
> *lost fewer lives,*
> *the leader, in that battle,*
> *had the Earl, sea-lord's kin,*
> *had an army of islanders,*
> *fighters from Shetland—*
> *his forces failed him.*

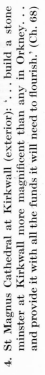

4. St Magnus Cathedral at Kirkwall (exterior): '... build a stone minster at Kirkwall more magnificent than any in Orkney... and provide it with all the funds it will need to flourish.' (Ch. 68)

5. St Magnus Cathedral (interior): 'Not long after that, the ground-plan of St Magnus' Church was drawn up and builders hired for the work. So rapidly did the building progress that more was done in the first year than in the two or three that followed.' (Ch. 76)

6. Orphir Church: 'Earl Paul made preparations for a great Christmas feast at his estate called Orphir . . . There was a great drinking-hall at Orphir, with a door in the south wall near the eastern gable, and in front of the hall, just a few paces down from it, stood a fine church.' (Ch. 66)

7. Mousa Broch, Shetland: 'Erland raised a force of men, abducted Margaret from Orkney, took her north to Shetland and settled down in the Broch at Mousa. . . .' (Ch. 93)

Now that the main part of Rognvald's fleet was on the run, Kalf and Earl Thorfinn made a joint attack on his ship, killing a number of his men. Seeing the desperate situation he was in and that he could never defeat the combined strength of Thorfinn and Kalf, Rognvald ordered the grappling ropes to be cut and made a run for it. This was late in the day and it was beginning to grow dark. That same night Rognvald made straight for the open sea and sailed east to Norway without a break until he came to King Magnus. The King gave him a friendly welcome, as he had done before, and invited Rognvald to stay with him: and for a while, that is what Rognvald did.

27. PREPARATIONS

Coming back now to Earl Thorfinn, the morning after the battle he sent men to scour all the islands in search of fugitives, killing a good many of them, though some gave themselves up and were given quarter. Thorfinn laid all the islands under his rule and ordered everyone to pay him allegiance, including those who had sworn oaths of fealty to Rognvald. After that he took up residence in Orkney, though since he had a large following he had to send to Caithness for provisions. He had Kalf Arnason go and stay in the Hebrides to make sure of his authority there.

After Rognvald had spent some time with King Magnus in Norway, he told the King that he wanted to go back to Orkney. The King heard him out, but then advised him against taking the risk until winter had passed, the ice had melted and the sea was navigable. After that, he said, he would provide Rognvald with all the ships and men he might need. In reply Rognvald said that he wanted to avoid sacrificing the King's men, for if he attacked Thorfinn and Kalf with a large army their position in the islands was too strong for him to succeed without heavy loss of life.

'I've made up my mind to sail with a single ship,' he said, 'and the best crew I can get. My hope is that there'll be no news of me until I arrive. Things will then go one of two ways: either we'll take them by surprise and win what we'd never have managed with a whole army, or else, if people find out about us, we can still put our trust in the open sea.'

King Magnus said he could go if he wanted and come back

whenever he liked. After that, Rognvald got his ship ready.
All his men were hand-picked so he had a very fine crew,
including several of the King's retainers. As soon as they were
ready they put to sea. It was early in winter.

28. THORFINN'S NARROW ESCAPE

Earl Rognvald put in at Shetland, where he learned that
Thorfinn was in Orkney with quite a small force, no trouble
being expected in the middle of winter: so Rognvald went
straight to Orkney. Earl Thorfinn was on Mainland, suspecting
nothing. As soon as Rognvald had landed he set out for the
place where he had been told Thorfinn was staying and took
him completely by surprise. The first Thorfinn and his men
knew about it was that the attackers had blocked every door
of the house. It was night-time and most of the men had gone
to sleep, but the Earl was still drinking. Rognvald and his
men set fire to the house, and when Thorfinn realised what was
happening, he sent some of his men to the door to ask who
was responsible. They were told Earl Rognvald had arrived.
The men ran for their weapons, but could put up no resistance
as there was no way of getting out, and soon the house was
ablaze. Thorfinn told his men to ask if they could go outside
and Rognvald agreed to allow all the womenfolk and slaves
out of doors, but said he thought that most of Earl Thorfinn's
men would be better off dead. Those who were given quarter
were helped out of the fire. The house was burning down fast
by now.

Earl Thorfinn broke out through a wooden partition-wall
and escaped carrying his wife Ingibjorg in his arms. The night
was pitch dark and he got clear under cover of the smoke
without Rognvald's men suspecting anything. That same
night Thorfinn rowed over to Caithness in a small boat.

Rognvald burned the farmhouse to ashes, along with all
those who had not been let out, and everyone was convinced
that Earl Thorfinn had perished there. After that, Rognvald
travelled to every part of the islands and laid them all under
his authority. Then he sent envoys over to Caithness and the
Hebrides claiming all the territories formerly ruled by Thorfinn. No one offered any resistance.

Thorfinn stayed secretly with friends at several places in
Caithness and there was no hint of a rumour that he had
escaped from the burning.

29. DEATH OF ROGVNALD

Earl Rognvald took up residence at Kirkwall and gathered in all the provisions he needed for the winter there. He had a great retinue and lived in grand style. Just before Christmas he went with a large band of men over to Papa Stronsay to fetch malt for the Christmas ale. After they had spent all the evening on the island, roasting themselves at the fire, the man who was looking after it said that they were running out of firewood.

Then the Earl made a slip of the tongue and this is what he said: 'We shall have aged enough when this fire burns out.' What he meant to say was that they would have baked enough. He realised his mistake immediately.

'I've never made a slip of the tongue before,' he said, 'and now I remember what my foster-father King Olaf said at Stiklestad when I pointed out a mistake of his, that I'd not have long to live if ever my own tongue made a slip. Perhaps my uncle Thorfinn is still alive after all.'

And that was the moment they realised that the house had been surrounded. Earl Thorfinn had arrived. At once his men set fire to the house, heaping a great woodpile in front of the door. Earl Thorfinn allowed everyone except Rognvald's men to leave, and then, when most of the people had been helped out, a man came to the door wearing a long nightshirt. Thorfinn told his men to give the deacon a helping hand, but the man put his hand on the pile of wood and vaulted over beyond the whole circle of men, landing some distance away, then vanished into the night. Thorfinn told his men to go after him, saying it must have been Rognvald.

'He's the only man capable of doing that,' said Thorfinn.

They set out to look for him and split up into several groups. Thorkel the Fosterer searched the shore. Suddenly they heard a dog bark among the rocks down by the sea. Rognvald was carrying his lap-dog with him and it was this that betrayed him. They killed him on the spot among the rocks. Some say Thorkel the Fosterer killed him because no one else would do it; but then, he had sworn to do anything Thorfinn believed would add to his power.

Thorfinn and his men spent the rest of the night on the island and killed every one of Rognvald's companions. In the morning they took the cargo boat, loaded it with malt, went aboard and ranged Rognvald's shields along the prow. They made sure to let no more men be seen than had gone with

Rognvald, then sailed to Kirkwall where everyone assumed it must be him and came to meet the ship, most of them unarmed. Earl Thorfinn had some thirty of them seized and put to death, mostly King Magnus' friends and retainers, but he spared the life of one, telling him to go back to King Magnus in Norway with the news.

30. EARL THORFINN AND KING MAGNUS

Rognvald's body was carried to Papa Westray for burial. Everyone agrees that of all the Earls of Orkney he was the most popular and gifted, and his death was mourned by many.

Earl Thorfinn now claimed control of the whole of Orkney and there was no one to challenge his right. News of Rognvald's death reached Norway early in the spring. King Magnus considered it a great loss and swore at once to avenge him in good time. But just then he was engaged in a major conflict with Svein Ulfsson who had recently taken the throne of Denmark. This was about the time that Magnus ceded half of the kingdom to his uncle, Harald Sigurdarson, who had just come back to Norway; and after they had been ruling jointly for a year they raised a levy of men and ships, meaning to attack Denmark. They were lying at anchor off the Sel Isles when two longships came gliding into harbour right up to King Magnus' ship. A man wearing a white-hooded cloak stepped aboard the King's ship and walked aft to the poop-deck where the King sat eating. The man greeted him with a bow, reached out for some bread, broke a piece off and ate it. The King acknowledged his greeting and, seeing him eat the bread, offered him the cup. The stranger took it and spoke.

'Mess-mate,' he said. 'Let's make a truce.'

The King looked at him. 'Who are you?' he asked.

'I'm Thorfinn Sigurdarson,' answered the man.

'You mean Earl Thorfinn?' said the King.

'That's what they call me there in the west,' he replied. 'I'm here with two ships, twenty benches apiece and fitted out with all the best I could afford. If you'll accept my help I'd like to join you in this expedition. My whole case is in God's hands and yours, my lord.'

By now, others had come up and were listening to their conversation. The King said nothing for a moment, then he made his reply.

'To tell you the truth, Thorfinn,' he said, 'I'd intended, should we ever meet as we now have, to make sure you never told the story of how we parted. But as things are, it would never do for a man in my position to have you killed, so for the present you'll stay with me and I'll tell you later on what terms we might be reconciled.'

Thorfinn took leave of the King and went back to his own ship.

For quite a long time the King lay at anchor off the Sel Isles, with more troops joining him from Oslo Fjord. As soon as he got a favourable wind he meant to set sail for Jutland. Thorfinn spent long hours talking to the King, who now treated him in a friendly fashion and, indeed, often consulted him about the plans for his campaign.

The Earl went one day aboard the King's ship and up to the poop-deck. King Magnus invited Thorfinn to sit next to him and once he was seated they began to drink and enjoy themselves. Then someone wearing a red tunic, tall and manly-looking, came up to the poop-deck and greeted the King, who responded warmly. The newcomer was one of his retainers.

'It's you I've come to see, Thorfinn,' said the man.

'What do you want with me?' Thorfinn asked.

'I want to know whether you mean to pay me for the loss of my brother,' he said. 'You had him killed at Kirkwall with more of King Magnus' men.'

'Perhaps you haven't heard,' said the Earl, 'that I'm not in the habit of paying compensation for the men I've killed. You'll learn that I seldom kill anyone without good reason.'

'I don't care how you've treated other people as long as you pay compensation for the one death I want set right. Anyway, I myself was humiliated there and I lost some of my possessions too. It's my duty to claim compensation, both for my brother and for myself, and I mean to get it. The King can forgive and forget what people do against him if he wants, as long as it doesn't worry him when his men are led out and slaughtered like sheep.'

'I see the one thing that saves me is not being in your power,' said the Earl. 'Aren't you the one I set free?'

'That I am,' said the man. 'You could have had me killed with the rest.'

'Then the old saying is true,' said the Earl, ' "Many a trap for the unwary." I never expected to suffer from being too easy on my enemies. Now I'm being paid for letting you off, but you wouldn't be abusing me in front of the King today if I'd had you killed along with your mates.'

King Magnus gave the Earl a sharp glance.

'Earl Thorfinn,' he said, 'this isn't the first time you think you killed too few of my retainers: nor the first time you failed to pay compensation.'

The King's face was flushed red as blood. Thorfinn got quickly to his feet, raced down from the poop-deck and so over to his own ship. After that things stayed quiet for the rest of the evening.

Next morning people woke to discover a favourable breeze blowing, so at once they started rowing out of the bay. The King sailed south to the Kattegat with all his ships. During the forenoon Thorfinn kept his ship well away from the shore, then towards evening altered course towards the open sea, and there's nothing to tell of him until he reached Orkney and took charge once more of his earldom.

King Magnus and Harald sailed to Denmark and spent the summer there, but King Svein wouldn't risk facing them and stayed at Skaneyr with his troops. During the summer King Magnus fell ill, and this led to his death. He made a public declaration, bequeathing the whole realm of Norway to his uncle Harald Sigurdarson.

31. PILGRIMAGE

Earl Thorfinn was now sole ruler of Orkney and the other territories he had won. Kalf Arnason never left his side. From time to time the Earl would go on viking expeditions to the west of Scotland and to Ireland and also spent some time in England as leader of the King's bodyguard.

When Thorfinn heard that King Magnus had died, he sent envoys east to King Harald in Norway with a message of goodwill, saying that he wanted the King's friendship. The King gave a favourable reply to the message and promised Thorfinn his friendship. As soon as the Earl heard the King's reply he got ready for a voyage and put to sea with two ships of twenty benches apiece and over a hundred men, all hand-picked. He sailed east to Norway and met the King in Horda-land, where Harald gave him a friendly welcome and presented him on parting with generous gifts.

From there Thorfinn sailed south along the coast all the way to Denmark where, after a land journey, he met King Svein at Aalborg. The King invited Thorfinn to stay with him and feasted him in grand style. Then Thorfinn announced his intention to visit Rome. In Saxony he met the Emperor Henry who gave him a warm welcome and many fine gifts, including a number of horses.

The Earl began his pilgrimage and travelled to Rome, had an audience with the Pope and received absolution from him for all his sins. After that Thorfinn started back home and arrived safe and well in his own earldom.

By now he was finished with piracy and devoted all his time to the government of his people and country and to the making of new laws. He had his permanent residence at Birsay, where he built and dedicated to Christ a fine minster, the seat of the first bishop of Orkney. Thorfinn was married to Ingibjorg the Earl's-Mother. They had two sons who survived childhood, one called Paul and the other Erlend, tall, handsome men, shrewd and gentle, taking rather more after their mother's side of the family. The Earl was very fond of them, as were all his people.

32. DEATH OF EARL THORFINN

Earl Thorfinn ruled all his lands till he died, and it's said on good authority that he was the most powerful of all the Earls of Orkney. He won for himself nine Scottish earldoms, along with the whole of the Hebrides and a considerable part of Ireland. In the words of Arnor the Earl's-Poet:

> *The raven-feaster ruled*
> *right from Dublin—*
> *what I say is certain*
> *—to the Giants' Skerries.*

Earl Thorfinn was just five years old when his grandfather Malcolm, King of Scots, gave him the title of earl, and for seventy years he held that rank. He died towards the end of the reign of Harald Sigurdarson and was buried at Christchurch, Birsay, the very church he had built. The Earl was greatly mourned in the lands he had inherited, though in those regions he had taken by force people thought it very oppressive to live under his rule, so most of the places he had conquered broke away and the people there looked for protection from those who held the lands by birthright. It was soon clear what a great loss his death was. These verses were composed about the battle between Earl Rognvald Brusason and Earl Thorfinn:

> *Ill-fortune followed*
> *when the Earls fought,*

many a hard lesson learned,
many a life lost;
where the spear-shower fell,
there fought our friends;
many a dear one that day
lay dead at Roberry.

The bright sun will blacken,
Heaven's bowl break
asunder, earth sink in dark
seas, mountains soar
through ocean ere
the islands bear another
like Thorfinn: help him,
Heaven, this hero.

33. EARLS AND NOBLEMEN

After Thorfinn's death his sons took over the earldom. Paul, the elder of the two, was also very much the one in charge. They did not divide the earldom and were for the most part on friendly terms. Ingibjorg the Earls'-Mother married Malcolm, King of Scots, known as Long-Neck. Their son was Duncan, King of Scots, father of William, who was a great man and whose son William the Noble every Scotsman wanted for his king.

Earl Paul Thorfinnsson married a daughter of Earl Hakon Ivarsson and they had a number of children. One was a son called Hakon, then there was a daughter, Thora, who was married in Norway to Halldor, the son of Brynjolf Camel. They had a son, also called Brynjolf, the father of Halldor who married Gudrid Dag's-Daughter. The second of Earl Paul's daughters was called Ingirid and she married Einar Vorse-Raven. Paul's third daughter was Herbjorg, the mother of Ingibjorg the High-Born, who married Sigurd of Westness. Their sons were Hakon Pike-Staff and Brynjolf. Herbjorg also had a daughter, Sigrid, who was the mother of Hakon the Child and of Herborg, whom Kolbein Heap married. The fourth daughter of Earl Paul was Ragnhild, and she was the mother of Benedikt, father of Ingibjorg, mother of Erling the Archdeacon. Ragnhild also had a daughter called Bergljot, who married Havard Gunnason, and their sons were Magnus, Hakon Claw, Dufniall and Thorstein. All these people belong to the families of the Earls and noblemen of Orkney, and will later come into our story.

Earl Erlend Thorfinnsson married a woman called Thora, the daughter of Sumarlidi Ospaksson. The mother of this Ospak was Thordis, daughter of Hall of Sida. Earl Erlend and his wife had two sons, Erling and Magnus, and two daughters, Gunnhild and Cecilia. The latter married a man called Isaac and they had two sons, Eindridi and Kol. Erlend also had a natural daughter, Jaddvor, who had a son called Borgar.

34. DEATH OF KING HARALD

Some time after the brothers Paul and Erlend began ruling in Orkney, King Harald Sigurdarson came west from Norway with a great army. He landed first in Shetland and sailed from there to Orkney, where his army grew considerably, and both Earls decided to join him. So he set off for England, leaving behind Queen Ellisif and their daughters Maria and Ingigerd. He landed in a district called Cleveland and took over Scarborough, then put in at Holderness, where he fought and won a battle.

On the Wednesday before St Matthew's Day he fought a pitched battle against the Earls Valtheof and Morcar, in which the latter was killed. On the following Sunday the stronghold which stood by Stamford Bridge surrendered to King Harald and he went ashore to occupy it, leaving behind his son Olaf, the Earls Paul and Erlend, and Eystein Heathcock, a relative of his by marriage. He was confronted on the march by the large army of King Harold Godwinson, and was killed in the battle which followed. After his fall, Eystein Heathcock and the Earls of Orkney came ashore and launched a fierce attack in which Eystein Heathcock perished along with almost the whole Norwegian contingent. When the battle was over, Harold Godwinson gave leave to Olaf, the son of Harald Sigurdson, and the Earls, to sail away from England with all the troops who had not run off. So in the autumn Olaf put out from Ravenseer and sailed to Orkney.

On the same day that King Harald was killed, indeed at the very same hour, his daughter Maria died quite suddenly, and people said of them that they shared one life. Olaf spent the winter in Orkney on the friendliest terms with the Earls, his kinsmen—their mother Ingibjorg and King Olaf's mother

Thora were cousins. In the spring Olaf sailed east to Norway,
where he was made joint-king with his brother Magnus.

For quite a long time the brothers Paul and Erlend ruled
over Orkney in harmony and goodwill, but as for their sons,
while Magnus was a quiet sort of man, Hakon and Erling
grew up to be very arrogant, though tall, strong and talented
in many ways. Hakon Paulsson wanted to be foremost among
the brothers' kin and considered himself more highly-born
than the others, being the grandson of Earl Hakon Ivarsson
and of Ragnhild, the daughter of King Magnus the Good.

In everything, Hakon wanted his friends to have a larger
share than those who sided with the Erlendssons, while
Erlend wasn't going to see his sons back down to anyone there
in the islands: so it came to a point where the cousins could no
longer see eye to eye and the whole situation was growing
ominous. The fathers did their best to bring the family
together and a meeting was arranged, but it soon became clear
that each of the Earls favoured the case of his own offspring,
and so there was no agreement. Bad feeling sprang up between
the brothers and they parted on hostile terms, which many
people considered a great pity.

35. HAKON PAULSSON GOES TO SWEDEN

Afterwards, men of goodwill stepped in and tried to bring
them together. At a meeting between the parties held on
Mainland, an agreement was reached for the division of
Orkney into two parts, just as in the time of Thorfinn and
Brusi, and so matters stood for some time.

Once Hakon had reached manhood he was always going
on raiding expeditions, growing more arrogant than ever,
particularly towards those who served Erlend and his sons.
This led to a fresh quarrel between them and they set on each
other with large numbers of men. Havard Gunnason and the
rest of the Earls' noblemen came between them with peace
terms, but Erlend and his sons would have no settlement as
long as Hakon remained in the islands. Because the Earls'
friends thought the quarrel a very serious matter they
pleaded with Hakon not to stand in the way of peace and
asked him to leave Orkney for the time being. The counsel
of good men prevailed and the two sides came to an agreement.

Hakon set out from Orkney, sailing first to Norway where
he visited King Olaf the Peaceful. This was towards the end
of Olaf's reign. Hakon stayed with him for some time, then

sailed east to Sweden where he got a good reception from King Ingi Steinkelsson. There Hakon met a number of his friends and kinsfolk and was paid the greatest respect mainly on account of his maternal grandfather Hakon Ivarsson, who had been exiled by Harald Sigurdarson but granted power in Sweden by King Steinkel, in whose opinion he stood high, as indeed he did with everyone. Hakon Ivarsson had another grandson, also called Hakon but nicknamed the Norseman, who was the father of Eirik the Wise, King of Denmark after Eirik Eymuni. For a good while Hakon Paulsson remained in Sweden with the King, who thought highly of him, but after a time he began to feel homesick for Orkney.

In Sweden, Christianity was in its infancy, so there were still a good many people practising paganism in the belief that by it they would gain wisdom and knowledge of many things yet to happen. King Ingi was a devout Christian and every heathen was abhorred by him. He made great efforts to put down the evil practices which had been for long a part of heathen worship, but other leading men and landowners grew so resentful when their barbarism was criticised that they installed another King who still adhered to the pagan rites, the Queen's brother Svein, nicknamed the Sacrificer.

On account of him, Ingi was forced into exile and went to West Gotaland, but eventually managed to trap Svein inside a house and burnt him there. After that he brought the whole country under his control and put an end to many of the barbaric practices.

36. HAKON CONSULTS A SOOTHSAYER

During his stay in Sweden, Hakon Paulsson got to hear of a certain wise man who could see into the future, though it is not known whether he used sorcery or other means. Hakon grew very curious to meet this man and see what he could learn about his destiny, so he set out to look for him and traced him eventually to one of the settlements on the coast. The wise man would go from feast to feast, telling the farmers how the season would turn out and certain other matters as well. When he got in touch with the man, Hakon asked if he would ever come to power and what kind of fortune he could expect. The soothsayer asked who he was, and Hakon gave him his name and information about his lineage, including the fact that he was a grandson of Hakon Ivarsson.

'Why do you want to consult me about your future?' the

soothsayer asked. 'Your ancestors paid little attention to people like me, as I'm sure you know. In fact it might be as well for you to learn your destiny from your kinsman Olaf the Stout, since you all have such confidence in him, though it's my opinion that he'll never condescend to tell you what you want to know, nor do I think he's the man of might you make him out to be.'

'I'm not speaking ill of him,' said Hakon. 'But I don't think I deserve to get knowledge out of him—not that he hasn't the power to give it me. The reason I've come to you is this: I don't think either of us need feel envious of the other on the ground of any particular talents or beliefs we might have.'

'I'm glad you feel you can place so much trust in me,' said the man, 'more than you and your kin give to your professed faith. It's very odd how these believers behave, fasting and keeping vigil in the hope of being told whatever it is they're so keen to know; yet for all their efforts, the more there is at stake, the less they find out. Now people such as myself, who don't load ourselves with penances can quite easily discover all the important things our friends want to know, so that they're not kept in the dark. And that's the way it will be between us two, as I'm obliged to you for showing that you'd rather learn the truth from me than from the priests King Ingi puts all his trust in. Come back in three days and then we'll see whether I can tell you any of the things you want to know.'

With that they parted. Hakon found a place to stay locally and three days later he went to see the soothsayer again. This time the man was alone in a house. When Hakon came in, the soothsayer rubbed his forehead and sighed heavily and said what an effort it had cost him to find out about what Hakon wanted to learn. Hakon replied that he wanted to hear about his destiny right away.

'If you want to know your future,' said the man, 'it will take me a long time. You're destined for great things and your life will be a source of stirring events. My feeling is that you'll end up as sole ruler of Orkney, though you'll most likely think you've waited long enough for it. I think your offspring will rule there as well, and as for the journey you're about to make west to Orkney, momentous events will result from it, matters of great consequence. During your life you'll be the cause of a crime for which you'll barely be able to atone—perhaps never—to that god you believe in. The trail of your life stretches deeper into the world than I'm able to see, but I think your bones will be laid to rest somewhere here in the

76

North. Now I've told you all I'm going to for the present.
What you make of your visit you'll have to decide for yourself.'

'You've told me some remarkable things,' said Hakon, 'that
is, if they're right. But I think my life may turn out better
than you've predicted. Maybe your vision isn't all that true.'

The soothsayer told him he could believe whatever he liked,
but that everything would happen as predicted.

37. NEWS FROM ORKNEY

After that, Hakon went back to King Ingi, but stayed only a
short while, then asked the King's leave to go abroad. First
he went to Norway to see his kinsman King Magnus, who gave
him a warm welcome. While he was there news arrived from
Orkney that Earl Erlend and his sons had control of everything
there and were on good terms with everyone, while his father
Paul took little part in governing the earldom.

Hakon gathered from those islandmen he had best reason to
trust, that the people of Orkney, who had been enjoying peace
and quiet for a long time, were not at all keen for him to go
there. They were afraid that if Hakon were to turn up, bad
feeling and violence would be the result. He thought the
matter over and came to the conclusion that, were he to
arrive there without a large force of men, his kinsman would
most likely defend their lands against him and his life would
be in danger. So he decided to ask King Magnus for help in
bringing him to power in Orkney.

38. PERSUASION

All this happened after King Magnus had Steigar-Thori and
Egil put to death and had freed the land from all such
troubles. Hakon was shrewd enough to gather from conversation with Magnus that he was an ambitious man and greedy
for power in other lands. So Hakon put it to him that it would
be a princely thing to do if he were to take an army abroad,
plundering and conquering in Orkney just as Harald Fine-
Hair had done. If King Magnus were to gain control of the
Hebrides, added Hakon, it would be easy for him to raid
from there in Ireland and Scotland and, once these western
regions were his, he could get reinforcements from Norway and
lead an army against the English.

'And that's how you can take revenge for your grandfather, Harald Sigurdarson,' said Hakon.

As they talked the scheme over, Hakon could see that it appealed to Magnus, who remarked that Hakon had spoken well, like a true leader, and that his words had been very much to the King's liking.

'But bear this in mind, Hakon,' he added, 'should I let myself be persuaded by your arguments to undertake this western expedition, don't be surprised at how harshly I deal with countries there: I mean to treat them all alike.'

When Hakon heard the King's last words he didn't like the sound of them at all, and wondered what lay behind them. After that he stopped urging the King to set off on any expeditions, not that Magnus needed much persuasion at this point, for immediately after this conversation he sent out an order to all parts of his kingdom levying men to go abroad and made it known publicly that he planned to lead these troops overseas to the west no matter what might happen. All through the land, men got ready for the campaign. King Magnus took his son Sigurd with him on the expedition, a mature lad for his eight years.

39. THE BATTLE OF THE MENAI STRAIT

When King Magnus sailed west from Norway, the brothers Paul and Erlend were ruling over Orkney. The King had a large army, with a good many landholders in his retinue, including Vidkunn Jonsson, Sigurd Hranason, Serk of Sogn, Dag Eilifsson, Skopti of Giske, Ogmund, Finn, Thord, Eyvind Elbow the King's marshal, Kali, son of Sæbjorn, son of Thorleif the Wise who was maimed by Hallfred, and Kali's son, Kol. Kali was a great sage, a fine poet and very close to the King.

As soon as King Magnus arrived in Orkney he seized the Earls, Paul and Erlend, sent them east to Norway, and made his own son Sigurd overlord of the islands with regents to govern the earldom. Magnus went on to the Hebrides and with him the Earls' sons, Hakon Paulsson and the Erlendssons, Magnus and Erling. As soon as King Magnus landed in the Hebrides he attacked and took control of Lewis. In the course of the expedition he took over the whole of the Hebrides and captured Logmann, the son of Godrod, King of the Western Isles.

From there he sailed south to the coast of Wales and fought a fierce battle in the Menai Strait against two Welsh earls, Hugh the Stout and Hugh the Proud. When the troops were getting their weapons ready for battle, Magnus Erlendsson settled down in the main cabin and refused to arm himself. The King asked him why he was sitting around and his answer was that he had no quarrel with anyone there.

'That's why I've no intention of fighting,' he said.

'If you haven't the guts to fight,' said the King, 'and in my opinion this has nothing to do with your Faith, get below. Don't lie there under everybody's feet.'

Magnus Erlendsson took out his psalter and chanted psalms throughout the battle, but refused to take cover.

It was a long, hard battle, fought first with bows, then hand-to-hand. For a good while no one could tell which way the tide would turn. King Magnus was using a handbow and there was another archer with him, from Halogaland. Hugh the Proud was putting up a brave fight, and was so well-armoured that only his eyes were exposed, so King Magnus suggested to the archer that they should both shoot at Hugh together, and that is what they did. One arrow struck Hugh's nose-guard, but the other entered the eyehole and pierced his head, and there Hugh the Proud fell. The King got the credit for it.

The Welsh lost a great many troops and in the end they had to run. King Magnus had won a famous victory, but many brave men of his had been killed and a good many wounded. This verse was made about the battle:

> *As blood beat on helms*
> *so did blades on breastplates:*
> *the bow of Agder's prince*
> *was bravely bent.*
> *On shields the arrow-storm*
> *spattered; as men fell,*
> *deftly the lord of Hordar*
> *dealt the earl's death-blow.*

After this King Magnus took possession of Anglesey, which lies as far south as any region ever ruled by the former Kings of Norway and comprises a third part of Wales. Kali Sæbjarnarson received a good many wounds, but none of them immediately fatal. Then King Magnus sailed back north, hugging the coast of Scotland.

40. MAGNUS ERLENDSSON ESCAPES

King Magnus had made Magnus Erlendsson his cup-bearer and he used to serve at the King's table, but after the Battle of the Menai Strait, King Magnus took an intense dislike to him and said he had behaved like a coward. One night when King Magnus' fleet was lying at anchor off the Scottish coast, Magnus Erlendsson saw a good chance of getting away and escaped from the King's ship. He prepared his bunk so that it looked as if someone were sleeping in it, then slipped overboard and swam ashore. As soon as he got there he began running towards a wood, wearing nothing but his underclothes, stumbling and scratching himself badly as he had no shoes on. When he could walk no further, he climbed up into the branches of a great tree, bound up one of his feet and hid there in the branches for some time.

In the morning, as the King's men were sitting at breakfast aboard his ship, the King asked where Magnus Erlendsson was: still asleep in his bunk, they told him. The King ordered someone to go and wake him, saying that they'd find sleep wasn't the only reason he was lying longer in bed than the rest of them. The man who went to his berth found him gone, so the King told his men to make a search and ordered the bloodhounds to be released. The dogs were set loose, took the scent immediately, raced to the wood and stopped under the oak-tree where Magnus was hiding. One of the hounds ran in a circle round the tree, baying. Magnus had a stick in his hand and threw it at the dog, catching it on the flank. The bloodhound put its tail between its legs and fled back to the ship with all the other dogs following. The King's men could find no trace of Magnus, who managed to hide in the forest for some time. Eventually he emerged and later became one of the retainers of King Malcolm of Scotland with whom he stayed quite a while, spending periods in Wales from time to time with a certain bishop and in various places with friends in England. As long as King Magnus was alive, Magnus Erlendsson did not go back to Orkney.

41. KING MAGNUS IN THE HEBRIDES

King Magnus was making his way north along the Scottish coast when messengers from King Malcolm of Scotland came to offer him a settlement: King Malcolm would let him have all the islands off the west coast which were separated by water navigable by a ship with the rudder set. When King Magnus reached Kintyre he had a skiff hauled across the narrow neck of land at Tarbert, with himself sitting at the helm, and this is how he won the whole peninsula. Kintyre is thought to be more valuable than the best of the Hebridean islands, though not as good as the Isle of Man. It juts out from the west of Scotland, and the isthmus connecting it to the mainland is so narrow that ships are regularly hauled across. From there, King Magnus sailed to the Hebrides and sent some of his men over to the Minch. They were to row close to the shore, some northwards, others south, and that is how he claimed all the islands west of Scotland.

Then the King declared that he was going to spend winter in the Hebrides, but those whom he thought had the most urgent reasons could go home. Hearing this, his men grew eager to get back and kept grumbling about having to stay abroad. The King had a word with his counsellors, then went to visit the wounded. He came to Kali Sæbjarnarson and asked him about his wounds. Kali said they were not healing too well and that he had no idea of how things would turn out. The King asked him his advice.

'Isn't it true that your friends are abandoning you?' asked Kali.

The King said he didn't think so. Kali advised him to call his troops together for a roll-call and, when the King did so, he found there were a good many absentees. He told Kali about this, and Kali said:

> How are princely gifts repaid
> by your powerful friends?
> Westward our craft's timbers
> creak, my King.

The King replied:

> I wasted all my wealth
> on these wanton fools;
> seaward let my cold keel
> climb, ill-companioned.

After that the King kept a sharp look-out for men who wanted to go away and, apart from those who had gone already, no one was allowed to leave. During his stay in the Hebrides, King Magnus arranged the betrothal of Bjadmunja, daughter of King Myrkjartan of Connaught, to his son Sigurd. The boy was nine years old at the time and the girl five.

That winter, Kali Sæbjarnarson died of his wounds. His kinsman Sigurd Sneis, a landholder in Agder, had been killed in the Battle of the Menai Strait.

42. DEATHS OF EARLS PAUL AND ERLEND

Early in the spring, King Magnus put out from the Hebrides and sailed first to Orkney, where he heard that Earl Erlend had died and been buried at Trondheim. Earl Paul was buried at Bergen.

Later that spring in Orkney, King Magnus gave Earl Erlend's daughter Gunnhild in marriage to Kol, son of Kali Sæbjarnarson, in compensation for the death of his father. Her dowry consisted of some property in Orkney including a farm at Paplay.

According to some people, Erling, the son of Earl Erlend, was killed in the Battle of the Menai Strait, but Snorri Sturluson says he met his death with King Magnus in Ulster.

Kol Kalason became one of the King's landholders and travelled with him east to Norway, where he and his wife Gunnhild settled down on his estate at Agder. They had two children, a son called Kali and a daughter Ingirid, both very promising youngsters and lovingly brought up.

43. DEATH OF KING MAGNUS

After ruling Norway for nine years, King Magnus sailed west over the sea to plunder in Ireland. He spent the winter in Connaught and was killed the following summer in Ulster, on St Bartholomew's Day. As soon as the news of his father's death reached Sigurd in Orkney, he set out for Norway where he was accepted as joint ruler along with his brothers Eystein and Olaf. He left the daughter of the Irish king behind in Orkney.

A year or two after King Magnus was killed, Hakon Paulsson came to Norway from Orkney and the Kings gave him the title of earl, as well as all the authority pertaining to his birthright. Then he went back west and took over power in Orkney. As long as King Magnus had been alive, Hakon had always been his follower and went with the King on a campaign to Gotaland in the east, as described in a poem on Hakon Paulsson.

44. ORKNEY DIVIDED AGAIN

Shortly after Earl Hakon came to power in Orkney, Magnus the son of Earl Erlend returned north from Scotland to claim his inheritance. The farmers were pleased, Magnus being well-liked.

He also had many friends and kinsmen there who were very keen that he should rule the earldom. His mother was married at the time to a man called Sigurd and their son was Hakon Karl: they had a farm at Paplay.

When Earl Hakon heard that Earl Magnus had come to the islands he gathered a force of men and refused to give up the land. But friends intervened to settle their differences, and so it was arranged that, subject to the approval of the King of Norway, Hakon would give up half the earldom. Magnus set off at once east to Norway and met King Eystein, since Sigurd was' away at the time visiting the Holy Land. King Eystein gave him a friendly welcome and handed over to him his patrimony, half of Orkney and the title of earl. Then Magnus sailed west over the sea to his earldom and was well received by friends, kinsmen and all. He and Hakon got on excellently together with the aid of well-wishers, and there was peace and goodwill in Orkney as long as their friendship lasted.

45. AN APPRECIATION OF ST MAGNUS

St Magnus, Earl of Orkney, was a man of extraordinary distinction, tall, with a fine, intelligent look about him. He was a man of strict virtue, successful in war, wise, eloquent, generous and magnanimous, open-handed with money and sound with advice, and altogether the most popular of men. He was gentle and agreeable when talking to men of wisdom and goodwill, but severe and uncompromising towards thieves and vikings, putting to death most of the men who plundered the farms and other parts of the earldom. He had murderers and robbers arrested, and punished the rich no less than the poor for their robberies, raids and other transgressions. His judgments were never biased, for he believed divine justice to be more important than social distinctions. While he was the most generous of men to chieftains and others in powerful positions, he always gave the greatest comfort to the poor. He lived according to God's commandments, mortifying the flesh throughout an exemplary life in many ways which, though revealed to God, remained hidden from the sight of men.

His intentions were clear when he asked for the hand of a girl from the noblest family there in Scotland, celebrating their wedding and afterwards living with her for ten years without allowing either to suffer by way of their lusts, and so remaining chaste, without stain of lechery. Whenever the urge of temptation came upon him, he would plunge into cold water and pray to God for aid. Quite apart from his glorious virtues, many were the qualities that he revealed to God alone and concealed from mankind.

46. DISAGREEMENT

Earl Magnus and his kinsman Hakon had joint charge of the defences of Orkney for some time, and on the whole they stayed on friendly terms. A poem composed in their honour tells how they fought against a chieftain called Dufniall, their second cousin, and killed him; also that they put to death a man of importance, Thorbjorn, at Burra Firth in Shetland; and indeed there are more records in the poem of their achievements, showing that they worked well together, though no details are given here.

When the kinsmen had been ruling the earldom for some time, it so happened, as it often does, that malicious tongues set out to destroy their friendship, and it was to Hakon that the more luckless men were drawn, for he was very envious of the popularity and splendour of his cousin Magnus.

47. PEACE MEETING

There were two men staying with Earl Hakon, Sigurd and Sighvat Sock, who were particularly active in making trouble between Hakon and his cousin. With the aid of other troublemakers, they brought things to a head with their slanders, so that once more the two kinsmen started gathering forces and launching heavy attacks on one another.

Then the two of them sailed over to Mainland, where the people of Orkney had their place of assembly, and both sides formed up in battle order. Most of the noblemen of the isles were with them and many were friends to both, so they did their best to reconcile them, going between them with courage and goodwill.

The meeting took place in Lent, and so many helpful people made a particular effort to prevent any serious trouble between them, refusing to aid one side or harm the other, that, in the end, the Earls swore oaths and shook hands on an agreement.

Shortly afterwards Earl Hakon, with fraud and flattery, fixed a day for a meeting with the blessed Earl Magnus to ensure that their newly agreed peace could be neither distorted nor destroyed. The meeting to confirm the peace and goodwill between them was to take place on Egilsay that spring, during Holy Week. Utterly trusting, honest and without ambition, Earl Magnus agreed happily to this arrangement. Each of them was to have two ships, and an equal number of men, and both swore to keep whatever agreement the wisest men might arrange between them.

After the celebration of Easter, they got ready for the meeting. Earl Magnus called around him all the people he knew to be the best-natured and likeliest to improve matters between him and his cousin. He had two ships, with the agreed number of men and, when he was ready, off he went to Egilsay. As they were rowing away upon a calm, smooth sea, a breaker suddenly rose high over the ship he was steering and crashed down upon the spot where he was sitting. His men were astonished to see such a breaker rise up from a calm sea: no one had seen anything like it before, and there was deep water below them.

'It's not surprising that you should be worried by this,' said the Earl, 'for I think it forebodes of my death. It may be what was prophesied about Earl Hakon will turn out now to be true. We'd better reckon with the possibility that cousin Hakon isn't going to be entirely honest with us at this meeting.'

The Earl's men were disturbed by what he had said, to hear him predict his own imminent death, and they asked him not to place his trust in Earl Hakon but to watch out for his own safety.

'On with the journey,' the Earl replied, 'let it turn out as God wills.'

48. TREACHERY

Now we come back to Earl Hakon, who gathered a large force of men and took with him as many fully-manned warships as he would have taken for battle. When all his army was assembled, he made it clear to them that he meant to settle the business between Earl Magnus and himself once and for all, and there was going to be no more joint rule over Orkney. Many of his men were delighted with this idea and had plenty of harsh things to say, the most unpleasant coming from Sigurd and Sighvat Sock.

So they started to pull hard on the oars and made good headway. Havard Gunnason, friend and adviser to the Earls and loyal to them both, was on Hakon's ship, which is why Hakon concealed his schemes from him as Havard would never have agreed to them. As soon as he learned of the Earl's intention, Havard jumped overboard and swam to an uninhabited island.

Earl Magnus was the first to arrive with his men on Egilsay and, when they saw Earl Hakon approaching, they realised he had eight ships with him. It was clear to Magnus that he could expect treachery. He went ashore with his men up to the church to pray and there he spent the night. His men told him that they would protect him.

'I don't want to risk your lives saving my own,' said the earl, 'and if there's not to be peace between me and my kinsman, then things must go according to God's will.'

It seemed to his men that everything was turning out as Magnus had predicted when the breaker crashed on them. Either by divine revelation or plain wisdom he knew the length of his own life-span, but he would not run away from his enemies nor put a distance between himself and them; he only prayed devoutly and had Mass sung for himself.

49. ST MAGNUS MAKES THREE OFFERS

In the morning Hakon and his men hurried ashore, ran straight to the church and searched it thoroughly without finding Earl Magnus, who had gone in the opposite direction into hiding with two other men. All the same, when the holy Earl Magnus saw people searching for him, he shouted out, telling them where he was and not to bother looking elsewhere. When Hakon caught sight of Magnus, he and his men rushed towards him, shouting and clashing their weapons. As they came up he was at his prayers. When he had finished he crossed himself and, stout-hearted as ever, spoke to Earl Hakon.

'You've not done well, kinsman,' he said, 'to break your oaths, though probably the cause lies in other people's sinfulness rather than your own. Now, I'll offer you three choices and you can take your pick, for I'd not have you violate your oaths by killing me, an innocent man.'

Hakon's men asked what he was offering.

'First, that I should go on a pilgrimage to Rome, or even as far as the Holy Land, to visit sacred places. I'd take two ships with me to carry all we need, do penance for both our souls, and swear never to return to Orkney.'

They soon said no to this.

'Then,' said Magnus, 'since I'm in your power, and have committed many a sin against Almighty God, send me with two companions over to our friends in Scotland. I could be kept under guard and you'd see to it that I didn't escape.'

This too was quickly turned down.

'There's still one offer left for me to make,' said Magnus. 'God knows that I'm more concerned with the welfare of your soul than with saving my life. For your own sake, have me mutilated in any way you choose, rather than take my life, or else blind me and lock me in a dungeon.'

'I'll accept these terms,' said Hakon, 'and make no further conditions.'

The chieftains with him jumped to their feet.

'We're going to kill one or the other of you,' they said. 'From this day forward we're having no more joint rule.'

'Better kill him then,' said Hakon. 'I don't want an early death; I much prefer ruling over people and places.'

That's how Holdbodi, an honest farmer from the Hebrides, described their conversation. He was one of Magnus' two companions when he was captured.

50. THE MARTYRDOM OF ST MAGNUS

As cheerful as if he'd been invited to a feast was the illustrious Earl Magnus. After this conversation he spoke neither in anger nor resentment, but knelt down to pray, covering his face with his hands and shedding many tears in the sight of God.

Once it had been decided that the saintly Earl Magnus was to die, Hakon told his standard bearer Ofeig to do the killing, but he refused angrily: so Hakon ordered his cook Lifolf to kill Magnus. Lifolf started to weep out loud.

'This is nothing to weep over,' said Magnus. 'A deed like this can only bring fame to the man who carries it out. Show yourself a man of spirit and you can have my clothes according to the old laws and customs. Don't be afraid, you're doing this against your will and the man who gives you the order is a greater sinner than you are.'

At this, Earl Magnus took off his tunic and gave it to Lifolf, then asked for leave to pray. This was granted, and he prostrated himself on the ground, committing his soul to God and offering himself as a sacrifice. He prayed not only for himself and his friends but for his enemies and murderers, forgiving them with all his heart for their crimes against him. He confessed his own sins before God, praying that his soul might be washed clean by the spilling of his own blood, then placed it in God's hands. He asked that he might be greeted by God's angels and carried by them into the peace of Paradise. Some people say that Mass was sung for him and that he received the sacrament. As this friend of God was being led to his execution, he spoke to Lifolf.

'Stand in front of me and strike me hard on the head,' said Magnus, 'it's not fitting for a chieftain to be beheaded like a thief. Take heart, poor fellow, I've prayed that God grant you his mercy.'

With that he crossed himself and stooped to receive the blow. So his soul passed away to Heaven.

51. THE FIRST MIRACLE

The place where this happened was rocky and overgrown with moss, but soon God revealed how worthy Earl Magnus was in His eyes, for the spot where he was killed turned into a green field. In this way God showed that it was in the cause of justice that Magnus had died, and that he had reached the verdant fields of Paradise, called the Land of the Living. Earl Hakon would not allow Magnus' body to be taken to church.

Earl Magnus died two days after St Tiburtius' Mass, and had been joint ruler of Orkney with Hakon for seven years. Since the death of King Olaf, seventy-four years had gone by, and the rulers of Norway at the time were Kings Sigurd, Eystein and Olaf. It was 1091 years after the birth of Christ.[1]

52. ST MAGNUS' BURIAL

St Magnus' mother Thora had invited both Earls to come to a feast after the peace meeting and now that the holy Earl

[1] The chronology is faulty here. St Magnus died many years later, probably on April 16, 1117.

Magnus had been killed, Earl Hakon came to that feast. Thora herself attended to the guests, serving drink to the Earl and the very men who had taken part in the killing of her son. When the drink was beginning to take effect on the Earl, Thora came up to him.

'I was expecting the two of you,' she said, 'but now only you have come. Will you do something to please me in the eyes of God and men? Be a son to me and I shall be a mother to you. I'm sorely in need of your mercy, so let me have my son taken to church. Hear my prayers now, just as you yourself would hope to be heard by God on the Day of Judgment.'

The Earl fell silent and started to think it over. She had made her request with such gentle tears to be allowed to bring her son to church, that now he began to feel the burden of his crime. He looked at her, and wept himself.

'Bury your son,' he said, 'wherever you wish.'

Soon after that Earl Magnus' body was carried to Mainland and buried at Christ Church, which Earl Thorfinn had built. Not long after the burial, a bright heavenly light was often seen over Magnus' grave. Then people in peril started praying to him and no sooner did they pray than their troubles came to an end. People would sense a heavenly fragrance near his grave, and the sick recovered their health, so ailing people started coming from both Orkney and Shetland to keep vigil at the grave of the holy Earl Magnus and there they were cured of their ills. However, as long as Earl Hakon was alive no one dared to make all this public. Also, the story goes that in general the men most deeply involved in the betrayal of the holy Earl Magnus died cruel and violent deaths. This took place when William was Bishop of Orkney, the first resident bishop in the islands, and the episcopal seat was at Christ Church, Birsay. William was bishop for sixty-six years, but for a long time he doubted the saintliness of Earl Magnus.

After the killing of Magnus, Hakon took over the whole of Orkney and made all those who had previously served Magnus swear oaths of allegiance to himself. Hakon grew to be a powerful ruler and made those of Earl Magnus' friends who had been most hostile to him pay heavily for it in tribute. Some years later, Hakon set out on a long journey overseas and travelled south to Rome. His pilgrimage took him beyond to Jerusalem, where he visited the holy places and bathed in the River Jordan as is the custom of palmers. After that he returned to his realm and ruled over all Orkney.

He grew to be a fine administrator and brought firm peace

to the land, making new laws for Orkney which the farmers found they liked much better than the ones they'd had before. That was how his popularity began to grow and, in time, the people of Orkney would have no one but Hakon and his offspring to rule over them.

53. DEATH OF EARL HAKON

At the time Earl Hakon ruled Orkney there was a farmer called Moddan, a rich and well-born man, living in the Dales of Caithness. His three daughters were called Helga, Frakokk and Thorleif. Helga Moddan's-Daughter was Earl Hakon's mistress and they had a son Harald, nicknamed Smooth-Tongue, and two daughters, one called Ingibjorg who married Olaf Tit-bit, King of the Hebrides, and the other called Margaret.

Frakokk Moddan's-Daughter was married to a man in Sutherland called Ljot the Renegade. They had a daughter, Steinvor the Stout, who married Thorljot of Rack Wick. Their sons were Olvir Brawl, Magnus, Orm, Moddan and Eindridi, and they also had a daughter Audhild. Frakokk had yet another daughter, Gudrun, who married Thorstein the Yeoman, called the Whistler, and their son was Thorbjorn the Clerk.

Earl Hakon had another son, Paul, nicknamed the Silent, a reserved man and well-liked, though he got on badly with his brother once they grew up.

Earl Hakon Paulsson died in his bed in Orkney and his death was felt to be a great loss, his latter years having been very peaceful. The farmers had grave doubts as to how the brothers Paul and Harald would get on together.

54. THORKEL THE FOSTERER IS KILLED

After Earl Hakon's death his sons took charge of the realm, but they soon fell out and divided the earldom in half, which led to serious rifts between the chieftains, who formed up in two opposed camps.

Earl Harald held the fief of Caithness from the King of Scots and spent much of his time there, though sometimes he would stay in Scotland to the south, where he had a good many kinsmen and friends.

On one occasion when Earl Harald was in Sutherland, a man called Sigurd, nicknamed the Fake-Deacon, came to him claiming to be the son of Adalbrikt the Priest. Sigurd was on his way from Scotland where he had been an honoured guest of David, King of Scots. Earl Harald gave Sigurd a good welcome and Sigurd went with him to Orkney along with Frakokk Moddan's-Daughter, whose husband Ljot the Renegade had just died. She and her sister Helga had a lot to say in the government of Earl Harald. Sigurd the Fake-Deacon was on intimate terms with all of them. His mistress at the time was Audhild, daughter of Thorleif Moddan's-Daughter, and they had a daughter called Ingigerd who later married Hakon Claw. Audhild had been married to Eirik Strife and they had a son called Eirik Stay-Brails.

As soon as Sigurd and Frakokk arrived in the islands, the people of Orkney started forming factions, with each Earl gathering round him all his friends. The two closest to Earl Paul were Sigurd of Westness, who was married to the Earls' cousin Ingibjorg the Noble, and Thorkel Sumarlidason, nicknamed the Fosterer, who spent much of his time with the Earl. Thorkel was closely related to Earl Magnus the Holy and was exceptionally well-liked. Earl Harald's friends suspected that Thorkel might cause trouble between the brothers on account of the losses he had suffered under their father, Earl Hakon. So it came about that Earl Harald and Sigurd the Fake-Deacon attacked Thorkel the Fosterer and killed him. Earl Paul was outraged at this when he learned about it and, wasting no time, gathered his forces. Earl Harald quickly got to hear of this and did the same. Friends of both were told what was going on and intervened in the hope of bringing about a settlement, and in fact everyone played a part in trying to get them to come to terms. Earl Paul was in such a rage that he refused any reconciliation until those who had taken part in the killing had been banished from the islands and, since the farmers thought the tension between the Earls such a serious threat, they all spoke up in favour of a settlement. The outcome was that Sigurd was banished from the islands along with all those whom Earl Paul thought most responsible for the killing. Earl Harald paid compensation for Thorkel's death and the agreement between the brothers also stipulated that they should pay more attention to their bonds of kinship, and spend time together at Christmas and other major festivals.

Sigurd the Fake-Deacon left the islands and travelled south to Scotland where he stayed for a while with Malcolm, King of Scots, held in the highest regard and greatly respected for all his manly talents. After spending some time in Scotland he travelled on to the Holy Land.

55. DEATH OF EARL HARALD

During the reign of the brothers Harald and Paul, a Christmas feast was arranged on Earl Harald's estate at Orphir and, as he was to provide for them both, he was busy with the preparations.

Their mother Helga and her sister Frakokk were staying there at the time and happened to be sitting in a small room getting on with their needlework, when Earl Harald came into the room. The sisters were sitting on the cross-dais and a newly made linen garment, white as snow, was lying between them. The Earl picked it up and saw that in many places it was stitched with gold thread.

'Whose is this treasure?' he asked.

'It's meant for your brother Paul,' answered Frakokk.

'Why take such pains making clothes for him?' asked the Earl. 'You're not so particular when you make mine.'

The Earl had only just got up and was wearing nothing but a shirt and linen breeches, with a tunic thrown over his shoulders. He cast it off and began unfolding the linen garment, but his mother grabbed hold of it and told him that there was no reason to be envious just because his brother had some fine clothes. The Earl snatched it back and was about to put it on when the sisters pulled off their bonnets, tore their hair and said that if he put on the garment his life would be at risk. Though they were both in tears he didn't let that stop him, but no sooner was the garment upon his body than his flesh started to quiver and he began to suffer terrible pain. He had to go to bed and it wasn't long before he was dead. His death was deeply mourned by his friends.

Immediately after Harald's death, his brother Paul took over the entire earldom with the approval of every farmer in Orkney. Earl Paul realised that the precious robe put on by Earl Harald had been meant for himself and for that reason he would not let the sisters stay on in the islands, so they went off with all their dependents, first across to Caithness and from there to Frakokk's estates in Sutherland.

It was there that Frakokk reared Erlend, the son of Harald Smooth-Tongue, while he was still a boy. There was another boy there too, Olvir Brawl, the son of Thorljot of Rack Wick and Steinvor Frakokk's-Daughter. He grew to be an exceptionally big and powerful man, a great trouble-maker and a killer. Others brought up there were Thorbjorn Clerk, son of Thorstein the Yeoman and Gudrun Frakokk's-Daughter,

Margaret the daughter of Earl Hakon and Helga Moddan's-Daughter, and Eirik Stay-Brails.

All these people were high-born and thought well of themselves. They all believed that they had a just claim on the earldom of Orkney which had once belonged to their kinsman Earl Harald. Frakokk had two brothers, Angus the Generous and Earl Ottar of Thurso, a man of great character.

56. LEADING FAMILIES

Earl Paul was now sole ruler in Orkney and was very well-liked. He was a man of few words and had little to say at public assemblies, sharing the governing of the earldom freely with other men. He was modest, treated his subjects with kindness and generosity, and was unsparingly open-handed to his friends. He was unwarlike and lived quietly throughout much of his life.

In Orkney at the time there were many well-born people descended from the Earls. Farming at Westness on Rousay was a man of distinguished lineage called Sigurd, married to Ingibjorg the Noble whose mother Herbjorg was Earl Paul Thorfinnsson's daughter. Their sons were Brynjolf and Hakon Pike, and both father and sons were among the chieftains of Earl Paul.

Magnus, Hakon Claw and Dufniall, the sons of Havard Gunnason and Bergljot, daughter of Ragnhild, daughter of Earl Paul Thorfinsson, were also friends of Earl Paul.

A man called Erling who farmed at Tankerness on Mainland had four sons, all of them fine men.

There was a man called Olaf Hrolfsson farming on Gairsay, though he had another estate at Duncansby in Caithness, a man of distinction and much respected by Earl Paul. His wife Asleif was a woman of good birth, great intelligence and strong character. Their sons were Valthjof, Svein and Gunni, all excellent men, and there was also a daughter, Ingigerd.

Sigurd, the Earl's kinsman-in-law, married Thora the mother of Saint Magnus the Holy, and they had a son, Hakon Karl, a great leader like his father.

Farming on North Ronaldsay was a distinguished woman called Ragna, and she had a very able son, Thorstein.

There was a farmer at Rapness on Westray called Kugi, a rich and intelligent man. There was a rich and dependable farmer called Helgi living at a certain hamlet which used to be there on Westray, and yet another farmer on Westray was Thorkel Flayer, a very able man, but overbearing. His sons were Thorstein and Haflidi, both unpopular men.

On Swona in the Pentland Firth the farmer there lived in poverty, but he had two sons, Asbjorn and Margad, who were men of great mettle.

On Fair Isle there was a farmer called Dagfinn.

Farming at Flydruness on Mainland there was a man called Thorstein whose sons were Thorkel Hook-Eye and Blann, all three of them overbearing men. At Knarston, Jaddvor the daughter of Earl Erlend farmed with her son Borgar, and they weren't very popular.

Jon Wing farmed at Upland of Hoy in North Hoy and his brother Richard at Brekkur on Stronsay, both able men and related to Olaf Hrolfsson.

A man called Grimkel farmed at Glaitness.

All these people figure in the story later.

At that time, William was Bishop of Orkney, with his episcopal seat at Christ Church, Birsay, where there were so many miracles resulting from the saintliness of Earl Magnus when people kept vigil over his grave, though because of Earl Paul's power the stories were not freely aired. Besides, Bishop William rather blunted the edge of these stories about Earl Magnus by calling it sheer heresy to spread them around.

And now for a time we shall give the narrative a rest and say something instead about the lofty miracles God has performed for the worthy sake of the holy Earl Magnus.

57. MIRACLES

There was a farmer in Shetland called Bergfinn Skatason, who was blind. He ferried two cripples, Sigurd and Thorbjorn, south to Orkney and all three of them kept vigil at the grave of Earl Magnus. The Holy Earl revealed himself to them and with the help of God gave them back their health. Bergfinn started seeing so well that he was able to tell one hand from the other, and the two cripples straightened up. A little later, before the anniversary of Earl Magnus' death, twenty-four sick people kept vigil at his grave and all got back their health. Then a number of people said to the bishop that he should have a word with Earl Paul and get his permission to open up the grave and translate the holy relics of Earl Magnus, but whenever the matter was raised the bishop's response was cool.

It happened one summer that Bishop William went east to Norway. On his return he was late setting out and reached Shetland in the autumn shortly before winter. The weather deteriorated and gales raged, but the bishop wasn't happy there and was eager to get back home. With the coming of winter, blizzards blew up and the ship's captain suggested that the bishop might make a vow, that if they got favourable weather he would no longer oppose the translation of Earl Magnus' holy relics. The bishop agreed to honour the vow if the weather improved sufficiently for him to sing Mass back home at his episcopal seat on the Sunday of the following week. As soon as he had sworn the vow, the weather improved and they got such a favourable wind for Orkney that he was able to sing Mass at home the very next Sunday. However, even when such tokens were given him, he was still unwilling to believe in the saintliness of Earl Magnus and, in addition, all those who preached it were abominated by Earl Paul.

One day the bishop was praying alone in Christ Church at Birsay and as he stood up to leave he suddenly went blind and could not find his way to the door. For a long time he tried to get out. Then he was seized with a great terror, went to Earl Magnus' grave and prayed there in tears, vowing that he would translate the holy relics of Earl Magnus whether Earl Paul liked it or not. And after that, there at the graveside, he got back his sight.

Later the bishop summoned all the leading men of Orkney to a meeting and announced that he intended to open up the grave of Earl Magnus. When they started digging they found that the coffin had already almost reached the surface. Once the bishop had them washed, the bones of the Earl shone brightly, and a knuckle bone that the bishop tested three times in consecrated fire wouldn't burn, but took on the colour of gold. Some people say that the bone also took on the shape of a cross. Many were the miracles worked there by the holy relics of Earl Magnus. Then on St Lucy's Day his relics were enshrined and placed above the altar, after he had been lying in his grave for twenty-one years, and a law was passed that both the day of his translation and the day of his death should be celebrated. For a long time the holy relics of Earl Magnus were kept there.

On Westray, it happened that a good farmer called Gunni dreamed St Magnus came up and spoke to him.

'Tell Bishop William that I want to leave Birsay and go east to Kirkwall,' he said. 'I believe that in his mercy Almighty

God will grant me this, that the sick will be cured of their ills if they go there with true faith. When you describe this dream, speak out boldly.'

After Gunni woke up, he thought it best not to tell of the dream because he was afraid Earl Paul would hate him for it, but the following night Earl Magnus appeared again in a dream, this time very angry.

'Go to Birsay and tell about your dream,' he said, 'when most people are near by. If you don't go, you'll be punished in this world and even worse in the next.'

Gunni woke up badly shaken. He set out right away for Birsay, where he told his dream at Mass to the whole congregation, in front of Earl Paul and many other important people. A number of them pleaded with the bishop to comply and translate the holy relics east to Kirkwall as·Earl Magnus intended. Earl Paul sat as silent as if he had his mouth full of water and flushed deep red.

Afterwards, Bishop William led a grand procession east to Kirkwall, taking along with them the holy relics of Earl Magnus, and placed the reliquary above the high altar of the church that stood there at that time. In those days the market town of Kirkwall had only a few houses. A good many miracles happened there immediately after these events.

A little later, Bergfinn Skatason made a second trip south from Shetland to keep a vigil by the holy relics of Earl Magnus, taking along with him his son Halfdan who suffered from leprosy. Earl Magnus revealed himself to them both and placed his hands upon them, whereupon Halfdan was completely healed and Bergfinn's sight improved so much that he could see well.

To the north in Shetland there was a man called Amundi whose whole body was leprous. He travelled to Kirkwall and kept vigil at the shrine of Earl Magnus the Holy, asking for help and health. Earl Magnus, that holy servant of God, appeared to him in a dream and laid his hands upon Amundi's whole body, whereupon, waking, he found himself completely cured, with nothing at all wrong with him. Everyone praised God and the Holy Earl Magnus.

There was a farmer in Orkney called Thorkel, who fell from the top of his barley rick right down to the ground, badly injuring one side of his body. He was carried to the shrine of the blessed Earl Magnus and there he recovered his health completely.

There was a man called Sigurd from the Faroes in the north

whose hand was so crippled that all the fingers were bent into the palm. He went to Kirkwall and was completely healed.

In Shetland there was a man called Thorbjorn, son of Gyrd, who was insane, but when he was taken to Earl Magnus he was cured immediately.

There was a man called Thord Dragon-Jaw, a tenant of Bergfinn's in Shetland. He was threshing corn in a barley-shed on the eve of St Magnus and St Lucy when just about sunset the farmer, Bergfinn, came to the barn and told them to stop work.

'It's not often you think I'm working too late,' said Thord.

'St Magnus' Mass is tomorrow,' said Bergfinn, 'and we should observe it with all the respect we can.'

Then he went away, but Thord kept working away harder than ever. Shortly after that Bergfinn came back and spoke to Thord very angrily.

'If you work on holy days,' he said, 'I shall take it as an act of spite. Stop at once.'

Bergfinn went off again in a temper, but Thord kept on working just as before. The household were sitting at table after their meal and just about to start drinking when in came Thord wearing terrible rags and immediately started drinking. He'd taken only one full cup when suddenly he went out of his mind and had to be held and tied up. For six days he stayed that way, then Bergfinn made a vow on his behalf, offered half a mark of silver to the shrine of Earl Magnus, and a three-night vigil by Thord. That very night, following the evening on which the vow was made, Thord was completely cured.

Two men, one from Orkney and the other from Caithness, stole some gold from the shrine of St Magnus. The Caithness man, named Gilli, was drowned in the Pentland Firth, and the man from Orkney went insane, telling in his madness of what they had done. Then a vow was made on his behalf that he would go on a pilgrimage to Rome if he were to recover at the shrine of Earl Magnus. He was taken there and recovered at once.

Then there was a Shetlander called Ogmund. A cross-beam fell on his head and fractured the skull badly. Bergfinn made a vow on his behalf, casting lots to determine whether to promise a pilgrimage to Rome, the freeing of a slave, or a gift of money to the shrine of Earl Magnus, should the man recover. It so happened that money was to be given to the shrine of Earl Magnus, and at once Ogmund was healed.

His uncle Bergfinn gave the shrine half a mark as he'd promised.

There was a woman north in Shetland called Sigrid Sigurd's-Daughter who had been blind from infancy. When she was about twenty her father took her to the shrine of Earl Magnus and made her keep vigil there, giving a great deal of money to the shrine, whereupon she regained her sight.

Yet another woman from Shetland called Sigrid broke her leg badly, yet when she was taken to Magnus she was completely healed.

A third Shetland woman called Sigrid, from the isle of Unst, was staying with Thorlak of Baliasta, and on the eve of Magnus' Mass she kept sewing after the others had stopped. Thorlak asked her why she was working so late and she said that she would stop right away, but after Thorlak had left she kept on sewing just as before. When Thorlak came back again he asked why she was behaving so wickedly.

'Clear out,' he said, 'you're not going to work in my house.'

She said there was only a little more to be sewn, but kept working till dark, sitting on her bed. When the fire had been lit and people were settling down to eat and drink, she went insane and had to be tied up, staying mad until Thorlak had made a vow on her behalf. He cast lots to discover what he should promise, a pilgrimage to Rome, freedom for a slave, or a gift of money to the shrine of the holy Earl Magnus. Thorlak took her there, she recovered her health, and later went on a pilgrimage to Rome.

In England, there were once two men staking money heavily on a game of dice and one of them had lost a great deal. Next he staked a cargo-boat and everything else that he had, against all that he'd lost. The other man was first to throw and got two sixes, which the man we're speaking of didn't think too promising, so he made a vow to the holy Earl Magnus asking him not to let him lose all his possessions, then he threw. One of the dice broke and he got two sixes and an ace, so that he collected everything at stake, and later on gave a lot of money to Earl Magnus.

There was a woman on Mainland called Groa who went out of her mind and was taken to the holy Earl Magnus, where she recovered and spent the rest of her life there praising God.

There was a man called Sigurd Tandrason farming north in Shetland, who was possessed by the Devil, so they sewed him up in a cowhide and carried him south to Kirkwall to the holy Earl Magnus where he recovered. Everyone there praised God and his holy and beloved friend, Earl Magnus.

Now we come to an end of the tales of lofty miracles performed by God for the sake of the holy Earl Magnus of Orkney and close this particular account with the prayer that he who wrote this record, he who has told it, and all who listen to it may enjoy from that holy knight of God, Earl Magnus, blessings and the answer to their prayers for the remission of their sins and for everlasting joy: also from our Almighty Lord Jesus Christ, succour and mercy, peace and rejoicing, both now and in the future, from Him who was, is and ever shall be the one and only true and eternal God, who gives, wills and commands all good things: for ever and ever, Amen.

58. KALI KOLSSON

As we've written earlier, Kol stayed on at his estates in Agder and didn't go back to Orkney. He was a man of exceptional intelligence, and his son Kali grew up there showing great promise. Kali was of average height, well-proportioned and strong-limbed, and had light chestnut hair. He was very popular and a man of more than average ability. He made this verse:

> *At nine skills I challenge—*
> *a champion at chess:*
> *runes I rarely spoil,*
> *I read books and write:*
> *I'm skilled at skiing*
> *and shooting and sculling*
> *and more!—I've mastered*
> *music and verse.*

Kali spent a great deal of time with his kinsman Solmund. He was the son of Sigurd Sneis who had been a royal steward in Tonsberg, a great chieftain with a large following and an estate in East Agder. The two kinsmen were much the same age.

59. KALI AND GILLIKRIST

When Kali was fifteen he went in the company of traders westward to England, with valuable merchandise aboard, and they sailed to a town called Grimsby. There was a large gathering of people there from Orkney, Scotland and the Hebrides.

In Grimsby Kali met a man who called himself Gillikrist and kept asking them all about Norway; it was mostly to Kali that he talked and they grew to be close companions. He told Kali in confidence that his real name was Harald and that his father was King Magnus Barelegs, though his mother's kin were from the Hebrides and Ireland. He asked Kali what kind of reception he might expect were he to go to Norway, and Kali said he thought it likely that King Sigurd would give him a good welcome unless other people spoiled things for him. When they parted, Kali and Gillikrist exchanged gifts and promises of true friendship wherever they should meet again. Gillikrist told his secret to no one else.

60. DRINKING IN BERGEN

After that Kali went back east in the same ship. They made landfall at Agder, then sailed north to Bergen, where Kali made this verse:

> *Five weeks we've waded*
> *through wetness and filth,*
> *mud wasn't missing*
> *in the middle of Grimsby:*
> *now our spirits are soaring*
> *as our fine ship skims,*
> *its bow bounds, an elk*
> *of the billows, to Bergen.*

When they reached the town there was quite a gathering of people there from the north and south of the country, and many too from overseas, bringing all sorts of good things with them. Kali and his shipmates started having a good time round the taverns. Kali was something of a dandy and was stylishly dressed now that he was just back from England. He had a high opinion of himself, as indeed others had of him, for he came from a good family and was a talented man.

In the tavern where Kali was drinking there was a young man of good birth called Jon, the son of Peter Serksson of Sogn and himself a landholder. His mother was Helga, the daughter of Harek of Sætersdale. Jon was a great one for clothes. The tavern they were drinking at belonged to a lady of good family called Unn. Jon and Kali grew to be close friends and they parted on the best of terms, Jon going south to his estates in Sogn and Kali east to join his father in Agder, where he also spent a great deal of time with his kinsman Solmund.

So it went on for several years, with Kali going on trading trips in the summer and wintering at home or with his kinsman Solmund.

61. HOW KALI GOT TO BE AN EARL

One summer, when Kali had sailed north to Trondheim, it happened that he was weatherbound at an island called Dolls, where there is a great cave called Dolls Cave in which people had the idea there was treasure hidden. The merchants made up their minds to explore the cave but found it very hard going. They came to a point where there was a lake stretching right across the cave which no on dared cross except for Kali and a man called Havard, one of Solmund's farmhands. They swam across the lake holding a rope between them, with Kali ahead carrying a blazing log in his hand and a tinder-box between his shoulderblades. They swam straight across the lake to the other side and came to a rocky place where the stench was vile, and they had difficulty striking a light. So Kali said they should go no further, but build a cairn to commemorate the event, and then he made this verse:

> *I've heaved up a high*
> *cairn here for the haunter*
> *of this dark den,*
> *seeking riches in Dolls Cave.*
> *I don't know who comes next,*
> *—will no one follow*
> *o'er the wide water,*
> *the weary crossing?*

After that they returned safe and sound to their men. They all made their way out of the cave and there's nothing else to tell of their journey because nothing else happened. They got back to Bergen and Kali went to the same tavern as before, the one owned by the good lady Unn. Jon Petersson was also there in the tavern with one of his retainers, Brynjolf, and many more of his men not mentioned by name.

One evening after Jon Petersson and Kali had gone to their beds, a number of the others stayed up drinking. A good many things were said as they got drunk and people began comparing one leader with another, arguing about which of

the landholders in Norway was the greatest. Brynjolf said that
Jon Petersson was the most talented and best-born young
man south of Stad, but Kali's companion Havard thought
Solmund just as good: indeed, he said that the men of Oslofjord
would rate him much higher. This led to a heated argument
and, when the ale began to talk, things got so bad that Havard,
leaping to his feet, grabbed a log, and gave Bjorgolf such a
blow on the head with it that he fell down unconscious.
Everyone rushed up, but somehow people got Havard out of
harm's way. He went to see Kali, who sent him south to a
priest at Alver called Richard.

'Give him this message from me,' said Kali, 'he's to look
after you till I go back east.'

Kali provided him with a boat and a guide, and they rowed
south to Græninga Sound. Then Havard spoke to his companion.

'Now we've managed to get beyond the sound of dogs
barking,' he said, 'let's take it easy here for a while and lie
down to sleep.'

The next thing to tell is that after Brynjolf had come to his
senses he was taken to Jon and told him what had happened,
including the fact that the man who hit him had been helped
to get away. Jon guessed the truth about the escape and
ordered a rowing skiff. Ten men boarded it, with Brynjolf in
charge, and they rowed off south to Græninga Sound, arriving
there after dawn. Then they sighted a ship ahead of them
beached on the sand.

'Maybe these people could tell us something about Havard,'
said Brynjolf.

They went ashore and there they came upon Havard and his
man, who had just woken up. Brynjolf wasted no time. He
drove his weapon right into Havard and killed him on the
spot together with his companion, then went back with his
men to Bergen where they told Jon the news, and soon it was
all over town. Kali took great offence over these killings and,
when people tried to mediate between the two, Jon said that
he wanted Kali alone to arbitrate on any issue about which he
felt offended. Apart from that, it was left to the King and the
two parties to decide the case. Kali accepted the terms, but
he and Jon were no longer friends.

Soon afterwards, Kali went east back to his home and told
his father the news and how things had turned out.

'It was a great surprise to me,' said Kol, 'when you agreed
to a settlement without having your kinsman Solmund there.

As I see it, the position you're in is tricky and there's little you can do but try to get a settlement: but that's not the kind of thing Solmund would have done had it been your farmhand and his shipmate who'd been killed.'

'What you say, father, is quite true,' said Kali. 'I was too hasty when I looked at the matter, and you were too far away to give me advice. This won't be the only time that you're proved a great deal wiser than me. But I was thinking that Solmund would be no closer to an honourable solution had I rejected the terms offered, and I don't see that Solmund or yourself should be so offended as to refuse Jon self-judgment in the case between you if he proposes it to you. Still, I rather doubt if it will come to that. I don't think I've any obligations to Brynjolf as long as I've made no promises and received no money.'

Father and son talked the matter over at great length, each of them trying to press home his own point-of-view, and after that they sent messengers to tell Solmund what had happened. Later, when Kali and his father met Solmund, Kol proposed sending messengers to Jon to try for a settlement, but Solmund and Havard's brother Hallvard wanted nothing less than blood-revenge. They said it would be out of the question to offer a settlement to the people of Sogn. All the same, Kol had his way on condition that he promised not to abandon the case till Solmund's honour had been satisfied: after that, Kol was to be given a free hand to arbitrate in the case.

However, when the envoys came back they said that their message had been given a cold reception and that Jon had flatly refused to pay compensation for anyone who was guilty of a punishable act. Solmund said that things had turned out just as he had expected, that the offer of a settlement to Jon was in no way likely to add to their honour. So now he asked Kol to think up a scheme which might help them.

'Is Hallvard willing to take any risks in avenging his brother?' asked Kol. 'Even so we may not gain very much.'

Hallvard replied that he would spare no effort to avenge his brother — 'even though lives may be at risk'.

'Then you must go north secretly to Sogn,' said Kol, 'to a man called Uni, who has a farm only a short distance from Jon's. He's an intelligent man but a little short of funds. For a long time, Jon has been making things difficult for him. Uni's a good friend of mine, but he's getting on in years, so I want you to take him six marks, properly weighed, that I'm sending him for this reason: he's to advise you how to get revenge on

Brynjolf, or on any member of Jon's household he values just as highly. If you can pull this off, then Uni is to go with you to Kyrpinga-Orm, my kinsman, and his sons Ogmund and Erling at Stole. Then I think you'll be as good as home. Tell Uni to sell his estate and move house here to me.'

Hallvard got himself ready for the journey and there's nothing to tell of it, nor of where he lodged, till he arrived one evening at Uni's under an assumed name. He exchanged news with Uni, but during the evening as people were sitting by the fire, the 'guest' kept asking in detail about all the important people in Sogn and Hordaland. Uni gave his opinion that there was no landed man greater than Jon for family background, and no greater bully either. Then he asked hadn't the people in the south some experience of the latter? This came as something of a surprise to the visitor.

The people started drifting away from the fire till there were only two of them left: then Uni spoke.

'Isn't your name Hallvard?' he asked.

'No,' said the guest, and repeated the name he'd given earlier in the evening.

'In that case I've nothing to worry about,' said Uni, 'but I'd have thought that if I happened to be called Brynjolf, you would be Hallvard. Well, let's go to our beds.'

At that the guest took hold of him.

'We mustn't go just yet,' he said, and with that he handed over the purse, saying that Kol had sent the silver with his best wishes — 'and for this reason, that you might advise me how to bring about my brother's revenge.' Then he explained the plans Kol had thought up.

'Kol certainly deserves a good turn from me,' said Uni, 'though I'm not sure how successful you'll be in getting your revenge on Brynjolf. He's expected here in the morning to collect his concubine and her clothes.'

Uni took him to the stable just outside the door and hid him in the manger. Hallvard had spent the whole night in the house, and this was just before people were about to get up.

Hallvard had been only a short while in the stable when he saw a brisk-looking man arrive at the farmstead, calling out that the woman should get ready. Hallvard realised who this must be and went outside, where Brynjolf was bundling up the woman's clothes and had put aside his weapons. No sooner had they met than Hallvard dealt Brynjolf his death-blow. Then he went back and hid in the stable. While the killing was taking place, the woman had gone inside to kiss

104

people goodbye and when she came out she saw what had happened. She ran back into the house, screaming out in terror, almost fainting, though she managed to tell people the news. The farmer Uni said that the visitor must have been a hired killer and ran outside to send someone to Jon and tell him what had happened. He kept calling on the others to search for the stranger, so that no one suspected him of his scheme.

Hallvard remained in the stable until the search was practically over, then at Uni's suggestion he travelled to Orm and his sons at Stole. From there they gave him an escort east to his home, where Kol and Solmund welcomed him warmly, now quite contented with everything. The news soon got around and people learned the truth. Jon was far from pleased.

The year passed and the following winter, shortly before Christmas, Jon set out thirty strong indicating that he was going to visit his uncle Olaf in Sætersdale, and that is what he did. He was given a warm welcome and had a talk with his uncle, telling him he planned to go from there to East Agder and see Solmund. Olaf discouraged him and said that Jon had nothing at stake even though he might have fallen out with Solmund, but Jon replied that he wouldn't put up with Brynjolf being unavenged. Olaf said that in his opinion Jon would have nothing to gain from further dealings with them, but Jon gathered another thirty men there and they set out sixty strong east over the mountains, hoping to take Kol and Solmund by surprise.

Shortly after Jon had left home, Uni travelled south to Stole to see Orm, and father and sons provided him with an escort south to Kol. He arrived at Christmas and told them he thought Jon was about to make an attack on them, so Kol sent out spies in every direction from which Jon could be expected to come. He also went to warn Solmund and the two kinsmen waited with a large force of men. When they got reports of Jon's movements they set out to face him, and started fighting as soon as they met, near a certain wood. Kol and Solmund had much the larger force and won the day, while Jon lost a good many of his men and ran off into the wood. He was wounded in the leg and it healed so badly that for the rest of his life he walked with a limp and was called Jon Foot. He got back home to the north during Lent, but his outing had made him a laughing-stock.

Winter passed, and in the summer Jon had Gunnar and

Aslak, two kinsmen of Kol's, put to death. A little later King
Sigurd visited the town and the troubles were reported to him.
Then he sent word to both parties, summoning them to him,
and they all came with their friends and kinsmen. Efforts
were made to reconcile them and, as things turned out, it was
decided that the whole issue should be referred to the King's
judgment. At that, both parties exchanged sureties.

King Sigurd made the settlement with the advice of the
very best men, and it was stipulated that Jon Petersson was
to marry Ingirid Kol's-Daughter, to strengthen their friendship by the bonds of kin. The killings were held to cancel each
other out. The attack on Kol and the wound suffered by Jon
were set against the loss of lives there in the east, and all
wounds were balanced off, the differences being compensated
for. Each side was to support the other at home and abroad.
But, apart from the agreement, King Sigurd granted Kali
Kolsson a half of Orkney (the other half being Earl Paul
Hakonsson's) and gave him the title of earl. He gave Kali the
name Rognvald because Kali's mother Gunnhild claimed Earl
Rognvald Brusason to have been the most able of all the Earls
of Orkney, and people saw this as a sign of good luck. This
part of Orkney had once belonged to Kali's uncle, Saint
Magnus.

After the settlement, those who had been enemies before
parted the best of friends.

62. NEW RULERS OF NORWAY

That winter King Sigurd spent in residence at Oslo, but in the
spring, during Lent, he fell ill and died the night after
Annunciation Day. His son Magnus was in town at the time
and summoned people to an assembly. He was immediately
adopted as king of the whole country on the same terms that
people had sworn to King Sigurd, and so Magnus took over the
royal treasury.

Harald Gilli was at Tonsberg when he heard about the death
of King Sigurd, and held a meeting there with his friends,
including Rognvald and his kinsmen. Rognvald had always
been his friend since they met in England, and he and his
father Kol had been Harald's principal sponsors when he had
to face an ordeal before King Sigurd, though they had the
backing of other landholders too, such as Ingimar Sveinsson
and Thjostolf Alason.

Harald and his supporters decided to convene the Haugar Assembly at Tonsberg, and there Harald was adopted as king over half of Norway. The oaths he had sworn giving up his inheritance before he had been allowed to undergo the ordeal were considered to have been made under duress. Soon people started flocking to his side offering him their allegiance, so he had plenty of support. Then he and King Magnus exchanged messages and after four days they came to a settlement on these terms, that each was to share half the kingdom, but King Magnus was to have King Sigurd's longship, dishes and other table-service and control of the treasury. All the same, he was far from satisfied with his share and made his dislike of all Harald's friends quite apparent. Nor did King Magnus want to acknowledge the gift King Sigurd had made to Rognvald of Orkney and the earldom, Rognvald being Harald's staunchest supporter in his dealings with Magnus, staying by his side until the whole affair had been settled.

For three years Harald and Magnus remained Kings of Norway without any serious breach, but in the fourth summer they fought a pitched battle at Farlev. King Magnus had about seven thousand two hundred men, Harald only about one thousand eight hundred. These were the chieftains alongside Harald: his brother Kristrod, Earl Rognvald, Ingimar of Ask, Thjostolf Alason and Solmund. King Magnus won the victory, Kristrod and Ingimar were killed, and King Harald fled. It was Ingimar who made this verse:

> *Trolls must have fixed*
> *my face towards Farlev:*
> *I was unwilling*
> *to wage this war.*
> *Arrows from elm-bows*
> *have eaten my flesh,*
> *never more shall I*
> *take my ease at Ask.*

King Harald's flight took him east to his fleet in Oslo Fjord, and from there he sailed to Denmark where King Eirik granted him charge of Halland and eight unrigged longships. Thjostolf Alason sold his estates, bought weapons and ships and in the autumn went to join King Harald in Denmark.

At Christmas, King Harald came to Bergen and lay at anchor over the festival, but after Christmas they attacked the town and met little resistance. King Magnus was taken

captive aboard his ship and maimed, and the whole land fell
into the hands of King Harald. In the spring he confirmed the
gift of Orkney and the earldom he had given to Rognvald.

63. PREPARATIONS

Immediately after this, Kol decided to send envoys to
Orkney, asking Earl Paul to surrender half of the islands, as
King Harald had laid down he must do. He said too that
they should become friends and act according to their kinship,
though, if Earl Paul were to refuse the envoys should go to
Frakokk and Olvir Brawl with an offer to share the land with
Earl Rognvald as long as they were ready to lead an army
against Earl Paul.

The envoys came to Orkney, saw Earl Paul and told him
their business.

'I understand this claim,' he said, 'and that there's a lot of
craftiness gone into the making of it. They've got the help of
the Kings of Norway to take the earldom from me, but I'm
not rewarding their dishonesty by handing over my land to
anyone with as feeble a claim as Rognvald's, and by denying
the claim of my nephews. There's no need to say anything
more about it. I'll defend Orkney with the aid of my kinsmen
and friends for as long as God lets me live.'

The envoys saw then how their mission would turn out, so
they went away over the Pentland Firth to Caithness and
from there to Sutherland. They saw Frakokk and told her
their business, that Earl Rognvald and Kol were ready to
give them half of Orkney if they'd fight Earl Paul for it.

'Kol's a wise man, that's a fact,' said Frakokk, 'and it's
clever of him to look for our support when we have so many
powerful friends and marriage connexions. Now that I've
married off Margaret Hakon's-Daughter to Earl Maddad of
Atholl, we've many a good claim to Orkney, for he's the best-
born of all the chieftains in Scotland, his father Melmar being
brother of Malcolm King of Scots, father of David the present
King. I'm not without influence myself and people think me
pretty shrewd, so it's unlikely that I'll be fooled by whatever
might happen in this conflict. But for a number of reasons I'm
very content to make this alliance with Rognvald and his
father. You can give them this message from me, that Olvir
and I will lead an army to Orkney against Earl Paul around
midsummer next year. Rognvald and his men are to join
us there and then we'll fight Earl Paul to the finish. Over

winter I'll gather an army in Scotland from my kinsmen, friends and in-laws.'

So the envoys went back east to Norway and told Earl Rognvald and his father how things were coming along.

64. FURTHER PREPARATIONS

That winter Earl Rognvald got ready for the voyage west, Solmund and Jon being among his chief men. They set out the following summer with a small but select band of fighting men and only five or six ships. They reached Shetland by midsummer but there was no word from Frakokk. Then a heavy gale blew up against them and they had to take shelter in Yell Sound, where the farmers gave them a good welcome and they began attending the feasts there.

As for Frakokk, she had set out from the Hebrides in the spring, she and Olvir having got together a number of men and about a dozen ships, mostly small and poorly manned. Around midsummer they headed for Orkney and their agreed appointment with Earl Rognvald, but they had to wait for a fair wind. Olvir Brawl was in command of the troops and it was decided that if all went well, he should get an earldom in Orkney. A good many of Frakokk's family were there with her.

65. EARL PAUL'S VICTORY

Earl Paul was at Westness on Rousay when he heard Earl Rognvald had landed in Shetland and learned about the troops gathered in the Hebrides against him. He sent word to Kugi of Westray and Thorkel Flayer, both very shrewd men, and to a good many of his other leaders. At the meeting the Earl consulted his friends, but there was no agreement about what should be done. Some wanted him to share the earldom with one or other of his enemies so that he wouldn't have both of them against him, while others advised him to go to Caithness, see his friends and kinsmen and find out how much support he could raise there.

'I'm not handing over my earldom to people now,' he said, 'from whom I've already refused a friendly offer. Apart from that, it doesn't seem to me proper behaviour for a chief to run off without putting anything to the test, so I'm going about it the other way. I'm sending men out tonight throughout all the islands to gather an army. We'll face Rognvald and his men right now and settle the matter between us before the Hebrideans get here.'

People decided to do as the Earl suggested.

There was a man with Earl Paul called Svein Breast-Rope, one of his retainers and very highly thought of by the Earl, with whom Svein used to spend the winter after going on viking trips during the summer. He was a tall, well built man, rather dark and with an unlucky look about him. He was keen on the old practices and had spent many a night in the open with the spirits. Svein was Earl Paul's forecastleman.

The chieftains who came to join Earl Paul that night were these: Eyvind Melbrigdason, with a fully-manned longship; Olaf Hrolfsson, with another ship, from Gairsay; Thorkel Flayer with a third, and Sigurd, who farmed there, with a fourth; the fifth ship was the Earl's. Now they sailed with these five ships over to Mainland, arriving there at sunset on the Thursday evening.

Overnight they gathered more men but could get no more ships. They meant to sail over to Shetland next day and confront Earl Rognvald, but early in the morning when it was light, just after sunrise, people came and told the Earl they had sighted some longships sailing north across the Pentland Firth, though they couldn't say whether there were ten of them or twelve. The Earl and his men decided that this must be Frakokk's fleet, and Earl Paul said they should attack them right away, but Olaf and Sigurd suggested more caution, since reinforcements could be reaching them at any moment. As they were rowing east of Tankerness, twelve longships came sailing towards them east from Mull Head, so the earl and his men roped their ships together. Then the farmer Erling of Tankerness and his sons came to Earl Paul and offered to help, but the ships were so crowded, they thought they couldn't pack any more aboard. So the Earl asked Erling and his men to spend the time, while there was no risk, in collecting rocks for them. Just as everything was ready, Olvir's fleet came up and attacked them with a larger number of ships, though they were smaller ones. But Olvir himself commanded a large ship, which he sailed right up to the Earl's, and a fierce battle began. Olaf Hrolfsson moved his ship towards the smaller craft of Olvir, and his stood so much higher that it took him very little time to clear three ships. Olvir laid so hard against the Earl's ship that the men in the bows were forced back behind the mast and, urging his men to board the ship, he was the first man himself to do so. Svein Breast-Rope was

fighting bravely at the head of Earl Paul's men and, when
Paul saw that Olvir had boarded his ship he shouted encouragement to his men and jumped off the raised deck into the bows.
Olvir saw this and picked up a throwing-spear, hurling it at
the Earl and striking his shield so hard that he fell on the deck.
There was a lot of shouting and just at that moment Svein
Breast-Rope picked up a large piece of rock. He flung it at
Olvir, hitting him such a blow on the chest that he was
knocked overboard into the sea. His men managed to get hold
of him and pulled him back aboard but he had been knocked
unconscious and nobody knew whether he was alive or dead.
Then some of Olvir's men ran to cut the grappling ropes and
get away, and every single one of them was driven off the
Earl's ship. They started rowing away and, though Olvir came
to and ordered them not to run, nobody took any notice of
what he was saying.

The Earl chased after them east of Mainland, then all the
way beyond South Ronaldsay into the Pentland Firth, but
when the gap between them began to widen the Earl turned
back. Five of Olvir's ships were left deserted at the place of
battle and these the Earl took, putting his own crews aboard.
The battle took place on a Friday. Next night the Earl had
his fleet refitted, then a large number of men came to join
him with two longships, so that by the morning he had twelve,
all of them well-manned. On the Saturday he sailed to Shetland,
arriving by night at Yell Sound and catching the men guarding
Earl Rognvald's fleet completely by surprise. Earl Paul had
them killed on the spot and took the ships and all the money
aboard for himself.

Next morning Earl Rognvald got to hear of this and gathered
his forces together, including a good many farmers, then went
down to the beach and challenged Earl Paul to come ashore
and fight. Earl Paul didn't trust the Shetlanders so he invited
the enemy to find some ships and fight him at sea. Earl
Rognvald and his men knew they had too few ships to stand
a chance against him, and that was how they parted. Earl Paul
sailed back with his fleet to Orkney and Earl Rognvald spent
the summer in Shetland, taking passage back in the autumn
on various trading ships. Their expedition was considered
something of a joke.

When Earl Rognvald got back home to his father, Kol
asked him whether he was satisfied with the way things had
gone. Rognvald said he thought his expedition had been a
disgrace and nothing to boast about.

'That's not the way I see it,' said Kol. 'I think your trip has been a success and that you've achieved a lot, now that the Shetlanders are your friends. A good effort is never wasted.'

'For you to praise this trip means only one of two things,' said Rognvald. 'Either you're less particular about matters than I thought, or you must know something about it that I don't. In future I'd be glad for you to do the planning and come along on the next trip with me.'

'I'm not going to make things easy for you,' said Kol, 'and at the same time stay in the background. If my advice is followed to the letter, you'll lose no credit.'

'I'll follow your advice gladly,' said Rognvald.

'This is the first piece of advice then,' said Kol. 'Send to King Harald and your other friends asking them to provide men and ships for you to sail west in the spring. Then we'll gather all the men we can muster over winter, and see to it that we either win Orkney or die there.'

'I'm not planning to go on many more journeys like the one I've just made,' said Rognvald, 'and I daresay those who went with me will feel the same.'

66. SVEIN ASLEIFARSON

After he had taken Earl Rognvald's ships, Earl Paul went back to Orkney with a victory he could be proud of, so he celebrated with a great feast, inviting all his most favoured chieftains. At the feast they decided to build a beacon on Fair Isle and set it alight should a fleet be seen approaching from Shetland. There was another on North Ronaldsay and on several other islands so that anyone could see all over Orkney if an enemy was coming.

Then people were appointed to raise levies in different parts of Orkney. Thorstein, son of Havard Gunnason, was in charge of North Ronaldsay. His brother Magnus had Sanday, Kugi had Westray and Sigurd of Westness, Rousay. Olaf Hrolfsson went across to Duncansby in Caithness and was in charge there. His son Valthjof was farming at the time on Stronsay.

Earl Paul presented his friends with gifts, and all of them promised him their undying friendship. He kept a large force together throughout the autumn until he heard that Rognvald and his men had cleared out of Shetland, and till Christmas nothing happened in the islands.

Earl Paul made preparations for a great Christmas feast at his estate called Orphir, and to it he invited a large number of important guests. One of these was Valthjof Olafsson, who set out in a ten-oared boat, but was drowned with his crew in Stronsay Firth on Christmas Eve. People thought it a sad loss, for he had been a very great man. His father Olaf had a large following in Caithness, among them his other sons Svein and Gunnar, and Asbjorn and Margad, the sons of Grim of Swona. Three days before Christmas Svein Olafsson had gone fishing with Asbjorn and Margad, both good men who used to travel with him wherever he went. His mother Asleif and Gunnar, his brother, had gone to visit friends nearby, and the following night, after they had left, Olvir Brawl arrived in Duncansby with a band of men who had been with him the previous summer on a viking expedition. They surrounded the house, set fire to it, and burned to death Olaf and five other men, though they allowed the rest of the household to go outside. Then Olvir and his men went off with all the property they could lay hands on.

Svein, who was later to be known as Asleifarson, came back home just before Christmas Eve and put out at once into the Pentland Firth, reaching Swona around midnight where he met Grim, the father of Asbjorn and Margad. Grim boarded his boat and they all ferried Svein over to Knarston on Scapa, where the farmer was called Arnkel and had two sons, Hanef and Sigurd. Svein gave Grim a gold ring and Grim went back with his sons. Then Hanef and Sigurd went with Svein over to Orphir, where he was given a good welcome and escorted to his kinsman Eyvind Melbrigdason. Eyvind led Svein up to Earl Paul who greeted him warmly and asked the news. Svein told the Earl that his father had been killed with all the details of how it had happened. The Earl was shocked at the news and said that the fault was largely his own. He asked Svein to stay with him and promised to add greatly to his honour. Svein thanked him for his offer and accepted it.

Just after that, people went to Vespers. The farmstead was a large one, standing on a hillside sloping down behind the farm buildings. Damsay is in the Bay of Firth, which lies on the other side of the hill. On the island there was a stronghold and the man in charge was called Blann, the son of Thorstein of Flydruness. There was a great drinking-hall at Orphir, with a door in the south wall near the eastern gable, and in front of the hall, just a few paces down from it, stood a fine church. On the left as you came into the hall was a large stone slab, with a lot of big ale vats behind it, and opposite the door was the living-room.

113

When people came back from Vespers they were led to their seats. The Earl had Svein Asleifarson placed next to him away from the door, and Svein Breast-Rope sat opposite him with his kinsman, Jon. After the tables had been taken down, visitors came with the news that Valthjof had been drowned. The Earl thought it a very sad affair and asked people not to do anything to annoy Svein Asleifarson over Christmas as he already had enough on his mind. In the evening after they had finished drinking, the Earl and most of his guests went to their beds, but Svein Breast-Rope spent the night there out in the open, as he often did. Next morning people attended Matins and then, after High Mass, they settled down to a meal.

After the Earl, Eyvind Melbrigdason was the senior man at the feast so he did not sit down, but served the two Sveins from two separate vessels, while the cup-bearers and boy attendants stood in front of the Earl's table. Then Svein Breast-Rope got the idea that Eyvind was filling up his cup more than that of Svein Asleifarson and even taking Svein Asleifarson's cup before he'd finished it, so he claimed that the other Svein was not playing fair at the drinking. For a long time there had been little love lost between Svein Breast-Rope and Olaf Hrolfsson, or between the two Sveins ever since Svein Asleifarson had reached manhood. After they had carried on drinking for some time they went out for Nones, then came back and drank toasts from horns. Next, Svein Breast-Rope wanted to exchange horns with his namesake, believing that Svein Asleifarson's was smaller. Eyvind thrust a large horn into the hand of Svein Asleifarson, who offered it to the other Svein. Svein Breast-Rope got into a temper and kept muttering, just loud enough for the earl and some others to hear: 'Svein will kill Svein, and Svein shall kill Svein,' but people hushed it up.

They kept drinking till Vespers and when the Earl went out Svein Asleifarson walked ahead of him, but Svein Breast-Rope stayed behind, still drinking. Eyvind came after them into the ale-room and asked Svein Asleifarson for a word in private.

'Did you hear what the other Svein said when you handed him the horn?' he asked.

'No, I didn't,' he replied.

Then Eyvind repeated what the other had said, adding that the Devil must have put the words into his mouth during the night.

'He means to kill you all right,' said Eyvind, 'so make sure you're the first to get a blow in, and kill him.'

114

Then Eyvind gave him an axe, telling him to stand in the shadow of the stone slab, strike Svein from the front if Jon walked ahead, but from the back if Jon walked behind.

The Earl went to church and no one paid any attention to Eyvind and Svein Asleifarson. Shortly after the Earl had gone out, Svein Breast-Rope and Jon followed. Svein Breast-Rope had a sword in his hand, for he always carried one even when everyone else was unarmed. Jon was walking ahead. There was a light at the door but it was very dark outside and as Svein Breast-Rope reached the outer door, Svein Asleifarson struck him on the forehead. He stumbled a little, but didn't fall, and as he straightened up he saw someone standing in the doorway. He assumed that this must be the one who had wounded him so he struck him on the head, splitting it open right down to the shoulders. But it was his kinsman Jon, and both of them fell to the ground.

At that moment Eyvind came up, took Svein Asleifarson into the room opposite the entrance and had him pulled outside through a skylight. Magnus Eyvindarson had a horse ready for him and accompanied him away beyond the farmstead as far as the Bay of Firth. There they boarded a ship, and Magnus took Svein over to Damsay and up to the stronghold there. Next morning Blann ferried him north to Bishop William on Egilsay, where on their arrival the bishop was saying Mass. After Mass Svein was taken secretly to the bishop and he told him all that had happened—the deaths of his father and Valthjof, and the killings of Svein Breast-Rope and Jon—then asked for the bishop's help. The bishop thanked him for killing Svein Breast-Rope and called it good riddance.

The bishop let Svein stay there for the rest of the Christmas season, and afterwards sent him to Tiree in the Hebrides to a man called Holdbodi Hundason, a great chieftain, who gave him a good welcome. He stayed there over winter and everyone thought well of him.

67. PREPARATIONS

Shortly after the killings at Orphir had taken place people ran out of the church and carried Svein Breast-Rope into the farmhouse. He was unconscious, not dead, but he died during the night.

The Earl ordered everyone to his seat so that he could discover who was responsible for the killings: then Svein

Asleifarson was found to be missing so he was assumed to be the killer.

Then Eyvind stood up and spoke.

'Anyone can see that Svein Breast-Rope must have killed Jon,' he said.

The Earl then said that no one should harm a hair of Svein Asleifarson's head, adding that there must be a reason for what had happened.

'But if he tries to avoid me,' said the Earl, 'he'll find himself in real trouble.'

People thought it most likely that Svein would have gone north to Paplay to see Hakon Karl, the brother of Earl Magnus the Holy, that great, gentle and moderate chieftain. For the rest of the winter the Earl heard nothing of the whereabouts of Svein Asleifarson, so he made him an outlaw.

In the spring the Earl travelled widely collecting rents throughout the Northern Isles. He made friends with all the most prominent people and was generally very free with his money. He came to Stronsay and gave to Thorkel Flayer the estate that had once belonged to Valthjof Olafsson, for finding out where Svein was staying.

'Evidently,' said Thorkel, 'the old saying that the king has many ears doesn't apply in this case. You may be only an earl but I think it amazing that you don't know where Svein is. I knew right away that Bishop William had sent him to Holdbodi Hundason in the Hebrides, and that's where he's been all winter.'

'What can I do about a bishop who does a thing like that?' asked the Earl.

'Don't put the blame for what's happened on the bishop,' said Thorkel. 'When Rognvald and his men come from the east you'll need every friend you've got.'

The Earl said that what he had to say was true.

From there the Earl travelled to North Ronaldsay where he attended a feast arranged by Ragna and her son Thorstein. Ragna was an intelligent woman and she and her son owned another farm, on Papa Westray. The Earl stayed the night there because the weather prevented him from going to Westray to visit Kugi.

The Earl and Ragna talked about a good many things and she told him that, though Svein Breast-Rope may have been a good fighting man, he was no loss to the Earl.

'You lost a lot of friends because of him,' she said, 'and if you want my advice on this very tricky problem you're facing, make all the friends you can and settle your differences. Better not hold this against Bishop William or any other of Svein Asleifarson's kin. Instead, hold back whatever anger you might feel against the bishop, send somebody to the Hebrides for Svein, pardon him and give him back his property, so that he might be the same to you as his father was. It's always been the way of great leaders to look after their friends and make them stronger and more popular.'

'You're a sharp woman, Ragna,' said the Earl, 'but you're not the Earl of Orkney yet and you're not going to rule in this land. You seriously expect me to bribe Svein to make a settlement, and think that will bring me victory!'

He made himself out to be very angry.

'Let God settle the matter between my kinsman Earl Rognvald and me,' he went on, 'and may each of us get what he deserves. If I've done him any wrong, now is the time for me to make up for it. But if he wants to attack my earldom, I'd call that man my best friend who would help me keep what power I have. I've never set eyes on Rognvald, nor knowingly offended him, and whatever my kinsmen may have done, everyone must see that I had no part in it.'

Many people said it would be unwise to fight Rognvald for the earldom, but none of them contradicted the Earl.

Late in the spring, Earl Paul had beacons built on Fair Isle and North Ronaldsay and on most of the other islands, so that each could be seen from the others. There was a man called Dagfinn Hlodvisson, a stouthearted farmer on Fair Isle, charged with the task of guarding the beacon there and setting fire to it if the enemy fleet were to be seen approaching from Shetland.

Earl Rognvald spent that winter at home in Agder on his estates and those of his father, sending messages to his kinsmen and friends; or travelling to see them, asking for help, both men and ships, on an expedition west. Most of them responded well to whatever he wanted. Early in March, Kol sent two cargo-ships abroad, one west to England to buy provisions and weapons, the other south to Denmark for all the things Kol needed as the one in charge of preparations. The two boats were supposed to be back by Easter, since the plan was to have everything ready for the expedition by the week following.

Earl Rognvald and his father had a longship each and Solmund had a third, while Kol had a provision ship. When they got to Bergen King Harald was there and gave Rognvald a fully-manned longship. Jon Foot had yet another, and there was a sixth, belonging to Aslak, son of Erlend of the Henn Isles and grandson of Steigar-Thorir: he also had a provision ship. So it was six large ships they had, with five cutters and three cargo-ships. While they were waiting off the Henn Isles for a favourable wind, a ship arrived from the west and they heard all the news from Orkney, including what preparations Earl Paul was making should Earl Rognvald arrive there in the west.

68. ROGNVALD'S VOW

While they were in the Henn Isles, Earl Rognvald had the horn sounded for a meeting, and there he talked about Earl Paul's preparations, as well as about the enmity shown him by the men of Orkney when they decided to deny him the family inheritance rightfully granted him by the Kings of Norway. He talked about this at length and with great eloquence: and he said that he meant his trip to Orkney to end either in victory or death. His men applauded his speech and promised him their loyal support. Then Kol got to his feet and spoke.

'We've heard reports from Orkney that everyone there wants to stand up against you and defend the realm beside Earl Paul. They'll be slow to abandon the hatred they've fostered against you, kinsman. Now, here's my advice: look for support where men will say the true owner of the realm granted it you, and that's the holy Earl Magnus, your uncle. I want you to make a vow to him, that should he grant you your family inheritance and his own legacy, and should you come to power, then you'll build a stone minster at Kirkwall more magnificent than any in Orkney, that you'll have it dedicated to your uncle the holy Earl Magnus and provide it with all the funds it will need to flourish. In addition, his holy relics and the episcopal seat must be moved there.'

Everyone thought it a great idea and the vow was solemnly sworn. After that they put out to sea before a fair wind and made land at Shetland, where they and the local people were delighted to see each other. They stayed there for a while and the Shetlanders had plenty of news for them from Orkney.

69. STRATAGEMS

One day Kol had a talk with Uni, whose name we've mentioned before. When he joined Kol after plotting Brynjolf's death he was getting on in years.

'Which would you rather do,' asked Kol, 'prevent the beacon

being kindled on Fair Isle or make sure another beacon isn't lit when that one is? I'm asking you this because I know you're more intelligent than most of the people here, even men of higher status than yourself.'

'I'm neither the man to give advice nor to issue military orders,' said Uni, 'I prefer the second alternative and I'll see to the arrangements myself.'

Shortly afterwards, Kol had a number of small ships fitted out and began sailing towards Orkney. There were no important men there apart from Kol himself. When they had travelled far enough to think they could be seen from Fair Isle, he had every ship hoist sail, though he ordered the oarsmen to keep pulling in the opposite direction so that the ships would move forward as little as possible, even in a good breeze. First of all he had the sails hoisted only up to half-mast, but later they were to hoist them higher, so that they would seem to have covered some distance. Kol said their sails would be noticed on Fair Isle and the ships would appear to be approaching faster than they were.

'Maybe they'll set the beacon alight,' he said, 'and go and report to the Earl themselves.'

When the beacon on Fair Isle was seen to be alight, Thorstein Rognuson had the beacon lit on North Ronaldsay, and so one after another was lit throughout the islands. All the farmers gathered around the Earl, making up a sizeable army.

When Kol saw the beacon ablaze, he ordered his men to turn back, saying that this trick might sow discord in certain places. With that he went back to Shetland and told Uni that now it was his turn.

Uni chose three young Shetlanders to come with him in a six-oared boat with provisions and fishing-tackle and rowed over to Fair Isle. He said he was a Norwegian married in Shetland and that he had these three sons. Then he said he'd been robbed by Earl Rognvald's men, and had harsh words to say about them. Uni got lodgings there and his three so-called sons started fishing, but he stayed at home looking after the catch. He got talking to people on the island, and in time they got to know him and like him.

70. DISCORD AMONG PAUL'S MEN

After Dagfinn had fired the beacon, he went to join Earl Paul, as we've said, and so did all the Earl's leading men. A close watch was kept on Earl Rognvald's movements and people thought it very odd there was no sign of his troops. They held their army in readiness for three days, but then the farmers started to grumble and say how stupid it had been to set fire to the beacons just because some fishermen and their boats had been sighted. Thorstein Rognuson was blamed for his mistake in lighting the beacon on North Ronaldsay, though he said there was nothing for him to do but light it when he saw the one burning on Fair Isle, and he put all the blame on Dagfinn.

'People suffer much more on your account,' said Dagfinn, 'than for anything you can blame on me.'

Thorstein told him to shut up, went for him with an axe and struck him a blow that killed him on the spot, then the others ran for their weapons and fighting broke out—this all happened on Mainland, not far from Kirkwall. Sigurd of Westness and his sons, Hakon Pike and Brynjolf, were on the side of Dagfinn's father; Hlodvir, and the kinsmen of Thorstein supported him. When the Earl was told he went to the scene but it took him a long time to separate them. Then Kugi of Westray made a long speech.

'You mustn't disgrace the Earl like this,' he said, 'fighting amongst yourselves. It won't be long before we'll be needing every man we can get. It's up to us to stay prepared and not squabble with one another. All this must have happened just the way our enemies hoped and planned, a trick of theirs to put the beacons out of action. So we can expect them any day and we'd better make our own plans. In this case, Dagfinn wasn't acting out of malice, though he shouldn't have been so rash.'

Here Kugi had hit on the truth, and he explained the situation in a long and sensible speech. Eventually it was agreed by both parties that the Earl should decide what ought to be done. The outcome was that they disbanded their force and the men went back home.

A man called Eirik was given responsibility for the beacon on Fair Isle, and after Uni had been there a little while he came to see Eirik.

'Would you like me to look after the beacon?' he asked. 'I've nothing else to do so I can sit there the whole time.'

Eirik agreed, but, when no one was around, Uni carried water to the beacon and soaked it so that it wouldn't burn.

71. ROGNVALD ARRIVES IN ORKNEY

Earl Rognvald and his men came to the conclusion that they ought to wait till the spring tide coincided with an easterly wind, for in those conditions it is virtually impossible to go between Westray and Mainland, though with the wind easterly one can sail from Shetland to Westray. And that's what Rognvald and his men did, arriving at Pierowall on Westray upon a Friday, and going to a man called Helgi who farmed there.

No beacon was lit because, when the sails had been sighted at Fair Isle, Eirik got himself ready to go off to join Earl Paul and sent someone else to Uni, asking him to light the beacon. Uni wasn't there when they arrived and, when they tried to light it, the beacon was so wet it wouldn't burn. As soon as Eirik heard this he realised what had happened and went to tell Earl Paul.

Once Earl Rognvald had landed on Westray, the people of the island gathered together, with Kugi and Helgi making the decisions for them. The first thing they did was to ask the Earl for mercy, and the outcome was that the people of Westray accepted Earl Rognvald as their overlord and swore oaths of allegiance to him.

72. ROGNVALD ON WESTRAY

On Sunday, Earl Rognvald attended Mass there in the village and was standing with his companions outside the church. Then they saw sixteen men, unarmed and with shaven heads, walking by, and thought them very oddly equipped. The Earl's men discussed who these people might be, and then the Earl made this verse:

> Sixteen I've seen
> stepping together; shaved
> their foreheads, no fur
> growth on their faces.
> We bear witness,
> west on this windswept isle,
> many a proud maid
> parades here, poll-pared.

After the week-end, Rognvald went with his men on a visit to the nearest settlements, where everyone submitted to him.

One night, it so happened on Westray that the Earl's men heard talk of a secret meeting being held by the islanders to hatch a plot against Rognvald. When he got these reports, the Earl set off himself for the meeting. Not only that, the

Earl's men had beaten up a number of the islanders: they had
taken Kugi and put shackles on him, claiming that he was the
one who had started all the trouble. When Rognvald came to
the meeting, Kugi cast himself down at the Earl's feet and
cried that his case should be left entirely in the hands of God
and the Earl. Then Kugi pleaded his case with eloquence and
there were plenty to back him up, but the Earl made his verse:

> Bent-iron I see bound
> about, night-beast, your
> legs, locking them
> from leaping away, Kugi:
> keep your word, care,
> Kugi, for your oath, don't
> you dare hold more dark
> councils, no more dodges.

The Earl spared the lives of all those involved and the
islanders bound themselves to new agreements.

73. THE BURNING OF THORKEL FLAYER

When the news began to spread of Earl Rognvald's arrival in
Orkney and how many had surrendered themselves to him,
Earl Paul held a meeting on Mainland and consulted with his
men, asking for guidance as to how this tricky situation might
be handled, but he got a mixed response. Some people advised
him to share the rule with Earl Rognvald, but most of the
leading men, and the farmers too, wanted him to buy Rognvald
off with money to go away, even offering to make contri-
butions of their own. Some wanted to put up a fight, saying
that it had proved successful in the past.

Earl Rognvald had his spies at the meeting and when they
came back he asked how things had gone. There was a poet
there who gave him this answer:

> I've heard men who hate us
> hide their true minds—
> great lord, among landed
> men I learned
> that many a warrior
> wants you, wolf-crammer,
> to keep ready your keels
> in Earl Paul's country.

After that Earl Rognvald sent envoys to the bishop asking him to mediate. The bishop sent for Thorstein Rognuson and Thorstein Havardsson of Sanday, with the request that they should try to reconcile the kinsmen. The bishop managed to arrange a fortnight's truce to help bring about a settlement. Then the islands were divided between the Earls and they came to an agreement over how the expenses were to be shared during this period. At that, Earl Rognvald went to Mainland and Earl Paul to Rousay.

At that time it happened in Orkney that two kinsmen of Svein Asleifarson, Jon Wing of Upland on Hoy, and Richard of Brekkur on Stronsay, attacked Thorkel Flayer at the farm once belonging to Valthjof and burned him to death in the house, along with eight other men. After that they went to see Earl Rognvald and told him that unless he took them in they would join Earl Paul with all their kinsmen. The Earl decided not to turn them away.

When Haflidi Thorkelsson heard about this, and that his father had been burned to death, he went to see Earl Paul, who took him in. Then Jon and his men gave their allegiance to Earl Rognvald, who soon had a large following and enjoyed great popularity.

Earl Rognvald gave Jon, Solmund, Aslak and a good many more of his supporters leave to go home, but they decided to wait and see how things would turn out.

'I think that if it's God's will for me to take over rule in Orkney,' said Rognvald, 'He'll strengthen me through my uncle, the holy Earl Magnus, and keep me in power even though you go back to your estates.'

After that they went back home to Norway.

74. EARL PAUL CAPTURED

Early in the spring Svein Asleifarson had put out from the Hebrides and had sailed to see his friends in Scotland. He spent quite a long time at Atholl with Earl Maddod and Margaret Hakon's-Daughter, talking over a good many matters with them in private. It was there that he heard about the fighting in Orkney, and this made him very keen to go there and see his kinsmen. First he travelled to Thurso in Caithness, taking with him a man of good family called Ljotolf, who had been with him most of the spring. They called on Frakokk's brother, Earl Ottar of Thurso, and Ljotolf did his best to reconcile Ottar and Svein over all the troubles that Frakokk had been the cause of, with the result that Ottar paid out compensation on his own behalf. He also promised his friendship to Svein, who in turn promised Ottar that he would support Erlend, the son of Harald Smooth-Tongue, in his claim over his patrimony in Orkney, at any time he might wish to follow it up.

Svein exchanged his ship for a cargo-boat and put out with thirty men aboard. He had a north-westerly wind as he sailed across the Pentland Firth, hugging the west coast of Mainland as far as the Eynhallow Sound, then along the Sound and home to Rousay.

At the far end of the island is a large headland with a great deal of rocky debris at its foot where otters used often to be seen among the rocks. As they were rowing across the Sound, Svein spoke.

'Some people are there on the headland,' he said. 'Let's put in and find out what's happened, but first I want you to make a few alterations to the set-up. We'll spread out our sleeping bags. Twenty of you are to get into them while the other ten row. Let's go very quietly.'

When they came closer to the headland, the men there shouted for them to row on to Westness and give Earl Paul whatever they had on board, thinking that they were talking to some merchants.

Earl Paul had stayed overnight at Westness for a feast at Sigurd's. He'd got up early and gone to the southern end of the island to hunt an otter which was on the rocky shore beneath the headland. His party were about to go back to the house for a morning drink.

The men in the cargo-boat rowed up to the shore and exchanged news with the others, telling them where they had come from and asking where was the Earl. The men said he was there on the headland with them. Svein and the others lying in their sleeping-bags heard this, and Svein told them to put in at a certain place out of sight of the headland, saying they should arm themselves and kill the Earl's men as soon as they could, which is what they did, killing nineteen men there, though six of Svein's men were killed too. They took Earl Paul by force and led him back to the boat. Then they altered direction, sailed the same way back west of Mainland, right between Hoy and Graemsay, then east of the Swelchie, into the Moray Firth and right up the Firth to the Oykel. There Svein left his ship with twenty men in charge, taking the rest of them with him to Atholl, where they were given a warm welcome by Earl Maddod and Margaret, Earl Paul's sister. Earl Maddad gave Earl Paul his own high-seat. When they had settled down, Margaret came in with a crowd of women and kissed her brother, after which entertainers were brought to amuse the guests. Earl Paul was rather subdued, not surprisingly in view of the problems he had on his mind. There's no record of what Earl Paul and Svein said to each other while they were together, though Earl Maddad, Margaret and Svein went on one side to have a word in private. In the evening, after the drinking, Svein and his men were led to a separate bed-chamber and locked inside, and every night they spent there the same thing happened.

75. END OF EARL PAUL

One day Margaret announced that Svein Asleifarson was to go to see Earl Rognvald in Orkney and ask which he would prefer as his co-ruler, Earl Paul or Harald, the son of herself and Maddad, three years old at the time. Earl Paul overheard them.

'I'll tell you what I have in mind,' he said, 'to leave my earldom for good and go so far that nobody will ever have heard tell of such travels. I'll never go back to Orkney again. I can see God's vengeance in this for all the robberies my kin is guilty of, but if God thinks the earldom is mine to give, Harald can have it as long as he can hold on to it. As for myself, I'll need a little money so that I can settle down in some monastery or other, where you can keep an eye on me and see to it that I don't get away. And, Svein, I want you to go to Orkney and tell them I've been blinded, and maimed as well, because my friends will come and visit me if they know I'm a fit man. It could be, too, that I'd be persuaded to go back to my realm with them, since my guess is that they'll feel our parting to be a greater loss for them than it really is.' Nothing more of the Earl's speech is known.

After that Svein Asleifarson set off for Orkney, but Earl Paul stayed behind in Scotland. This is Svein's account of what happened, but according to some people, the story was a lot uglier: Margaret hired Svein Asleifarson to blind her brother, Earl Paul, then put him in prison, and later on hired someone else to kill him. We can't say which comes nearer the truth, but this much is known, that he never came back to Orkney and never gained power in Scotland.

125

76. A MEETING AT KIRKWALL

In the meantime at Westness, when Earl Paul did not return
home, the farmer, Sigurd, sent some men to look for him and,
when they came to the rocky foreshore, they saw the bodies
lying there. They thought the Earl must be among the dead
and hurried back to tell the news. Sigurd went to the scene at
once to investigate, and there they identified nineteen of the
Earl's men along with six other bodies they couldn't recognise.

Then Sigurd sent messengers to Egilsay, reporting to the
bishop what had happened. The bishop set out at once to see
Sigurd and they had a talk about it. Sigurd guessed that it
must have been done with the connivance of Earl Rognvald,
but the bishop answered that time would show Earl Rognvald
had not betrayed his cousin Earl Paul.

'It's my guess,' said the bishop, 'that other people are
responsible for this crime.'

Borgar, the son of Jaddvor Erlend's-Daughter, was farming
at Gaitnip and he had noticed not only how the cargo-boat
had put in but also that it went back southwards. When he
told people about this they thought it must be some scheme of
Frakokk and Olvir Brawl. But when it became generally
known in the islands that Earl Paul had vanished without
trace or any word, people started looking for protection, mostly
turning to Earl Rognvald and swearing oaths of loyalty to
him. However, Sigurd of Westness and his sons Brynjolf
and Hakon Pike said they would not swear oaths to anyone
until they knew what had happened to Earl Paul and whether
or not he might be expected to return. There were others who
refused to swear oaths to Earl Rognvald, but some said that
if nothing had been heard of Earl Paul by a certain date they
would submit. Once Earl Rognvald realised that he was up
against a large number of important people, no condition the
farmers laid down was a matter for blunt refusal. As time
went by, more people came to join him at every one of the
assemblies he held regularly with the farmers.

It happened one day, when Rognvald was holding one of
these meetings with the farmers, that the people there saw
nine armed men walking to the assembly from Scapa. As these
men came closer, people saw that one of them was Svein
Asleifarson, and were curious to know what news he had.
Svein had gone north to Scapa by ship, left it there, and
travelled on foot to Kirkwall. As the men came up, Svein's
friends and kinsmen crowded round him asking the news, but

he had little to say apart from telling someone to fetch the bishop.

The bishop gave him a good welcome, for they were old friends, and the two men went aside for a talk. Svein told the bishop all about his travels, saying nothing but the truth, then asked for his advice on this rather tricky affair.

'It's a very serious matter indeed that you've just told me about, Svein,' said the bishop, 'and I think it's beyond our powers to deal with your case. But I want you to wait here while I put it before the assembly and Earl Rognvald.'

The bishop went to the assembly to ask for a hearing and on getting it he gave an account of Svein's case—why he had left Orkney and how Earl Paul had blamed him for the killing of that most wicked of men, Svein Breast-Rope. The bishop pleaded with Earl Rognvald and the whole assembly to make a truce with Svein.

'For myself,' the Earl answered, 'I can promise Svein a three-day truce, but it strikes me, bishop, from the look on your face, that you and Svein are about to tell us some great news that hasn't yet been made public. I want you to take Svein into your care and be responsible for him and tomorrow I'd like a word with him.'

'Yes, indeed,' said the bishop, 'he's very eager to speak to you as soon as possible, and he wants to become your retainer too, if you'll have him.'

'I don't think I've an overabundance of friends in the land,' said the Earl, 'but before I say yes to that we'll need to discuss the matter further.'

At that the four of them went aside for a talk, Earl Rognvald, his father Kol, the bishop and Svein Asleifarson. Svein explained all the ups and downs of his relationship with Earl Paul, then all four agreed to send most of the people away from the assembly.

Next morning the Earl addressed the assembly and gave people permission to return home. When most of them had gone he ordered every single one that was left to come and see him, though first of all he had them all promise to keep the peace with Svein while he had his say. Later that morning, Hakon Karl, brother of the holy Earl Magnus, was given the task of telling Sigurd of Westness and his sons about Earl Paul's travels and also that he was not to be expected back and had been mutilated.

'It's a great shock to me to hear that the Earl has gone for good,' said Sigurd, 'but I find his maiming the hardest thing of all to bear. If it hadn't been for that, I'd gladly have sought him out, no matter where.'

And afterwards, Sigurd told his friends that if he'd had the strength he wouldn't have let Hakon get away unhurt after telling that story, so greatly had it troubled him.

Once they heard the news, all the people of Orkney submitted themselves to Earl Rognvald, who now became sole ruler of the land that had once belonged to Earl Paul.

Not long after that, the ground-plan of St Magnus' Church was drawn up and builders hired for the work. So rapidly did the building progress that more was done in the first year than in the two or three that followed. Kol was principal supervisor of the construction and had the most say in it. As the building progressed, the Earl began to use up his assets, so very heavy were the costs, and he asked for his father's advice. Kol suggested that Rognvald should make it law that the Earls had inherited all the estates, yet allow the heirs to pay a fee for them, but this was thought rather severe. Then Earl Rognvald called the farmers to an assembly and offered them the chance to buy their estates, so that there would be no need to pay any fee, and to this they all agreed, so both sides were content. The Earl was to be paid one mark for every piece of ploughland in Orkney, after which there was no shortage of money for the church and the building was carried out with the greatest care.

77. HARALD MADDADARSON MADE AN EARL

After Earl Rognvald had been ruling over Orkney for two years he held a Christmas feast on his farm at Knarston. On the sixth day of Christmas a ship was seen sailing north across the Pentland Firth. The weather was fine and the Earl and many others were standing outside watching the ship. One of the men there was called Hrolf and he was the Earl's court-priest. As soon as the men landed they set off from the ship, and the Earl's men reckoned that there must be some fifteen or sixteen of them. Leading the group was a man wearing a blue cloak, his hair tucked into his cap. The centre of his chin was shaved but his moustache grew long over the lip and on the cheeks. People thought this a very odd looking man, but Hrolf explained that he was Bishop Jon of Atholl in Scotland, so they set out to meet them and gave the bishop a great welcome. The Earl set the bishop on his own high-seat and he himself served at table as cupbearer.

Next morning the bishop celebrated an early Mass, then went off to see Bishop William on Egilsay and stayed there till the tenth day of Christmas, after which the two bishops set out in a grand procession to see Earl Rognvald and state their mission. They told him about the private arrangement between Svein Asleifarson and Earl Maddad, that Harald Maddadarson would be given the title of earl and half of Orkney but that Earl Rognvald would rule over them. Even when Harald reached manhood, if there was a disagreement, Rognvald was to have his way. Svein was present and bore out what the bishop said.

They agreed with the Earl to hold a meeting in Caithness during Lent; later they concluded the agreement by sealing it with sworn oaths of all the best men of Orkney and Scotland. Then Harald Maddadarson went out to Orkney with Earl Rognvald and was given the title of earl.

Thorbjorn Clerk, son of Thorstein the Yeoman and Gudrun Frakokk's-Daughter, travelled with Earl Harald to Orkney. He was a shrewd and forceful man, acted as Harald's foster-father, and was very much his master. Thorbjorn got married in Orkney to Ingibjorg Olaf's-Daughter, sister of Svein Asleifarson. Sometimes he lived in Orkney and sometimes in Scotland. He was a very brave man, but in general a great bully.

Svein Asleifarson took over all the estates that had been the property of his father Olaf and brother Valthjof. He grew to be a powerful chieftain and always kept a large retinue. Svein was a shrewd man and had a talent for seeing into the future, but he was ruthless and violent. At the time, no two men were held in greater respect than Svein and his brother-in-law Thorbjorn, and they were on very close terms.

78. THE BURNING OF FRAKOKK

One day Svein Asleifarson had a word with Earl Rognvald, asking for men and ships so that he could take his revenge on Olvir and Frakokk for the burning of his father Olaf.

'Don't you think, Svein,' said the Earl, 'that we've little to fear now from Olvir and old Frakokk, who's hardly capable of much?'

'As long as they're alive they'll always cause trouble,' said

Svein, 'and after all I've done for you I wouldn't have expected you to refuse me this small favour.'

'How much do I have to give you to satisfy you?' asked the Earl.

'Two ships,' answered Svein, 'both well fitted-out.'

The Earl said that Svein would get what he asked for, and after that Svein prepared for the voyage, sailing south as soon as he was ready to the Moray Firth with a north-easterly wind as far as Banff, a market town in Scotland. From there he made his way beyond Moray to the Oykel, then on to Atholl where Maddad provided him with guides who knew the mountain and forest route he might choose. From Atholl he travelled by forest and mountain above all the settlements till he reached Helmsdale in the centre of Sutherland.

Olvir and Frakokk had posted spies in every direction from which they might expect trouble from Orkney, but they didn't bargain for an attack from this one and had no idea the men were there until Svein led them down the hillside behind Frakokk's farmstead. There Olvir Brawl faced them with sixty men, but though it didn't take long for the fighting to begin there was little resistance. Olvir and his men were unable to get away into the forest so they retreated down to the farmhouse, where there was fearful slaughter. Olvir managed to run to Helmsdale River and from there up the mountain, over to the west coast and across to the Hebrides. Now he is out of the story.

After Olvir had escaped, Svein and his men went to the farmstead and looted everything they could lay their hands on, then set fire to the house and burned everyone inside to death. That is how Frakokk died.

Svein plundered all over Sutherland before he and his men went back to their ships. Throughout the summer they lay out at sea, making raids on Scotland, and in the autumn got back to Orkney. Svein came to see Earl Rognvald who gave him a great welcome. Then Svein went across to Duncansby in Caithness, where he spent the winter.

Then Svein had a message from Holdbodi of the Hebrides asking for his help against a chieftain from Wales, a man called Robert, of English descent, who had arrived in the islands, driven Holdbodi off his estate and stolen a great deal of money. Svein wasted no time. As soon as he got word he sailed over to Orkney and asked Earl Rognvald for men and ships. The Earl wanted to know what was in his mind this time, so Svein told him that he'd had a request for help from the last man he could refuse, since that man had given the greatest help when Svein needed it most and when everyone else seemed to be against him.

'Not many Hebrideans are to be trusted, so better part while you're still friends,' said the Earl. 'Still, you must do whatever your sense of honour requires: I'll give you two ships, both fully-manned.'

Svein was pleased with that and set off right away for the Hebrides, but there was no sign of Holbodi till he reached the Isle of Man, to which Holdbodi had escaped. When Svein reached Man, Holdbodi was very glad to see him, for the Welshman had caused a great deal of damage on the island, killing and looting as he had all over Southern Europe. A man of good family called Andres had been killed by him and had left a widow, Ingirid, and a son called Sigmund. Ingirid was a lady of wealth and property, so Holdbodi advised Svein to ask her to marry him, but when he put the question to her she said that, if Svein wanted to marry her, he had to take revenge for her husband Andres. Svein said he could do the Welsh a bit of damage.

'But as for blood-debt,' he said, 'I'm not so sure how well I'll do.'

At that Svein and Holdbodi set out on a raiding expedition with five ships. They attacked Wales, going ashore at a place called Jarlsness, and created havoc there. One morning they came to a settlement which offered hardly any resistance. The farmers ran for their lives as Svein and his men looted the whole settlement and burned six farms before breakfast. An Icelander with Svein made this verse:

> Barns were burnt by us,
> —we bled them,
> the farmers; Svein
> ravaged six at sunrise.
> Savage, he sought
> to serve them, carried
> enough coal to kindle
> their cottages.

After that they went back to their ships and spent the rest of the summer sea-raiding and winning a great deal of plunder. The Welsh chief ran off to Lundy Island where there was a good stronghold. Svein and his men laid siege to it, but after a while they saw they were getting nowhere so in the autumn they went back to Man.

79. END OF A FRIENDSHIP

Over winter Svein celebrated his marriage with Ingirid and lived in grand style. In the spring he started gathering forces and went to see Holdbodi asking for his support, but Holdbodi only made excuses, saying that his men were busy at one thing or another, some of them on trading trips, so Svein got nothing out of him. But the truth of the matter was that Holdbodi and the Welshman had come to terms in secret and settled their differences with gifts of money.

Svein didn't let that stop him and set out with three ships, but got little in the way of loot during the first part of the summer. Later, however, they went south to Ireland and seized and robbed a merchant ship belonging to the monks of the Scilly Isles. He plundered all over the place in Ireland and in the autumn returned to Man with plenty of loot.

Svein Asleifarson had not been there long before he heard a rumour that Holdbodi was being disloyal to him. Svein said this couldn't be true, but one night during the winter his watchmen came and said they were under attack. Svein and his men went for their weapons and rushed outside, where they saw a large force of men carrying firebrands coming towards the farmstead. Svein and his men ran to the top of a nearby hillock and there they took their stand. They had a trumpet and, when they began sounding it, the place was so thickly populated that men came running from all directions and the attackers fell back. Svein and his men chased and routed them, killing a good many, though before they broke off there were plenty of wounded on both sides. The leader of these raiders was Holdbodi. He saved his skin by running away back to Lundy Isle where he got a good welcome from the chief and stayed on with him.

Svein went back home but kept a strong force and stayed on the lookout, as he put little trust in the Hebrideans. Late in the winter he sold his estates for cash and in the early spring set out north for Lewis. He had done a fair amount of pillaging on this expedition.

80. SVEIN AND THORBJORN RECONCILED

While Svein Asleifarson had been in the Hebrides, Earl Rognvald had gone over to Wick in Caithness to attend a feast given by a man called Hroald. Hroald had a brave-looking son called Svein. While the Earl was at this feast, Thorbjorn Clerk and his men came north from Scotland with the news that his father Thorstein the Yeoman had been killed by an earl called Valthjof. People were wondering what Earl Rognvald and Thorbjorn had to talk about at such length, for because of it the Earl was barely attending to his own affairs. Thorbjorn went back from Wick to Orkney accompanied by the Earl, who had Svein Hroaldsson as his cup-bearer. Thorbjorn had spent some time in Scotland before all this and had had two of the men who had been with Svein Asleifarson at Frakokk's burning put to death.

In the summer, when Svein Asleifarson came back from the Hebrides, he went home to his estate on Gairsay without visiting Earl Rognvald as he usually did at the end of viking expeditions. When the Earl heard that Svein had gone straight home, he asked Thorbjorn why Svein had not been to see him.

'It's my guess,' said Thorbjorn, 'that Svein is angry with me for having killed the men who were with him at Frakokk's burning.'

'I don't want you two at loggerheads,' said the Earl.

After that the Earl went over to Gairsay to arrange a settlement between them, an easy enough task since they both wanted the Earl himself to fix the terms. So he reconciled them and the settlement lasted for a long time.

81. EARL ROGNVALD'S POETRY

About that time an Icelandic ship put in at Orkney with a man aboard called Hall, the son of Thorarin Broad-Belly. He took lodgings with Thorstein and Ragna on North Ronaldsay, but he was not happy there and asked Thorstein to help him find a place with Earl Rognvald. They went to see him but the Earl would not take Hall in. When they got back, Ragna asked how things had gone and Hall made this verse:

> *I sent your son, Ragna,*
> *seeking work for me*
> *at court — cleverly*
> *he accomplished it:*
> *the generous gentleman*
> *rejected me: said he'd all*
> *the soldiers he needed,*
> *'so go swallow your sausages'.*

A little after this, Ragna went to see Earl Rognvald on
some business. She was wearing a red head-dress made of
horse-hair, and when the Earl saw that, he made a verse:

So, no sweet-talk:
time surely was when
the queenly ones covered
heads with a kerchief?
Now this merry matron
ties a mare's
tail—she's teasing me—
to her top-knot.

'This bears out again the old saying,' answered Ragna.
' "No man knows all": this comes from a stallion, not a mare.'
Then she took a silk kerchief and as she put it upon her head
she carried on talking about her business. The Earl was rather
cool at first, but as time went on he began to soften towards
her and she got what she wanted, a place for Hall amongst the
Earl's retinue, where he stayed for a long time after that.
Together they composed *The Old Key of Metres*, using five
verses to illustrate each metre: but in these days only two are
used as the poem was thought too long.

82. SVEIN AND THORBJORN
FALL OUT

It is said that when Svein Asleifarson heard Holdbodi had
arrived in the Hebrides, he asked Earl Rognvald for troops
to avenge himself. The Earl gave him five ships, one commanded by Thorbjorn Clerk, another by Haflidi, son of
Thorkel Flayer, a third by Dufniall, son of Havard Gunnason,
a fourth by Richard Thorleifarson, and a fifth commanded
by Svein himself.

As soon as Holdbodi heard about Svein's movements he
ran from the Hebrides. Svein and his men killed a lot of people
there, plundering and burning in a number of places. They
picked up plenty of loot, but couldn't catch up with Holdbodi,
who never came back to the Hebrides.

Svein wanted to spend the winter in the Hebrides, but
Thorbjorn was keen to go home, so in the autumn they sailed
north to Caithness and put in at Duncansby. As they were
about to share the loot, Svein announced that everyone should
have the same, apart from himself, and he was to have the

leader's portion since he had been commander-in-chief over all the troops and also because he was the one for whom the Earl had sent along support. He added that he was the one who had a quarrel with the Hebrideans, not them. Thorbjorn said that he had done as much as Svein to earn his share and had been just as much of a leader. All the other captains wanted to have equal shares, but Svein had his own way since he had much the greater support there in Caithness.

Thorbjorn went out to Orkney to see Earl Rognvald and told him about how things had gone between Svein and the other captains, who were in a fury because he had robbed them of their share.

The Earl said this would be neither the first nor the last time that Svein showed himself unjust and a bully.

'Still,' he said, 'the day will come for him to pay for his injustice. Don't make a fuss about this, I'll give you as much from my own pocket as you're losing to him. Another thing, I don't want you to make demands on him over this matter: I'd be glad if worse troubles weren't to arise because of him.'

'God reward you, my lord, for all the honour you show me,' said Thorbjorn, 'I promise not to argue with Svein about this, but I'll never again be his friend and I'll find some other way to humiliate him.'

After that he divorced Ingirid, Svein's sister, and sent her over to her brother in Caithness. Svein gave her a kindly welcome, but took this as a personal insult, and now there was a feeling of profound ill-will between the two men. So the old saying was once again borne out, 'Evil beware evil'.

While Svein was in the Hebrides, he had put Margad Grimsson of Duncansby in charge of the stewardship he himself held under Earl Rognvald. Now, Margad was a vicious troublemaker and his bullying didn't make him very popular. Those who suffered most from his injustice took refuge with Hroald and this led to bad feeling between Hroald and Margad. Not long after, Margad went south to Wick on business with twenty others and before he came back he set on the farmer Hroald, and killed him at his own home along with a number of his men. Then he and his companions went to Duncansby and joined Svein. Svein gathered his forces and went over to Lambaborg, ready to take a stand. It was a safe stronghold and they stayed put there, sixty strong, fetching in all the provisions and other things they needed. The fortress stood on a sea-cliff with a stoutly-built stone wall to landward. The cliff stretched quite a distance along the coast. They committed

many a robbery in Caithness, taking the loot into their stronghold, and so became thoroughly unpopular.

83. FROM CAITHNESS TO EDINBURGH

News of this reached the ears of Earl Rognvald and Svein
Hroaldsson, and Svein asked the Earl for support so that he
could seek redress in this case. There were plenty of men there
to back him up and the upshot was that Earl Rognvald set out
for Caithness with chieftains Thorbjorn, Haflidi Thorkelsson
and Dufniall Havardsson, all those most ill-disposed towards
Svein. When they got to Duncansby they found that Svein
had left, but they were told he was at Lambaborg, so there
the Earl led his men.

When they came up to the stronghold, Svein asked who was
in charge of these troops and they told him Earl Rognvald.
Svein asked the Earl why he had come and the Earl asked him
to hand over Margad. Svein asked if Margad's life would be
spared. The Earl said he was making no promises.

'I don't much feel like surrendering Margad to Svein
Hroaldsson,' replied Svein Asleifarson, 'or to any other
enemies of mine with you now. But as for you, my lord, I'll
gladly be reconciled.'

'Listen to the way the traitor talks!' answered Thorbjorn
Clerk. 'After plundering the Earl's land and living the life of a
thief and outlaw, he says he wants to be reconciled with Earl
Rognvald. It's a poor repayment to the Earl for all the
honours that he's heaped on you, and given the chance, you'll
do just the same to others.'

'No need for you to lay it on, Thorbjorn,' said Svein,
'nothing will be done because of anything you might say. My
own feeling is that before you and the Earl break up your
partnership, you'll find your own way to repay him for all that
he's heaped on you. Nobody who has dealings with you will
get much in the way of luck.'

Earl Rognvald ordered them to stop the slanging-match.

After that they laid siege to the fortress, cutting off all
supplies, but for a long time they were unable to storm it.
When provisions were running low, Svein Asleifarson called his
men together to discuss matters and they all said the same
thing, that they wanted to be guided as long as possible by his
advice. So Svein made this speech.

'As I see it,' he said, 'the least respectable thing we could
do would be to starve here, then surrender to our enemies. It's

all turned out as might have been expected. Compared with Earl Rognvald, we're short on luck and wisdom. We've tried for peace and a settlement for my comrade Margad and we've got neither. On the other hand, I know that there are others here who have a chance of coming to terms, but personally, I don't care to put his head under the axe. I know it's unfair that so many should have to suffer because of his problems, but I can't bring myself to abandon him, not just yet.'

After that, Svein tied together all the rope they could find and during the night they lowered Svein and Margad from the wall of the stronghold down into the sea. They started swimming and managed to get ashore beyond the end of the cliff, then travelled south through Sutherland to Moray and from there to Banff. They met some Orkneymen there who had a cargo-boat, captained by two men called Hallvard and Thorkel. Altogether there were ten in the crew, a dozen after Svein and Margad had gone aboard. They sailed south of Scotland as far as the Isle of May where there was a monastery at the time with an abbot in charge named Baldvini. For seven days Svein and his companions lay weatherbound there, claiming to be Earl Rognvald's envoys on their way to see the King of Scots. The monks doubted their story and suspected them of being robbers, so they sent to the mainland for help. As soon as Svein and his men realised this, they looted the monastery and boarded their ship, then sailed up the Firth of Forth and paid a visit to David, King of Scots at Edinburgh, where he gave Svein a friendly welcome and invited them to stay. Svein told the King all the circumstances of his visit, including what had happened between him and Earl Rognvald before they parted and how they had plundered on the Isle of May. Svein and his men stayed for some time with the King of Scots and were granted fine hospitality.

King David sent messages to those who had been robbed by Svein on his travels, letting each man assess his losses and compensating everyone with money for the damage done. King David offered to send for Svein's wife from Orkney and give him such status in Scotland as would make him well content. But Svein told the King what his own wishes were, that Margad should stay with the King and that David should send word to Rognvald asking him to make peace with Svein. Svein said he wanted to leave the decision entirely in the hands of Earl Rognvald, and added that he was always happy for them to be on good terms and miserable when they were not.

'This Earl must be a fine man,' said King David, 'and not

only that, it seems that as far as you're concerned, he's the only one whose affairs matter: you mean to pay no attention to our offer, and to gamble on his good faith?'

Svein said he never wanted to lose King David's friendship, but that he must ask him this favour, and the King said he would grant it. He sent messengers north to Orkney carrying gifts, asking the Earl to make peace with Svein. Later, Svein travelled north to Orkney himself, but Margad stayed behind with the King. When King David's envoys came to Earl Rognvald, he welcomed them and the gifts they brought, and promised to make things up with Svein. Then he received Svein into full friendship and settlement and Svein went home to his estates.

84. AN ACT OF REVENGE

After Svein and Margad had escaped from the stronghold, those who were left behind agreed to surrender it to Earl Rognvald. He asked them what was the last thing they knew of Svein and Margad, and they told him the whole story. The Earl heard them out.

'It's a fact,' he said, 'there's nobody quite like Svein, at least not among any we're likely to find here with us. A trick like that shows a strong, brave heart. You may have got yourselves involved in this trouble with Svein, but I'm not going to treat you badly. You're all free to go in peace.'

Then the Earl went back home to Orkney and sent Thorbjorn Clerk in a troop forty strong to Moray Firth to look for Svein and Margad, but there was nothing at all to learn. Then Thorbjorn told his men they were behaving a bit strangely.

'Here we are,' he said, 'rambling around after Svein while we know Valthjof, my father's killer, lives somewhere near here with hardly any men to back him up. If you're willing to join me in an attack on him, I promise you this: if we get any loot, you won't be robbed of your share as you were by Svein. Everything will be yours and you can give me whatever you think fit. I'm more interested in fame than money.'

After that they went to the house where Valthjof was attending a feast, surrounded it and without more ado set it on fire. Valthjof and his men rushed to the door asking who had started the fire and Thorbjorn told them who he was. Valthjof offered to pay compensation for the killing of Thorstein, but Thorbjorn told him there was no point in asking for any settlement. For a while, Valthjof and his men defended themselves bravely, but when the fire grew too much for them they rushed outside and there was little fight left in them, they were so worn down by the heat. Earl Valthjof fell there, along with thirty of his men. Thorbjorn took a great deal of plunder and kept his promise faithfully to his men. After that they went back to Orkney to see Earl Rognvald, who was very pleased with their expedition. Things were quiet and peaceful now in Orkney.

At that time there was a very able man called Kolbein Heap farming on Wyre in Orkney. He had a fine stone fort built there, a really solid stronghold. Kolbein was married to Herbjorg, sister of Hakon Child whose mother was Sigrid, daughter of Herborg Paul's-Daughter. Their children were Kolbein Karl, Bjarni the Poet, Sumarlidi, Aslak and Frida, all outstanding characters.

85. POETRY AND FISHING

In those days the sons of Harald Gilli were ruling in Norway. Eystein was the eldest, but since Ingi was the legitimate son the landholders had more respect for him and he let them have their own way in everything. The landholders who mostly shared power with him at that time were Ogmund and Erling, the sons of Kyrpinga-Orm. They persuaded King Ingi to extend a generous invitation for Earl Rognvald to come to Norway, since the truth was that the Earl had been on the very friendliest terms with Ingi's father. They asked the King to do all he could to win the Earl's affection, so that he would be a closer friend to Ingi than to his brothers, no matter what might happen between them. The Earl was in fact a close kinsman of the brothers and a good friend of them all.

When the invitation reached Earl Rognvald he wasted no time but started getting ready at once for the voyage, being very keen to go to Norway and visit his friends and kinsmen. He asked Earl Harald, who was nineteen years old at the time, to come along with him for pleasure and interest. When the Earls were ready they sailed east with some merchants and the very best of company, reaching Norway early in the spring. At Bergen they met King Ingi who gave them a great reception. Rognvald stayed there most of the summer, meeting a good many of his friends and kinsmen.

During the summer Eindridi the Young came back from Constantinople where he had been working as a mercenary for quite some time. He had plenty to tell people about it and they thought it great entertainment to ask him all about those foreign parts. The Earl often talked with him and one day, during their conversation, Eindridi spoke up.

'It seems very odd to me, Earl,' he said, 'that you don't want to go to the Holy Land yourself and are content to listen to people's reports about it. Men of ability like you are just the kind who ought to go there. It would bring you great respect if you were to mix with people from the noblest families.'

After Eindridi had spoken, there were plenty of others to back up his words and urge the Earl to be their leader on the expedition. Erling had a lot to say on the subject and promised to join in as long as the Earl would take charge. With so many of the most respected men persuading him, the Earl agreed to the expedition and, once the Earl and Erling had made their decision, a number of men from the very best families wanted to join too, including the landholders Eindridi the Young, who was to act as guide, Jon Petersson, Aslak Erlendsson and Guthorm Mjolukoll of Halogaland. It was stipulated that none of them, apart from the Earl, should have a ship with more than thirty oars and that his would be the only one to be ornamented. This was to ensure that no one would envy anyone else for having more men or a better equipped vessel. Jon Foot was given the task of building the Earl's ship for the voyage to the Holy Land and fitting it out with the best of everything.

In the autumn Earl Rognvald went back home, intending to stay in his realm for two years. King Ingi gave him a pair of longships, rather small but very handsome and fast, designed more for rowing. One of these, called the *Bog Cotton*, Rognvald gave to Earl Harald. The other was called the *Help*, and with these two ships the Earls sailed west across the sea. Earl Rognvald had received other fine gifts from his friends, too. They put out to sea on a Tuesday evening and sailed all night before a fair wind. On the Wednesday a fierce gale blew up and that night they made landfall. It was dark by then, but they could see breakers on all sides. So far they had been sailing close together and now they had no choice but to sail both ships ashore with the risk of wrecking them, so that is what they did. The place was rock-strewn along a narrow strip of foreshore and sheer cliffs rose above it. All hands were saved but they lost a lot of cargo, though some of it drifted ashore during the night. As usual Earl Rognvald bore up

better than anyone else and he was so cheerful he kept
twiddling his thumbs and making up poetry all the time. He
took a ring from his finger and made this verse:

> *I set this serpent*
> *circle, this hammered*
> *form on finger-branch,*
> *fashioning a verse*
> *for the girl who grants me*
> *(she gleams in gold*
> *of old giants) such joy,*
> *my thumbs dance a jig.*

After they had carried their baggage ashore they made their
way inland to look for buildings, as they were sure they had
landed in Shetland. They soon reached some farmsteads and
were billeted out at various places, where the people were
delighted at the Earl's arrival and asked him about his travels.
He made this verse:

> *The breaker battered*
> *our boats, cracked*
> *in sleet-storm our two*
> *sisters, our ships.*
> *Curling, the killer-wave*
> *crushed lives, the crew*
> *endured: the undaunted*
> *Earl's story won't die.*

The woman of the house brought Rognvald a fur for him to
use as a cloak. He stretched out his hands and took it with a
laugh, then said this:

> *Shivering in skin-cloak*
> *I seem less smart than*
> *when stepping in style*
> *from our sea-rinsed ship.*
> *The ocean's great maw*
> *ate up our overcoats,*
> *its surf drove our sea-horse*
> *smack into the cliff.*

A blazing fire was built up for them and they sat baking
themselves round it. A servant girl came shivering into the
room and mumbled something, but people couldn't understand what she was saying: then the Earl said that he understood her language:

You sit steaming, but Asa's
s-soaked to the skin;
f-f-far from the fire,
I'm freezing to death.

The Earl sent a dozen of his men to Einar of Gulberwick,
but he refused to take them in unless the Earl himself came
too. When the Earl heard about it he made this verse:

Einar would entertain
none but the Earl—
the bard speaks, brainwashed
with Odin's brew.
No honour in the oath
of egregious Einar: still,
one night, I saw swords
scatter sparks at his place.

It happened one day south in Shetland at Sumburgh Head
that a certain penniless farmer was still waiting for his mate
to join him long after all the other boats had put out, each as
soon as it was ready. Then a stranger wearing a white cowl
came up to the old man and asked him why he didn't go
fishing like the others. The farmer said that his companion
had not turned up.

'Would you like me to go out rowing with you, man?' asked
the stranger in the cowl.

'I would indeed,' said the farmer, 'but I want a share for the
use of my boat. I've a lot of children at home and I must do
all I can for them.'

So they rowed out beyond Sumburgh Head and round
Horse Island. There were strong currents where they lay, and
large whirlpools in which they were supposed to keep moving
while they fished from the current. The cowled man sat in the
bow pulling against the current while the old man tried to
fish, and he kept warning the stranger not to let them drift
into it, for then they'd be in real trouble; but the cowled man
paid no attention to the farmer's words and seemed not to be
worried even though the farmer was finding it a bit of a trial.
Shortly after that they were swept into the current and the
farmer was in an absolute panic.

'Just my miserable luck to take you rowing with me today,'
he said, 'now I'm going to drown here, and no one to help my
family, left penniless if I die.'

The farmer was so terrified, he started weeping with fear at the thought of dying.

'Cheer up, farmer,' said the cowled man, 'dry your eyes. He who let us drift into the current will bring us out of it as well.'

Then the cowled man pulled the boat out of the current, much to the farmer's relief. After they had rowed ashore and beached the boat, the farmer asked the stranger to start dividing the catch, but he told the farmer to share it out any way he pleased and said he only wanted the third belonging to himself. A good many people, men and women, many of them very poor, had gathered on the beach and the cowled man gave away to the poor every fish he had earned that day. Then he got ready to leave. He had to climb a slope where a number of women were sitting and, as he began to make his way up, his feet shot from under him where the rain had made it slippery and he tumbled down to the bottom of the slope. The first woman to notice this burst out laughing, whereupon others joined in, and when the cowled man heard them he made this verse:

> *Wittily the woman*
> *mocks my wear,*
> *but she laughs overlong,*
> *and may not laugh last.*
> *Early I sailed out,*
> *eagerly, and all fully*
> *furnished for fishing.*
> *Who'd figure me for an earl?*

Then he walked away and later on people found out that the stranger was Earl Rognvald himself. Since then it has been revealed to a number of people that Rognvald performed many an act both happy in the eyes of God and entertaining to men, and they realised the significance of the words in the verse, that not many people know an earl when he's dressed as a fisherman.

The Earl spent some time in Shetland, but went south to Orkney in the autumn and took up residence in his own realm. That same autumn, two Icelanders visited the Earl, one a poet called Armod, and the other Oddi Glumsson the Little, who was also quite a versifier. The Earl admitted both of them to his court, and at Christmas held a great feast to which he invited people and handed out presents. To the poet Armod he gave a gold-inlaid spear and asked him to make a verse in return. This is what Armod said:

Lavish must he be, the great
lord, no laggard
in paying the poet
for his praise-song.
Wisest in the world
is he, our watchtower:
gold-ingrained
his gift-blade for Armod.

One day over Christmas, people were seeing to the wall-hangings when the Earl turned to Oddi the Little.

'Make a verse,' he said, 'about the man pictured there on the hanging. Make it as quickly as I compose mine, and don't use any word in yours that I use.' Then the Earl said this:

Age-worn, the warrior
waits in the wall-drape,
from his old shoulder down
he lets the sword slide,
bow-bent, his legs won't
bear him again to battle,
never again will he go,
gold-rich, to glory.

Oddi said this:

See how the swordsman
squares himself to strike
from the wall-hanging,
weapon raised in warning:
make your settlement soon,
seamen—the back
bends for the blow—
quick, boys, make peace.

The Earl entertained Bishop William and a good many of his chieftains at the feast over Christmas and it was there that he announced his plan to go abroad and visit the Holy Land, inviting the bishop, who had studied in Paris, to join him. The Earl wanted very much to have him as interpreter and the bishop promised to go with him.

The men who decided to travel with Earl Rognvald were Magnus, son of Havard Gunnason, and Svein Hroaldsson, each in command of a ship. In addition, though of less importance, these men are named: Thorgeir Safakoll, Oddi the Little, Thorbjorn the Black and Armod, all of them the

Earl's poets; then there were Thorkel Hook-Eye, Grimkel of Glaitness and Blann, son of Thorstein of Flydruness.

When the two years of preparation were over, Earl Rognvald set out from Orkney early in the spring and sailed east over to Norway to find out how well-prepared the landholders there were for the journey. When the Earl reached Bergen, Erling Wry-Neck and the Earl's brother-in-law, Jon Foot, were waiting for him along with Aslak, while Guthorm arrived soon afterwards. Lying at the quayside was the ship Jon Foot had built for the Earl, with thirty-five rowing benches. It was magnificently constructed, everywhere carved and inlaid with gold upon prow and stern, wind-vanes and so on and there was no ship to compare with it in value.

During the summer Eindridi kept coming to town saying every time that in a week he would be ready to leave. The others took a poor view of having to wait so long, and some of them didn't want to wait for him at all, saying that people had made the voyage without having Eindridi with them. But some time after that, Eindridi came to town and announced that he was ready. The Earl, he said, could put out to sea as soon as he thought the weather was right. There came a day when they appeared to have a fair wind, so they left the harbour and hoisted sail. But the breeze was in fact very light, and the Earl's ship made poor headway, needing as it did a strong wind. The other captains lowered their sails, not wanting to sail ahead of the Earl, but once they got out beyond the islands the wind grew stronger and began to blow so fresh that they had to reef sail on the smaller ships while the Earl's ship raced ahead.

Next, they saw two large ships astern, which soon caught up and passed them. One of them was a superbly built dragon-head, heavily inlaid with gold upon both stern and prow, brightly painted in the bows and all above the water-line. The Earl's men said that it must be Eindridi's ship.

'And he hasn't kept his word, sir,' they said, 'that only you were to have your ship ornamented.'

'He's so arrogant, that Eindridi,' said the Earl. 'Now I see why he didn't want to be compared with inferior people like us. Still, it's hard to tell whether his luck will travel faster or slower than he does. We're not going to plot our course according to his ambitions.'

Eindridi soon outsailed the rest in his bigger ship, but the Earl kept his whole fleet together and they had a good passage, arriving safe and sound in Orkney during the autumn. They decided then to remain there over winter, some at their own expense, others lodging with farmers, and many of them staying with the Earl. There was a great deal of brawling in Orkney that winter. The Norwegians and the men of Orkney fell out over both trade and women, and there was plenty of room for disagreement. The Earl had a hard time keeping an eye on them, for, though both groups felt they owed him a lot, they also thought they deserved every favour.

Coming back now to Eindridi and his men, they reached Shetland where his fine ship was smashed to matchwood and much valuable cargo lost, though the smaller ship survived. Eindridi spent the winter in Shetland, but sent some of his men east to Norway to order the building of a ship for the voyage to the Holy Land.

A man in Eindridi's crew called Arni Pin-Leg went south with nine others to Orkney and spent the winter there. He was a brave man but a great bully. Throughout the winter he and his men looked after themselves on a small island, and from one of Svein Asleifarson's tenants Arni bought some malt and animals for slaughtering, but when the man asked for payment Arni made excuses. The second time the man asked for his money all he got was abuse and before they parted, a blow with the back of Arni's axe.

'Now go and tell that champion of yours you're always threatening people with,' said Arni, 'let him put things right for you, that's all you need do.'

The tenant went off and told his story, asking Svein to get him a fair deal. Svein said little except that he was making no promises, but one day in spring he went off to collect his rents. He was with three others in an eight-oared boat, and their route took them past the island where Arni and his companions were staying. Even though it was low-tide, Svein suggested putting in there and went ashore alone carrying a small axe, telling the others to look after the boat and make sure that it didn't go aground.

Arni and his companions were in a house not far from the shore. Svein went up to it and walked inside, where Arni and the other four greeted him. He returned the greeting, then told Arni he ought to settle the matter with the farmer. Arni answered that there was no great hurry. Svein asked Arni as a special favour to settle the debt, but Arni said that was no reason for him to do it. Svein said that he was asking for very little and at the same moment he drove the axe into Arni's head right up to the handle and lost his grip on it. Svein ran

146

outside and, while some of Arni's companions tried to lift him up, others chased Svein down to the muddy beach. One of them outran the rest and started grappling with Svein. There were tangle-stems lying around on the mud-flat and grabbing one, Svein hurled it, mud and all, into the face of the one closest to him. While the man had both hands up to his eyes, trying to wipe away the mud, Svein jumped into the boat and sailed back to his estate on Gairsay.

Not long after that, Svein went over to Caithness on business and sent word to Earl Rognvald that he wanted to make a settlement over the killing of Arni Pin-Leg.

As soon as the message arrived, Earl Rognvald called together all those whose duty it was to take action over the killing of Arni and settled the matter with them to everybody's satisfaction, paying the compensation out of his own pocket. The Earl had to pay with his own money for many an act of violence committed over winter by the Norwegians and the men of Orkney, so badly did they get on together.

Early in the spring the Earl held a large assembly on Mainland, attended by all the leading men in his earldom. He announced that he was planning a journey abroad to the Holy Land and handing over his authority to his kinsman, Earl Harald Maddadarson. He asked them all to give Harald their full support while he was away, whenever Harald required it.

Earl Harald was about twenty years old at the time, a tall, strong man, with an ugly face but a shrewd character, and people thought him likely to make a good chieftain. After Rognvald had set out from Orkney, Harald's chief counsellor at first was Thorbjorn Clerk.

86. EARL ROGNVALD IN GALICIA

Earl Rognvald got ready to set out from Orkney early in the summer, though his preparations were delayed because he had to wait so long for Eindridi, whose ship ordered from Norway during the winter was late in arriving. But when everything was ready, they sailed from Orkney with a fleet of fifteen large ships captained by these men: Earl Rognvald, Bishop William, Erling Wry-Neck, Aslak Erlendsson, Guthorm Mjolukoll, Magnus Havardsson, Svein Hroaldsson, Eindridi the Young and five others whose names are not mentioned. They sailed south from Orkney to Scotland, then to England, and while they were off the coast of Northumbria, Armod made this verse:

High the wave heaves
while we tack off Humber,
the mast sways, in the swell
sink Veslu Sands:
sea-spray never soaks
the warrior at assembly,
nor stings the sight
of the sleepy citizen.

From there they sailed south beyond England and over to France, and there's nothing to tell of their travels till they reached a seaport called Narbonne. The news there was that the Earl in charge of the town, a man called Germanus, had died and left a beautiful young daughter, Ermingerd, who had now taken over her inheritance and was looking after it with the help of her kinsmen, all very noble men. They persuaded the Queen to invite Earl Rognvald to a splendid banquet, saying that if she were to welcome men of such high rank, travelling from such distant lands, it would add to her reputation far and wide. The Queen told them to see to the arrangements and, as soon as the decision had been made, envoys were sent to the Earl inviting him to the feast with as many companions as he wished. The Earl thanked her with pleasure and chose all his best men to go with him. There was lavish entertainment at the feast, and nothing that might be done in his honour was denied the Earl.

The Earl was sitting feasting one day when the Queen came into the hall escorted by a group of ladies and carrying a serving-bowl of gold. She was in her finest clothes, with her hair falling loose as is customary with virgins and a golden tiara upon her forehead. She served the Earl, while her companions began to entertain them with music. The Earl took her hand along with the bowl, and sat her on his knee, and for the rest of the day they had a great deal to say to one another. Then the Earl made a verse:

I'll swear, clever sweetheart,
you're a slender delight
to grasp and to cuddle,
my golden-locked girl.
Ravenous the hawk, crimson
-clawed, flesh-crammed—
but now, heavily hangs
the silken hair.

The Earl had a long stay and the best of hospitality, and the people of the town tried to persuade him to settle down there, hinting strongly that he could have the lady in marriage. The Earl answered that he wanted to complete the journey as planned, but promised to call in on his way back, when they could work things out as they wished.

After that, the Earl got ready for the journey and set out with his men. They sailed round Thrasness with a good wind, then sat and drank contentedly, and the Earl made this verse:

> *In the Earl's ear the words*
> *of Ermingerd will echo,*
> *enjoining us to journey*
> *by water to Jordan.*
> *But when the sea-riders*
> *race back from the river,*
> *as we navigate northward*
> *we'll call at Narbonne.*

Then Armod made this one:

> *I fear my fate*
> *turns my face from Ermingerd;*
> *many a man*
> *would match her if he might.*
> *Her brow's such a beauty—*
> *I'd bed her gladly, even*
> *once would be worth it,*
> *a wish come true.*

And Oddi the Little made this:

> *The elegant Ermingerd,*
> *queen over all,*
> *I guess we're not likely*
> *to govern that girl—*
> *she merits so much*
> *more, to my mind:*
> *God keep her safe*
> *and secure 'neath the sun.*

On they sailed till they came to Galicia in the west and, since the festive season was near, they decided to spend Christmas there. They asked the local people to set up a market so that they could buy food, but the supplies there were poor and the people found it difficult to feed so many. They also learned that a foreign chieftain had occupied a nearby castle and was

making the people suffer badly under his tyranny. He would
lead armed raids against them whenever they refused him
anything he asked for and would bully and badger them in
the most unpleasant ways. When the Earl tried to buy food,
the people made him an offer, that if he could find any way to
drive off the castle-dwellers, a market would be set up till the
beginning of Lent. Earl Rognvald and his men were to bear
the brunt of any attack, but all money taken from the enemy
was to be theirs.

The Earl put this proposal to his men and asked them what
they thought should be done. Most of them were in favour of
an attack on the castle-dwellers, as they expected plenty of
loot, so Rognvald and his men agreed to the terms of the local
people.

Shortly before Christmas, he called his men together for a
talk.

'We've been here for some time now,' said Rognvald, 'but
we've done nothing about the castle-dwellers and the people
are getting less keen to trade with us. I've a feeling they think
our promise to them was just empty talk. But to fail in our
promises is hardly honourable, so, kinsman Erling, as the
cleverest tactician here, you're to work out a scheme for taking
the castle, though I'd like every man to have his say on
whatever he thinks might get results.'

'I don't intend to stay silent,' answered Erling, 'but I'm no
master tactician. Much better consult people with more
experience, people accustomed to this kind of expedition, such
as Eindridi the Young. Still, they say you never catch a bird
without a shot, so let me make a suggestion and see what
comes of it. If you and the other leaders think it a tolerable
idea, why not all go into the forest today and each of us carry
a load of wood to the foot of the castle wall? It strikes me that
the mortar isn't firm enough to withstand the heat of a large
fire, so let's try working at it for the next three days and then
we shall see how things turn out.'

They did as Erling proposed, but by the time the work was
finished it was Christmas, so the bishop wouldn't let them
attack.

The chieftain in charge of the castle was a man called
Godfrey, shrewd but getting on in years, learned and widely
travelled, with a knowledge of several languages, but for all
that greedy and a bully. When he saw what the Earl's men
were doing he called his own men together and spoke to them.

'What the Norwegians are trying to do,' he said, 'seems to

me a clever scheme and a dangerous one for us. If the castle is attacked with fire, we'll find that the stone ramparts can't be relied on, and should these Norwegians get near us we can expect a tough fight, for they're strong, brave men. So I'd like to talk with you about what we might do to get ourselves out of the predicament we're in.'

All his men agreed to leave the decision to him and he spoke again.

'My first plan is for you to tie a rope round me,' he said, 'and lower me down from the castle wall, in ragged clothes. I'll make my way into the Norwegian camp to find out whatever I can.'

They did as he had suggested, and when Godfrey met Earl Rognvald's men he told them he was a beggar, speaking in French since that was the language they were most likely to understand. As he went from tent to tent begging for food, he realised that there was a great deal of envy and discord among the Norwegians, with Eindridi heading one faction and Earl Rognvald the other. Godrey went up to Eindridi and began talking to him, saying that the chieftain in the castle had sent him there.

'He wants to make an alliance with you,' said Godfrey, 'and hopes that you'll spare his life if the castle's taken. As long as you keep your part of the bargain, he'd rather you had his treasure than the people who wish him dead.'

They talked this over, along with a good many other matters. It was kept a close secret from the Earl and for a while there was no hint of a rumour. After Godfrey had spent some time with the Earl's men he went back to his own people. They didn't remove their possessions from the castle as they weren't sure the attack would succeed and, besides that, they couldn't trust the local people.

87. BEYOND GIBRALTAR

On the tenth day of Christmas, a day of fine weather, Earl Rognvald stood up and told his men to arm themselves and to blow the trumpets summoning everyone to the castle. The firewood was taken right up to the ramparts and piled all around. Then the Earl gave orders where each of his chief men was to attack; he himself and the men of Orkney from the south, Erling and Aslak from the west, John and Guthorm from the east and Eindridi the Young from the north. When they were all prepared for the assault, they set fire to the wood-piles, and the Earl made this verse:

> *Most admired of maidens,*
> *gold-decked at our meeting,*
> *Ermingerd the exquisite*
> *once offered me her wine—*
> *now fiercely we bear fire*
> *up to the fortress,*
> *assault the stronghold*
> *with unsheathed sword-thrust.*

They attacked ferociously with iron and fire, hurling a shower of missiles into the fortress, this being the only way they could assault it. The defenders held the ramparts none too decisively, as they had to protect themselves from the missiles, but they poured down burning sulphur and pitch, though this did little harm to the Earl's men. Eventually, as Erling had forseen, the ramparts started crumbling before the fire, leaving huge gaps where the mortar failed to hold.

A man called Sigmund Fish-Hook, stepson of Svein Asleifarson, fought more fiercely than any man there and took his stand ahead of the Earl, though he was barely grown to manhood at the time.

After the fighting had been going on for a while, the defenders withdrew from the ramparts. There was a southerly breeze, so the smoke drifted in the direction of Eindridi and his men. Once the fire had done most of its work, the Earl had water brought up to cool the hot stones and there was a lull in the fighting. Then Earl Rognvald made this verse:

> *Swordsman, with Agder's brave*
> *Solmund I spent one*
> *Christmas—out of many*
> *this mind remembers it.*
> *Now comes another—*
> *I'm still not unoccupied,*
> *storming from the south*
> *the stronghold walls.*

Then he made another:

> *Once the wine-serving*
> *wench understood me,*
> *the touches of my tongue;*
> *I was content.*

I loved that good lady,
but lime-bound stones
crumble: now I cram
the hawk with carrion.

Then Sigmund Fish-Hook made this one:

In Spring when you steer
to Orkney, say this,
bear on your way
these words to the woman:
that when the swords sang,
no grown man swung
blade closer to castle
than this young killer.

After that the Earl and Sigmund Fish-Hook decided to force their way into the castle and there was little resistance. A good many men were killed there, but those who were offered quarter surrendered to the Earl. Rognvald and his men took a great deal of loot, but could not find the leader and got little of value. There was a lot of talk about how Godfrey could have managed to get away and it wasn't long before suspicion fell most on Eindridi the Young, who must have helped him to get away into the forest under cover of the smoke.

Earl Rognvald and his men stayed only a short while after that in Galicia, and then sailed west of Spain, looting all over the pagan areas and winning a great deal of plunder there. They stormed a certain village where the natives held ranks firm and fought back, but in the end, for all their fierce resistance, the people there ran off leaving a number of dead. Then the Earl made this verse:

The Spaniards retreated
—time for a tryst soon
with a woman—war-weary
we proved worthy of Ermingerd.
Ballads of battle
we chanted, bragging: but
on the carrion field, only
a clutter of corpses.

Next they sailed south along the coast of Spain, running into a fierce gale which forced them to lie at anchor for three days. The weather was so rough they came near to wrecking their ships, and the Earl made this verse:

> *'While ship-stays don't*
> *snap, no storm strains*
> *me, lady, not while leathery*
> *anchor-line lasts out.'*
> *To my linen-decked lady*
> *my lips spoke this promise.*
> *Now, to the Straits*
> *the storm speeds us.*

They hoisted sail and tacked against a strong head-wind until they reached the Straits of Gibraltar, where Oddi made this verse:

> *Seven days with the gold*
> *scatterer I spent*
> *in my cups, content,*
> *the comrade of kings.*
> *But Rognvald and his raiders*
> *raced upon painted*
> *sea-stallion, bore*
> *shields to the Straits.*

And as they were tacking up to the Straits, the Earl made another:

> *From the arms of Ermingerd*
> *an easterly winter-squall*
> *sent us skipping: now*
> *let's adjust sails,*
> *lower and lash them*
> *to mid-mast, locked*
> *tight: to the Straits*
> *the storm speeds us.*

They sailed on through the Straits of Gibraltar, then the weather improved and, as they emerged, Eindridi the Young and six ships parted company with the rest. He sailed across to Marseilles but Earl Rognvald and his men held back, keeping close to the Straits. Many people remarked how Eindridi had openly admitted helping Godfrey to escape. The Earl told them to hoist sail and they set course over the sea towards the African coast. Then Earl Rognvald made this verse:

> *Constantly north-curving*
> *the coast: a roaring*
> *sea makes sport*
> *of our sturdy timbers.*

My verse flows—vain
your envy, villains—
seaward from Spain
slips my slim prow.

On they sailed, east over the sea beyond the land of the Saracens, and came close to Sardinia though they did not know there was land there. The sort of weather they had was like this: for long periods there was dead calm, with fog and sea mist, so they could see little from the ships, and progress was slow. Then one morning the fog lifted and when they got up and looked around they saw two islands, but when they looked again later on, one of the islands had disappeared. They reported this to the Earl.

'It can't have been an island,' he said. 'It must have been the kind of ship people in this part of the world use, called a dromond. From a distance, they seem as big as small islands. A sea-breeze must have sprung up where one of the dromonds was lying and the people aboard will have sailed off. They must be merchants of some kind.'

After that, the Earl asked the bishop and all the captains to come and see him.

'My lord bishop,' he said, 'and my kinsman, Erling, I'd like to ask you something. Can you think of any trick or tactics by which we might overcome the crew of that dromond?'

'I think you'll find it difficult to lay your ship alongside,' said the bishop. 'The best you'll be able to do will be to hook a broad-axe onto the gunwale, and then they'll have sulphur and boiling pitch to drench you with, head to foot. A shrewd man like you, sir, must see that it would be sheer madness to risk yourself and your men like that.'

Then Erling had his say.

'My lord bishop,' he began, 'maybe you can see more clearly than others that an attack by our ships on the dromond most likely won't bring us much success. But as I see it, if we tried to get in close under them and laid our ships broadside on, most of their weapons would fall clear of us, and even if things were to happen otherwise we could easily get away from them, since they're hardly going to chase us in the dromond.'

Then the Earl spoke.

'These are brave words,' he said, 'much after my own heart, and now I want this understood by captains and crews. Every man is to take his place and arm himself with his best weapons. After that we'll attack them. If they're Christian merchants, we'll give them the chance to make peace with us, but if, as I suspect, they're heathen, then in his mercy God Almighty will grant us victory over them. Whatever loot we get, we'll give a fiftieth of it to the poor.'

The men took up their weapons and got the ship ready for war, making the best of whatever they had. The Earl gave orders how each ship was to attack. After that they began pulling at the oars and made for the dromond as fast as they could row.

88. THE BATTLE WITH THE DROMOND

When the people aboard the dromond saw ships pulling towards them they suspected an attack and carried all their finery and jewels to the gunwales, where they began to make so much noise that the Norwegians took it for a challenge. Earl Rognvald laid his ship aft alongside the dromond on the starboard side while Erling laid his aft to larboard, and Jon and Aslak theirs forrard on either side. The other two were laid amidships, one on each side, all six of them broadside on. When they managed to get under the lee of the dromond it stood so high they couldn't reach the gunwale with their weapons. The people aboard the dromond kept pouring sulphur and boiling pitch over them but, just as Erling had foreseen, most of it fell beyond the ships, so they didn't have to protect themselves from it.

Since the attack was failing to give results, the bishop's and two other ships pulled away and on these they gathered together all the best archers. The ships were laid within shooting distance of the dromond and when they began to bombard it there was quite a battle. The people on the dromond brought out their protective armour, paying little attention to what the others were doing beneath them.

At this point Earl Rognvald called on his men to take their axes and break through the wooden hull of the dromond where it was least heavily plated with iron, and when the other crews saw what the Earl's men were doing they followed suit. Where Erling had laid his ship there was a huge anchor suspended from the dromond, with one fluke hooked over the gunwale but the shank pointing down towards Erling's ship. His forecastleman, Audun the Red, was helped up onto the anchor-stock and then he pulled others up after him so that they stood packed together there, chopping away at the timbers with all their might, well above

the spot into which the others were hacking. As soon as they'd
made a gap large enough for them to get through into the
dromond they boarded it, the Earl and his men onto the
lower deck and Erling's onto the upper. Once both parties
were aboard there was fierce fighting, the people on the
dromond being Saracens, whom we call infidels of Mohammed,
among them a good many black men, who put up strong
resistance. Erling got a nasty wound on the neck just above
the shoulder as he leapt aboard the dromond and it healed so
badly that for the rest of his life he carried his head to one
side, which is why he got the nickname Wry-Neck.

Once Earl Rognvald and Erling joined forces, the Saracens
fell back, retreating towards the prow, but the Earl's men
came racing up one after the other and the larger their force
grew, the harder they pressed.

The Norwegians noticed a man aboard the dromond both
taller and more handsome than the rest, and they took him
to be the leader. Earl Rognvald gave orders that no one was
to wound this man if they could get at him any other way.
They crowded round with shields and captured him, then
took him with several others aboard the bishop's ship.
Everyone else on the dromond they killed, getting plenty of
money and other valuable things. After most of the hard
work had been done they settled down for a rest, and the
Earl made this verse:

> Erling, honoured aimer
> of spears, eagerly
> advanced toward the vessel
> in victory, with banners
> of blood: the black
> warriors, brave lads,
> we captured or killed,
> crimsoning our blades.

Then he made another:

> Busy with this dromond
> business, our blades we
> blooded on the blacks—
> that was something like butchery!
> Of the slaughter, the spear
> storm, from south and
> north, at Narbonne,
> she will hear news.

They began to talk over what had just happened, each describing things as he thought he had seen them. One point of argument was who had been first aboard the dromond, and on this they could not agree. Some said that it was ridiculous for them all to have different versions of such a great event and, in the end, they decided that Earl Rognvald should have the last word and that everyone would then stick to this version. At that the Earl made this verse:

> *First aboard the black*
> *boat, the unbending*
> *Red Audun, rampaging,*
> *that stern ravager.*
> *Christ helped us crimson*
> *the carrion, the dark*
> *-blue bodies, piled*
> *black on the deck.*

When they had cleared the dromond they set it on fire and destroyed it. The tall man they had taken captive saw this and grew very distressed. His face turned pale and he wouldn't be still. Though they tried to talk to him, he said not a word, made no sign to them of any kind, and revealed nothing, no matter what they threatened him with or what favours they promised. When the dromond was ablaze it seemed to them as if a stream of fire were pouring into the sea. The captive was deeply affected by this sight. The Earl's men feared that they hadn't searched the dromond carefully enough for money and that all the gold and silver had melted in the fire.

From there Earl Rognvald and his men sailed south to the land of the Saracens, lying at anchor off one of their towns. They made a week's truce with the townspeople and traded with them, selling them silver and other valuables. No one would buy the tall captive, so the Earl gave him leave to go, along with five others. Next morning the man came back with a large company and told them that he was a Saracen nobleman: he said he had been presented with the dromond and all the money aboard as a parting gift and that it was a great pity they had destroyed both the dromond and a vast sum which would now benefit no one.

'But now,' he went on, 'you're completely in my power. What chiefly saves you is that you spared my life and tried to show me the respect you thought fitting. But I hope we never meet again, and so goodbye.'

Then he rode off into the country and Rognvald and his men sailed from there to Crete, weathering a fierce gale on the way. One night while Armod was standing watch, he made this verse:

> *From the prowed sea-prancer*
> *we peer, keep watch*
> *as the wave whips*
> *over our wood-walls.*
> *Now as the fopling*
> *falters with the fair-fleshed*
> *courtesan, I cast*
> *my eyes towards Crete.*

They lay off Crete till they got a fair wind for the Holy Land, then made Acre one Friday morning and walked ashore in such style and grandeur as was rarely to be seen in those parts. Then Thorbjorn the Black made this verse:

> *I was up in arms*
> *with the warrior of Orkney*
> *when in winter that crow-fattener*
> *went to war.*
> *Now swiftly and surely*
> *my shield's borne*
> *alongside the Earl*
> *to ocean-sprayed Acre.*

They stayed some time at Acre, then a disease broke out amongst them and many died of it, including Thorbjorn the Black. Oddi the Little composed these verses:

> *Thrusting round Thrasness*
> *with Thorbjorn, the longships*
> *of the landed-men sailed*
> *the soil of the sea-king.*
> *Bold as bears*
> *they paced the billows*
> *eastward to Acre*
> *with the Earl's best bard—*
>
> *but soon I saw him*
> *buried in the sand,*
> *the Earl's comrade*
> *carried to the churchyard;*
> *there he lies, stretched*
> *where a southern sun*

glares upon his grave
in stony ground.

Earl Rognvald set off from Acre and travelled with his men
to Jerusalem, visiting all the most sacred places in the Holy
Land. They all went and bathed in the River Jordan and,
with Sigmund Fish-Hook, Earl Rognvald swam across the
river. They began walking on the other side and came to a
certain copsewood where they tied some large knots, after
which the Earl made this verse:

> *In serpent-cold season*
> *of snow, let the wise*
> *lady's thoughts light*
> *on this lifeline:*
> *no lay-abed, I judge,*
> *will journey to Jordan*
> *here, the wide plain*
> *washed with warm blood.*

Then Sigmund made another:

> *I'll tie this link*
> *for the lumpish laggard*
> *who clings to his comfort*
> *while kinsmen take risks.*

The Earl said:

> *In the thicket we bind*
> *a bow for such bastards*
> *—dog-tired I dragged myself here—*
> *on St Lawrence's Day.*

After that they went back to Jerusalem and the Earl made
this verse as they were approaching the city:

> *A cross on this bard's*
> *breast, on his back*
> *a palm-branch; peacefully*
> *we pace the hillside.*

That summer, the Earl and his men set out from the Holy
Land, intending to travel to Constantinople, and in the
autumn they reached a town called Imbolum, where they
stayed for quite some time. There was a common expression
used in the town when people met in a narrow street. If one of
them wanted the other coming towards him to give way, he

would say 'Midway, midway'.[1] One evening, making his way out of town, Erling Wry-Neck was walking down the pier towards his ship, when some townspeople came towards him and said 'Midway, midway'. Erling paid no attention, being very drunk, but just as they met he tumbled off the pier and landed in the mud below so that his men had to run down after him, haul him up and take off every stitch of clothing he had on. When they saw the Earl next morning the men told him about it, but he just smiled and made this verse:

A filthy misfortune
befell my friend Erling,
mucked up with mud
for not shouting 'Midway'.
The King's own kinsman
wasn't covered in glory,
ditched at Imbolum
and dripping with dirt.

Shortly after, it happened that Jon Foot and his companions set out very drunk from the same town. Suddenly they realised that Jon was missing and some of them started looking for him in the other ships but he couldn't be found. During the night it was impossible to search for him ashore, but in the morning, as soon as it was light, they set off and discovered him near the city wall. He was dead and they saw wounds on him, but no one ever learned who had inflicted them. After they had prepared his body, he was given burial at a church.

Following that they put out to sea and there's nothing to tell of their voyage till they came north to Engilsness, where they lay at anchor for some time waiting for a good wind to carry them further north to Constantinople. They sailed with great care and in fine style, as they knew Sigurd the Pilgrim had done, and as they were travelling north over the waves Earl Rognvald made this verse:

Steer the sea-king's
stallion to Stamboul,
plough up the sea-plain
with the spraying prow.

[1] It has been suggested that this word, *miðhæfi*, is a corruption of a Greek expression—see *Orkneyinga Saga*, ed. Finnbogi Guðmundsson, 1965, pp. 233-4.

We'll add to the honour
of the emperor, take
our pay, then push forward
and tickle the wolf's palate.

89. FROM BYZANTIUM TO NORWAY

When Earl Rognvald and his men reached Constantinople they were given a great reception by the Emperor and the Varangians. At that time Menelias, whom we call Menula, was ruling Byzantium. He gave money freely to the Earl, and offered to hire them as mercenaries if they would agree to stay on there. They spent the winter there enjoying the best of entertainment. Eindridi the Young was there, treated with honour by the Emperor, but having little to do with Earl Rognvald and his men and trying to discredit them with other people.

Earl Rognvald set off from Constantinople that winter, sailing first to Durazzo in Bulgaria, and from there across the sea to Puglia where he disembarked, together with Bishop William, Erling and all the other noblemen in his retinue. They got themselves horses and rode on their way, first to Rome, then following the usual pilgrim route all the way to Denmark. From there they crossed to Norway, where people were very happy to see them. This journey became very famous and everyone who made it was considered all the greater.

While they had been off on their travels, Ogmund the Manly, brother of Erling Wry-Neck, had died. While both of them were alive, he had been considered the greater of the brothers. Without wasting any time, Erling joined King Ingi, being closer to him than to the King's brothers, and never left him as long as they both lived.

After the death of King Ingi, the leadership of his faction was taken over by Magnus, son of Erling and of Kristin, daughter of Sigurd the Pilgrim, though Erling himself was sole ruler throughout all Norway. King Valdemar of Denmark gave Erling the title of earl and he became a great chieftain, as is told in his saga.

Eindridi the Young came back to Norway several years after Earl Rognvald and joined up with King Eystein as he wanted nothing to do with Erling. After the death of King Eystein, Eindridi the Young and Sigurd, son of Havard the Yeoman of Ror, gathered forces and adopted as king Hakon the Broad-Shouldered, son of King Sigurd Haraldsson, and it was they who killed Gregorius Dagsson and King Ingi. At Sekk, Eindridi and Hakon fought a pitched battle against Erling Wry-Neck: Hakon was killed there and Eindridi had to run for his life. A little later, Erling had Eindridi the Young put to death east at Oslo.

90. ROGNVALD COMES BACK TO ORKNEY

Earl Rognvald spent much of the summer in Hordaland, where he learned all the news from Orkney, that there was a lot of hostility on the island and that most of the leading men had split up into two factions, very few being uncommitted and staying out of trouble. On one side there was Earl Harald and on the other, Earl Erlend and Svein Asleifarson. When the Earl heard this he composed a verse:

> *Many a bond broken*
> *by the best-born of men:*
> *intrigues have earned*
> *the anger of God.*
> *I'll pace warily,*
> *give no peace to the plotter,*
> *chance nothing, cherish*
> *the beard on my chin.*

Earl Rognvald had no ships at his disposal, so he went and asked his kinsmen and friends to build him a longship in the winter. They gave him a fair answer and promised him everything he asked for.

In the summer the Earl got ready to go back to his earldom in Orkney, but was late in leaving as there were a good many things to delay him. He took a passage on a merchant ship belonging to Thorhall Asgrimsson, an Icelander by birth who ran a farm south in Bishops Tongues. The Earl was well-attended by the fine retinue of men aboard with him. They made landfall in Scotland, where winter was almost at an end, and for a long time they lay off Tarbet Ness. Just before Christmas the Earl reached Orkney, where he was given a great welcome by his friends.

91. EVENTS IN ORKNEY

Now we have to explain what had happened in Orkney while Earl Rognvald was on his pilgrimage. That same summer the

Earl went abroad, King Eystein, son of Harald Gilli, came west from Norway with a large force. When he reached Orkney he sailed his fleet to South Ronaldsay, where he learned that Earl Harald Maddadarson had gone over to Caithness in a boat with twenty benches and a crew of eighty, and was lying at anchor off Thurso. As soon as he heard this, King Eystein manned three skiffs and sailed west over the Pentland Firth to Thurso, arriving so suddenly that the Earl and his men suspected nothing till the King's men had boarded their boat and taken the Earl captive. They led him before the King and the outcome was that the Earl redeemed himself with three gold marks and handed over authority to King Eystein, agreeing to be his liegeman for the remainder of his life: so the Earl became the King's subject under sworn oath.

From there King Eystein went looting in Scotland during the summer, and widely in England too, claiming to avenge the death of King Harald Sigurdarson. After that King Eystein went back east to his realm in Norway. There were conflicting opinions about this expedition of his.

Earl Harald remained in his realm of Orkney and most people liked him well. By this time his father Earl Maddad was dead and his mother Margaret had moved house to Orkney. She was a very beautiful woman but full of her own importance.

About this time David, King of Scots, died and his son Malcolm was adopted as King while he was still only a child.

92. SVEIN ASLEIFARSON AND THE EARLS

After Earl Ottar's death, Erlend, the son of Harald Smooth-Tongue, spent much of the time in Thurso, though he some-times stayed in Orkney or went off on viking trips. He was an exceptional man, talented in almost every way, open-handed, gentle, always ready to take advice and much loved by his men, of whom he had a large following.

There was a man called Anakol who had fostered Erlend and had more influence over him than anyone. Anakol was a viking, a ruthless man of Hebridean origins with a good family background, and he was Erlend's counsellor.

When Erlend heard that Rognvald had left his realm to travel to the Holy Land, he went to see his kinsman Malcolm, King of Scots, asking for the title of earl, and authority over Caithness, just as his father Harald had been granted by King David, Malcolm's grandfather. King Malcolm was still

a child and, because Erlend had plenty of high-ranking kinsmen there to plead his case, it came about that Erlend got his
title of earl and half of Caithness, his kinsman, Harald, having
the other. After that he went to visit his friends in Caithness,
then gathered forces and travelled to Orkney to seek recog-
nition.

As soon as he learned about Erlend, Earl Harald Maddadarson began to muster his own forces and gathered a good
number. Their kinsmen intervened and tried to bring about
a settlement, but when Erlend demanded half of Orkney from
Harald he refused to give it up, though a truce was fixed for
one year. It was decided that Erlend should go east to see
King Eystein in Norway and ask for the half of Orkney that
belonged to Earl Rognvald. Harald said that if the King
agreed, he would give it up. So Erlend sailed east to Norway
leaving Anakol behind in Orkney with some of his men.

Gunni Olafsson, brother of Svein Asleifarson, fathered a
child on Margaret, Earl Harald's mother, so Harald made him
an outlaw, and this created bad feeling between Harald and
Svein Asleifarson. Svein sent his brother Gunni south to
Lewis, to stay with his friend Ljotolf with whom Svein
himself had once lived. Ljotolf had a son called Fogl who
was staying with Earl Harald and he didn't get on at all well
with Svein. After Erlend had gone east to Norway, Earl
Harald travelled over to Caithness and spent the winter in
residence at Wick. Svein Asleifarson was at Freswick in
Caithness at the time, looking after the estate of his stepsons.
He'd first been married to Ragnhild Ogmund's-Daughter but
they were together only a short time. They had a son, Olaf, who
married Ingirid Thorkel's-Daughter, and their son was called
Andres.

On the Wednesday of Holy Week, Svein Asleifarson
happened to go up to Lambaborg with a few men and they
saw a cargo-boat travelling south across the Pentland Firth.
They guessed this must be Earl Harald's men sent to collect
the tributes in Shetland. Svein told his companions to come
down to the ships with him and sail out to the cargo-boat,
which is what they did, capturing it along with everything on
board and ferrying Earl Harald's men ashore. The men
travelled on foot to Wick and told the Earl all about it, but
he had little to say apart from remarking that he and Svein
were taking turns at making money. He billeted them out
over Easter, and the men of Caithness said that the Earl was
on well-trodden ground.

Immediately after Easter, Svein sailed out to Orkney with the cargo-boat and some rowing skiffs. When they reached Scapa they stole a ship from Fogl Ljotolfsson who had just come back north from visiting his father in Lewis and was on his way to see Earl Harald. On the same excursion they took twelve ounces of gold from Sigurd Klaufi, one of Earl Harald's retainers, who had brought the money to pay out at a certain farm, but the men to be paid happened to be in Kirkwall. Next, Svein went back to Caithness, then south to Aberdeen, where he saw Malcolm, King of Scots, now nine years old. Svein spent a month there enjoying the best of entertainment, and the King of Scots told him he could have all the revenues from Caithness that he'd had before falling out with Earl Harald. After that Svein got ready to set off again and he and the King of Scots parted the best of friends. Svein went to his ships and sailed them north to Orkney.

Anakol was at Deerness when Svein and his men came from the south and sighted their sails east of Mull Head. Gauti, the farmer at Skeggbjarnarstead, was sent to Svein with a request from Anakol for him to arrange terms with Fogl over the seizure of the ship, not simply because Fogl was related to Anakol but because he was staying with him. Gauti gave Svein the message and Svein asked them to meet him at Sanday, since that was where he meant to go; so that's where the peace-meeting took place. It was a long time before they could come to terms, and in the end it was agreed that Svein himself was to decide what compensation he should pay. After that, Anakol joined forces with Svein and undertook to arrange a truce between him and Earl Erlend when the Earl came back from Norway, for there was still bad feeling between them over the burning of Frakokk.

Svein and Anakol sailed to Stronsay and lay for several days off Huip Ness. Thorfinn Brusason was farming on Stronsay at the time—he was married to Svein's sister Ingigerd, whom Thorbjorn Clerk had abandoned. While they were lying off Huip Ness, Earl Erlend put in and at once Anakol and Thorfinn Brusason went to see him and tried to settle matters between him and Svein. The Earl responded moodily, saying that Svein had always been hostile towards him and his kin, not even keeping the agreement with Earl Ottar to help Erlend to power. Svein made an offer to the Earl of help and advice, but the negotiations went on all day without any agreement being reached, until Anakol and Thorfinn threatened to leave Orkney and join Svein unless the Earl came to terms with him. Then Erlend told them what King Eystein had declared in Norway, that he was to have that part of Orkney formerly ruled by Earl Harald. After he and Earl Erlend were reconciled, Svein suggested that they should go straight to Earl Harald before he learned about it from elsewhere and demand that part of the islands for Earl Erlend. They did exactly as Svein suggested and went to see Earl Harald, who was with his fleet off Cairston.

On the morning of Michaelmas Day, Harald and his men saw a longship coming towards them and, expecting trouble, they ran from their own ships into the fortress that used to stand there. There was a man called Arni Hrafnsson who was so scared, he ran from the Earl's ship all the way to Kirkwall before he realised, when he got stuck in the church door, that he still had his shield on his back—a man called Thorgeir was in the church when it happened. Arni's companions thought he was lost and searched for him two days.

Earl Erlend and Svein raced from their ships, chasing Earl Harald all the way to the fortress, and attacked it all day with iron and fire, but the people there made a stout defence till it grew dark and night separated the two sides. There were a good many wounded in both armies and had the attack lasted longer Harald's men would have had to surrender.

In the morning, farmers who were friendly to both sides came up and tried to bring about a settlement, but neither Svein nor Earl Erlend wanted one. However, in the end they agreed to a reconciliation with Harald on condition that he swore oaths that he would hand over to Earl Erlend his part of the islands and never claim it back. These oaths were sworn, and witnessed by a number of the most important men on the islands.

After that Earl Harald crossed over to Caithness and went south from there to join his kinsmen. This time few Orkneymen went with him.

Earl Erlend and Svein summoned the farmers to an assembly at Kirkwall, and numbers of them came from all over Orkney. Earl Erlend put his case to them, as did many of his friends and kinsmen, saying that King Eystein had given him authority over that part of Orkney formerly in Harald's charge, and asked them to accept him. In support of what he had told them, he carried with him letters from Eystein and, as it turned out, the farmers agreed to give their allegiance to Earl Erlend. So he laid the whole of Orkney under his rule and became its chieftain.

Part of the agreement between Erlend and the farmers was that, should it be Rognvald's fate to return to Orkney, Erlend would not try to hold on to his portion. On the other hand, should Rognvald claim more than half of Orkney, the farmers were to side with Erlend.

Svein Asleifarson spent much of his time with Earl Erlend, warning him constantly to be on his guard and not to trust Earl Harald and the Scots. Most of the winter they stayed aboard their ships, sending out spies, but, as it drew nearer to Christmas and the weather grew more severe, Svein went home to his estate. Now that they were parting he asked the Earl to be as watchful as ever, and so the Earl was, for he spent most of the time aboard his ships and made no preparations for a Christmas feast in any one particular place.

93. ABDUCTION AND ROBBERY

On the tenth day of Christmas, Svein Asleifarson was on Gairsay drinking with his men, when he started to rub his nose.

'I've got a feeling,' he said, 'that Earl Harald is on his way here to the islands.'

His men said that was hardly likely with such a gale blowing, but he replied that he knew that was the way they would think.

'So I'm not going to give Earl Erlend a warning based purely on intuition,' he said, 'though I doubt if I'm being very wise.'

That was the end of the conversation and they got on with their drinking just as before.

Earl Harald set out for Orkney at Christmas with four ships and a hundred men. He lay for two days off Graemsay, then put in at Hamna Voe on Mainland, and on the thirteenth day of Christmas they travelled on foot over to Firth. During a snowstorm they took shelter in Maeshowe and there two of them went insane, which slowed them down badly, so that by the time they reached Firth it was night-time. Meanwhile Earl Erlend had gone back to his ship after spending the day drinking in a nearby house. Earl Harald and his party killed two men there, one called Ketil, and took four prisoners— Arnfinn the brother of Anakol, a man called Ljot and two others—then Harald returned to Thurso along with Thorbjorn Clerk, but Benedikt and his brother Eirik went to Lambaborg taking Arnfinn with them.

The same night that Erlend got word of the attack, he sent

a messenger to Svein. Early next morning Svein launched his ships and went to see Earl Erlend, as the Earl had asked. For a good part of the winter they stayed aboard their ships. A message came from Benedikt and his brother Eirik, that Arnfinn would be set free only on condition that Erlend handed back the ship he had taken off Cairston. The Earl wanted to give up the ship but Anakol spoke against it, saying that Arnfinn would organise his own escape over winter—'no need for us to do what they ask,' he said.

On the last Wednesday before Lent, Anakol and Thorstein Rognuson set out twenty strong in a skiff over to Caithness, arriving by night. They hauled their skiff into a secret cove with a fortress above it, then made their way up near to the farmstead at Freswick, where they hid themselves in a copse. They had arranged things in the skiff so that it looked as if a man were lying in every space, and when someone came up to the skiff next morning it didn't appear at all suspicious. Anakol and his companions saw some people row away from the fortress and put in at the river mouth. Next they saw someone riding from the fortress with another man walking beside him, and realised that one of them was Eirik. Anakol divided his party into two, ten of them going down to the foreshore along the river to make sure no one got to the skiff, and the other ten up to the farmstead. Eirik reached the house just ahead of them and went into the hall. When he heard the sound of armed men, he ran through the hall to the far door trying to get to the skiff, but they were waiting for him there and took him prisoner. After they brought him to Earl Erlend in Orkney, messengers were sent to Earl Harald telling him Eirik would not be set free until Arnfinn and his companions were back safe and sound with Earl Erlend. Everything went as planned.

In the spring Earl Harald set out from Caithness north to Shetland, intending to kill Erlend the Young. Erlend had asked to marry Harald's mother Margaret, a proposal the Earl rejected. Erlend raised a force of men, abducted Margaret from Orkney, took her north to Shetland and settled down in the Broch at Mousa where everything had been made ready.

When Earl Harald arrived in Shetland, he laid siege to the Broch and cut off all supplies, but it's not an easy place to attack. Then people started trying to reconcile them. Erlend wanted Harald to let him have the lady in marriage, and in return he offered his support to the Earl, adding that what Harald needed most was to recover his realm and the best way would be to make as many friends as he could. There were plenty there to argue the same case and the upshot was that Erlend and Harald were reconciled. Erlend married Margaret, joined the Earl, and went with him in the summer to Norway.

When news of this reached Orkney, Earl Erlend and Svein got together over their plans. Svein wanted to go looting and make some money, and that's what they did, sailing south to the Moray Firth and plundering the east coast of Scotland as far south as Berwick-on-Tweed.

There was a merchant called Knut the Wealthy who spent much of his time at Berwick. Svein and his men took a fine, big ship belonging to Knut with a valuable cargo and Knut's wife, who was aboard too, then sailed south to the Bly Isles. Knut was at Berwick when he heard about the robbery and he offered the men of Berwick a hundred marks of silver to get his property back. Most of those who set out to look for it were merchants, sailing in fourteen ships. While Svein and Earl Erlend lay anchored off the Bly Isles, Svein warned them not to sleep under awnings, as he expected the men of Berwick to arrive in large numbers during the night. But as there was a cold wind blowing, they ignored his warning and everyone slept under awnings except for those on Svein's ship, where there were no awnings aft of the mast. Svein stayed on the raised deck wearing a fur cloak and sitting on a chest: that, he said, was how he meant to spend the night.

There was a man aboard Svein's ship called Einar Bandy-Legs, who said that the tales of Svein's courage were exaggerated.

'People talk about how much more manly he is than anyone else,' he said, 'and here he is, too scared to put up the awnings on his ship.'

Svein pretended he hadn't heard. The watchmen were stationed on the island and he heard them arguing about something they had seen. When he went ashore and asked them what they were arguing about, they said they were not sure what it was they could see, but he was exceptionally keen-sighted and looking closely he made out fourteen ships sailing together. He told the watchman to go aboard and warn the others what was going on, then went back to his own ship and told his men to wake up and throw off the awnings.

After that there was a great deal of shouting, most people calling to ask Svein what they should do. He told them to be quiet and to lay their ships between the island and the mainland.

'Wait and see if they sail past us,' he said, 'and if they don't, we'll just have to row against them as hard as we can.'

Other leaders were against this idea, saying the only solution was to sail off, so that's what they did.

'If you want to get away,' said Svein, 'tack out to the open sea.'

Svein was the last one ready to leave and Anakol waited for him, but, since Svein had the faster ship, he had to reef his sails and wait in turn for Anakol, not wanting to leave him behind with only one ship.

When Svein's ship was under full sail, Einar Bandy-Legs spoke up.

'Surely our ship's not moving, Svein?' he said.

'I wouldn't say that,' answered Svein, 'but if you're so scared that you can't tell whether or not the fastest ship under sail is moving, I trust you'll never question my courage again either.'

The men of Berwick sailed southwards past them, whereupon Svein and his men altered course towards the mainland. As they were approaching the Isle of May, Svein sent messengers to Edinburgh, telling the King of Scots about their plunder, but before they could reach the city twelve men on horseback came riding towards them with bags full of silver strapped to their saddles. When they met, the Scotsmen asked about Svein Asleifarson: they were told where he was, but were asked what business they had with him. The Scots said they'd heard Svein had been taken captive and the King of Scots had sent them with this money to pay his ransom. Svein's men told them the rumour was false, then went on to the King and explained their mission. The King was far from troubled about Knut's losses, but he sent Svein a fine shield and other valuable gifts. Then Earl Erlend and Svein went back to Orkney, arriving there quite late in the autumn.

It was during this summer that Earl Harald went to Norway, as we've mentioned already, and also when Earl Rognvald and Erling Wry-Neck came to Norway from Byzantium. Just before Christmas, Earl Rognvald returned to Orkney.

94. THE KILLING OF EARL ERLEND

At once people started going between Earl Rognvald and Earl Erlend, trying to arrange a settlement. The farmers referred to the particular agreement they had made with Erlend, that

he should not deny Rognvald his share of the islands. A
meeting was fixed between the Earls, to be held at Kirkwall,
and there they were reconciled two days before Christmas,
each of them swearing oaths to keep their agreement. The
terms were that each should rule one half of Orkney and
defend the islands jointly against Earl Harald or anyone else
who laid claim to them.

At the time Earl Rognvald was without ships and had none
till the following summer, when his ships came west from
Norway.

Things were quiet for the rest of the winter, but in the
spring Rognvald and Erlend made plans to face up to Harald
should he come west. Earl Erlend and Svein sailed for
Shetland, laying in wait in case he made land there; but Earl
Rognvald went over to Thurso, as they also thought it possible
that Harald might try landing there when he came west,
where he had so many friends and kinsmen. Earl Erlend and
Svein stayed in Shetland the whole summer, checking every
ship, so that no one could get from there to Norway.

In the summer Earl Harald put out from Norway with seven
ships. He landed in Orkney, but three of his ships were driven
off course to Shetland where they were seized by Erlend.
When Earl Harald arrived in Orkney he was given the news
that Earls Rognvald and Erlend had come to terms and were
to share the islands with one other. Harald thought there
was nothing in it for him, so he decided to go over to Caithness
and see Earl Rognvald before Earl Erlend and his troops
arrived from Shetland.

Erlend and Svein were in Shetland when they heard that
Earl Harald had arrived in Orkney. At once they set out for
Orkney with five ships, but they ran into dangerous tidal
currents and fierce winds at Sumburgh Roost and the ships
were separated. Svein and his men were driven up to Fair Isle
in two ships, and thought the Earl had perished. But when they
sailed south to Sanday they found the Earl waiting for them
there with the other three ships, and they were all very glad
to meet again. From there they went to Mainland, where they
learned that Earl Harald had crossed over to Caithness.

Now we turn to Earl Harald's travels: he had arrived at
Thurso with six ships, but Earl Rognvald was up in Suther-
land at his daughter Ingirid's wedding to Eirik Stay-Brails.
As soon as he heard that Earl Harald had arrived there, Earl
Rognvald left the wedding feast and rode to Thurso with a
large following. Eirik Stay-Brails was related to Earl Harald

and did all he could to bring the two Earls to a settlement. There were plenty of people to support his argument that, as kinsmen, foster-brothers, and former comrades-in-arms, they should never fall out with one another. Eventually a peace meeting and a truce were agreed upon. They were to get together at a certain castle in Thurso, and talk things over alone, though each was to have the same number of men stationed outside the castle. They had a long discussion and got on well together. This was the first time they had met since the return of Rognvald from his travels.

As evening drew on, Earl Rognvald learned that Earl Harald's troops were armed and approaching the castle, but Earl Harald said it was nothing to worry about. Then they heard the sound of fighting outside, and rushed out to find that Thorbjorn Clerk had turned up with a strong force and had attacked Earl Rognvald's men the moment they met. The Earls shouted for them to stop fighting and people came running from the town to keep them apart, but thirteen of Rognvald's men were killed there and he himself was wounded in the face. Then mutual friends intervened to reconcile them and eventually they came to terms, confirming their alliance yet again with sworn oaths. This happened four days before Michaelmas. Yet another decision was made to set out for Orkney that same night against Erlend and Svein, and so they sailed in thirteen ships west to the Pentland Firth, then across to South Ronaldsay, where they landed at Widewell Bay and walked ashore.

Earl Erlend and his men were aboard their own ships in Barth Wick and from there they could see the gathering on South Ronaldsay, so they sent spies over. They found out that the Earls had come to terms and that they would be given no chance to raid or get supplies in any way, so there was no hope of their getting food from the islands. Earl Erlend talked things over with his men and asked their advice, but it was agreed that whatever was to be done, the decision should be left to Svein. His plan was that, since they hadn't the strength to fight both Earls on the islands, they should sail over to Caithness that same night. In front of the whole army he announced that they were going to the Hebrides for the winter, and on the eve of Michaelmas Day they sailed into the Pentland Firth. As soon as they had landed in Caithness they poured into the settlements and rounded up droves of cattle for slaughter on the beach, then loaded the carcases onto their ships. A fierce gale was blowing and the weather was so bad the Pentland Firth was impassable most of the time, but when the storm abated Svein sent some men in a boat across to the islands with the news that Earl Erlend had been raiding in Caithness and was setting sail for the Hebrides as soon as weather permitted. When this reached the ears of Earl Rognvald he called a meeting and told his troops to be on their guard and to stay aboard their ships during the night.

'I expect Svein in Orkney at any moment,' he said, 'and all the more so when he talks about going somewhere else.'

Early in winter Svein and his men put out from Thurso and cruised west of Scotland in seven large, well-manned ships, rowing hard. After Svein's men had left Caithness, Earl Rognvald's spies went back with the news to Orkney and the Earls then shifted their fleet over to Scapa, Rognvald telling them to stay aboard their ships for a while.

When Svein had reached almost due west of the Point of Stoer, he told his men not to wear themselves out any more at the oars, but to change course and hoist sail. They thought the idea rather stupid, but did as they were told, and once they had done so the ships started gathering speed before the wind. There is nothing to tell of their voyage till they reached Orkney, where they put in at South Walls and learned that the Earls were off Knarston in Scapa with a fleet of fourteen ships. With Svein at the time were Erlend the Young, Eirik Stay-Brails and many other men of good family.

Thorbjorn Clerk had gone east to Paplay to see his father-in-law Hakon Karl, having married Ingigerd, Hakon's daughter. Four days before the Feast of Jude and Simon, Svein announced that he planned to attack the Earls that night. Others thought him ill-advised in view of the heavy odds against them, but Svein wanted his own way and since Earl Erlend was in favour of it that's how things went.

In the evening there was a blizzard with sleet. Earl Rognvald went ashore to visit his estate at Orphir, believing that he had nothing to fear. He had five companions and they reached Knarston during the storm. The farmer there was an Icelander called Botolf the Stubborn, a good poet, and he repeatedly invited Rognvald to stay the night. They went inside, were helped off with their wet clothes, and went to bed. Botolf was to keep a look-out.

That same night, Earl Erlend and his men took Earl Harald's force by surprise, for until they heard the war-cry they had suspected nothing. They seized their weapons and put up a stout defence, so a good many were killed, but the outcome was that Earl Harald had to beach his ship when there were only five fit men left aboard. Bjarni, a man of good family and the brother of Erlend the Young, was killed there along with a hundred others, and many were wounded. All the survivors jumped off the ships and ran ashore. Earl Erlend lost only a few men, but took fourteen of the Earl's ships there, as well as all the money on board.

When most of the hard work had been done, Erlend and his men learned that Rognvald had gone ashore that evening and walked as far as Knarston, so they did the same. Farmer Botolf was outside the door when they arrived and gave them a good welcome. They asked if Earl Rognvald was there and Botolf said that he had been there overnight. They were very insistent and kept asking where was he then, surely Botolf must know? Botolf stretched out his arm towards the fence, and made this verse:

> Out after eating-birds!
> Fine archers, the Earl's men:
> hard for the hen-bird,
> the head-shot on the hill.
> Excellent the aim
> of the elm-bows, savage
> the grouse-hunt, grim
> the guardian of the land.

Earl Erlend's men raced across the homefield, each of them with the thought that the fastest man would be the best, and the one most likely to overcome the Earl. Botolf went back inside, woke Rognvald and told him both what had happened during the night and what Erlend's men were up to as well. Rognvald and his men leapt to their feet, put on their clothes and set off right away for the Earl's estate at Orphir, where on arrival they found Harald in hiding. They put out to sea at once and sailed over to Caithness, each in his own boat, one of them with two companions and the other with three. Everyone who could get a passage went over to Caithness.

Erlend and Svein seized all the ships belonging to the Earls and a vast sum of money as well. Svein Asleifarson gathered together all the treasures taken from Rognvald's ship and sent them over to the Earl in Caithness. He urged Erlend to move their fleet over to South Walls where they could lie at anchor close to the Pentland Firth and see the moment anyone put out from Caithness. It was also thought a good place from which to make an attack, should the opportunity arise, but Erlend was persuaded by his supporters to go north to Damsay, where they spent each day drinking in a great hall, though in the evening they would rope their ships together and slept on board at night.

Three days before Christmas, Svein Asleifarson travelled east to Sandwick to visit his kinswoman Sigrid, and settle an issue between her and a neighbour called Bjorn. Before he set off, Svein warned Earl Erlend to sleep on board ship that night and not to let his absence make Erlend careless. Svein stayed one night with his kinswoman Sigrid.

One of Svein's tenants, a good friend of his called Gils, asked Svein to come and spend the night with him. Gils had brewed some ale and wanted to entertain Svein and his men. When they came to Gils' house, they were told that Earl Erlend had not gone to the ships the previous evening, and at once Svein sent Margad Grimsson and two other men to the Earl, asking him to pay attention to his warning that night, even though he'd not done so the night before.

'But I'm afraid I won't have to give advice to that Earl very much longer,' he added.

Margad and his companions saw the Earl and gave him Svein's message, but the Earl's men said Svein was a very odd character: one moment he thought there was nothing he couldn't do, then the next he was so scared he knew neither what to do for himself nor for anyone else. They said they weren't going to the ships, but meant to sleep in comfort ashore. The Earl said that they should do as Svein told them, and the upshot was that he and nineteen others went down to the ships while the rest stayed in houses ashore. Margad and his men lay out in a small creek not far from there. That same night, Earls Rognvald and Harald arrived, taking Earl Erlend so completely by surprise that neither the watchmen ashore, nor those on board, knew a thing until the enemy had boarded their ships.

Two men called Orm and Ufi were in the foc's'le room of Earl Erlend's ship. Ufi leapt to his feet and tried to rouse the Earl, but couldn't because Erlend was dead-drunk, so Ufi picked him up bodily and jumped overboard with him, then got into a dinghy floating beside the ship. Orm jumped over the other side and got ashore, but Earl Erlend and most of the others on board were killed.

Margad and his men were awakened by the war-cry and began pulling at their oars, rowing round the headland. In the bright light of the moon they could see the Earls pulling away and realised that the issue between them and Erlend must have been settled at last, so they rowed off and headed for Rendall. They sent people to Svein to tell him all that they had seen.

Earl Harald wanted to give Erlend's men quarter, but Earl Rognvald said that they should first wait and see if his body was found, or if he had escaped. Two days before Christmas they discovered the body—someone saw a spear-shaft sticking out of a heap of seaweed and closer inspection showed that the Earl had been run through with it. His body was taken to church and his men were spared, as were four of Svein's farm-hands who had also been taken prisoner.

There was a man called Jon Wing, nephew of the Jon Wing who figured earlier in the story. He had been staying with Hakon Karl and had made Hakon's sister pregnant before running off on a viking expedition with Anakol, but now he had been serving with Earl Erlend, though absent from the fight. All Erlend's men had made their way to Kirkwall, seeking sanctuary in St Magnus' Cathedral. Earls Rognvald and Harald went there, too, and a peace meeting was arranged, though Jon was not given terms by the Earls until he promised to marry the girl. Everyone there swore oaths of allegiance to the Earls, who were not too exacting in their demands. Jon Wing then joined Earl Harald and became his steward.

95. SVEIN ON THE RUN

After the death of Earl Erlend, Svein Asleifarson went over to Rendall to have a word with Margad and his companions and heard in detail of the events on Damsay. Then they all went together to Rousay, arriving at high tide, carried their tackle ashore and beached the ship. The men were billeted out at various settlements, then spies were despatched to find out what the Earls and the other powerful men were up to. With five men, Svein climbed a mountain, then down the other side, and under cover of darkness they crept up to a certain farm from which they could hear a great deal of noise. Inside were Thorfinn, his son Ogmund and their kinsman-in-law Erlend the Young. This Erlend was boasting to father and son that he had given Earl Erlend his death-stroke, and all three were going on about how bravely they'd fought. When Svein heard this he rushed into the house with his comrades behind him. He was the quickest and struck Erlend dead with a single stroke. They took Thorfinn prisoner and made off with him, leaving Ogmund wounded. Svein and his men went to Ting-wall, where his uncle Helgi was farming at the time, and stayed there in hiding for the first part of the Christmas season.

Earl Rognvald went to Damsay at Christmas but Earl Harald remained behind at Kirkwall. Rognvald sent messengers to Helgi of Tingwall telling him that if by any chance he knew of the whereabouts of his nephew Svein, Rognvald wanted to invite him over for Christmas and promised to do his best to reconcile Svein with Earl Harald. When Svein got the message he set out with five men to see Earl Rognvald and stayed the second part of the Christmas season with him.

After Christmas a peace-meeting was arranged between Svein and the Earls to settle all the outstanding issues between them. At the meeting, Earl Rognvald threw his weight on the side of a settlement between Svein and Earl Harald, though most people who were neither friends nor kinsmen of Svein, gave advice that was not well-meant and said he would always be causing trouble unless he was banished from the islands. All the same they came to this agreement, that Svein was to pay a mark of gold to each of the Earls and hand over half his estates together with a fine longship.

'This settlement will only work,' said Svein after the verdict, 'as long as I'm treated decently.'

Earl Rognvald refused his share of the fine imposed on Svein, saying that he had no intention of bullying him and valued his friendship more than his money.

After the settlement, Earl Harald went over to Svein's estate on Gairsay and used his grain-store and other property with little consideration. When Svein learned about this he complained to Earl Rognvald, calling it a breach of the agreement, and said that he wanted to go home and look after his property.

'You stay here with me, Svein,' said Earl Rognvald, 'and I'll send word to Harald asking for further talks about your disagreement, but I don't want you even to think of starting a quarrel with Harald. I know you're a strong man and a brave one, but face to face he'll prove more than a match for you.'

But Svein could not be dissuaded. He put out in a skiff with ten men and sailed to Gairsay, arriving there late in the evening. He saw there was a fire in the back room of the house. He went there, wanting to get some fire and burn down the house with the Earl inside, but a man called Svein Blakarason, the leading man in his company, was against it. He said it might well be that the Earl was not inside and, even if he was, Svein's wife and daughters would never be allowed to leave the house and it was out of the question to let them burn to death there.

So Svein and his men went up to the door of the house, but when they came to the inner door leading to the hall the men inside jumped to their feet and managed to close it. Svein now realised that the Earl was not there, but he gave quarter to all the Earl's men there after they had given themselves up, handed over their weapons to him and walked out unarmed.

Svein poured all his ale down the drain and took his wife and daughters away with him. When he asked his wife Ingirid where the Earl was, she refused to tell him.

'Don't speak then,' he said, 'just give me a nod.'

But again she refused, as she was related to the Earl.

After they had boarded the ship, Svein gave some of the men their weapons back, and that was the end of the settlement between him and Earl Harald.

Earl Harald had gone to hunt hares on a small island. Svein went over to Hellis Isle, where there are steep sea-cliffs and a great cave in them: at high tide the sea comes right up to the mouth of the cave.

Once Earl Harald's men got their weapons back from Svein they went straight to the Earl and told him how things had gone with Svein. The Earl ordered them to float his ship at once and row after Svein.

'We must settle the matter between us right now,' he said.

They started pulling at their oars and it wasn't long before each party saw and recognised the other. When Svein realised that the Earl was catching up, he spoke to his men.

'We'd better think of something to get us out of this,' he said, 'for I'm not so keen to meet him as matters stand, with the kind of odds we're clearly up against. So what we'll do now,' he said, 'is go to the cave and wait there to see what happens.'

And that's what they did. They got to the cave on the rising tide and hauled the boat up inside, since the cave slopes upwards into the cliff, and the sea rises right up to the mouth of the cave.

Earl Harald spent the day scouring the island for them, but found no trace, nor was any boat seen leaving the island, and this they thought very odd indeed, for it didn't seem likely that Svein had vanished into the earth. They rowed round the island searching for him, but as you'd expect, they still found nothing. They came to the conclusion that Svein must have reached some other island, so off they rowed in what seemed the likeliest direction.

Just as the Earl and his men were pulling away from the island the tide began to ebb away from the mouth of the cave and Svein and his companions were able to overhear their conversation. Svein left his own boat in the cave, took a cargo-boat belonging to some monks and sailed it over to Sanday. There they disembarked, pushing out the cargo-boat so that it drifted from beach to beach till it was wrecked.

Svein and his men walked up into the island as far as a farm called Voluness, the home of one of Svein's kinsmen called Bard. They asked for him to come outside for a quiet word, and Svein said he wanted to stay there. Bard agreed to let him have his way.

'But it's a risk I daren't take unless you stay hidden,' he added.

They went inside and found themselves alone in a room, separated from the rest of the household by a wicker partition. There was a hidden passageway to the room they were in, blocked with loose stones.

That same evening, Earl Harald's steward, Jon Wing, arrived with six other men. Bard the farmer gave them a friendly welcome and had a fire made for them to bake themselves by. Jon was blustering away about the news of the dealings between the Earls and Svein, having some very critical things to say of the latter and calling him a truce-breaker, to be trusted by no one.

'No sooner has he come to terms with Earl Harald,' said Jon, 'than he wants to go and burn him to death!'

He went on to say that there would never be any peace in the land until Svein was exiled from it, but Bard and Jon's companions spoke up for him. Then Jon started criticising Earl Erlend and said that his death was nobody's loss and that the Earl had been such a man of violence nobody could live in peace while he was around. Hearing this, Svein could take no more of it, grabbed his weapons, rushed into the concealed passage and pushed the stones out of his way with a great clatter, meaning to run for the hall-door. Jon was only wearing a shirt and linen breeches, but when he heard the racket that Svein was making, he strung his shoes together and raced away from the fire and the farmstead into the black and frosty night. Later that night he reached another farm, his feet so badly frostbitten that he lost several toes.

Svein gave quarter to Jon's companions, at the request of the farmer, Bard, and spent the rest of the night there. In the morning they set out in a skiff Bard loaned to Svein and went south to Barth Wick, putting in near a certain cave. In the daytime Svein would often sit drinking in some house, but at night he stayed aboard ship, always on guard against his enemies.

96. SVEIN AND EARL ROGNVALD

Early one morning Svein and his men sighted a big longship sailing from Mainland to South Ronaldsay, and at once Svein recognised it as the one usually commanded by Rognvald himself. It headed straight for the spot where Svein's skiff was beached and five of the crew disembarked there. Svein and his men were at the top of a nearby hill and from there they began pelting the Earl's party with stones, whereupon, seeing this, those on board grabbed their weapons. Next, Svein and his men set off running down the hill towards the shore, floated the skiff and jumped aboard. The longship was already beached and firmly aground. As Svein and his men were rowing the skiff past the longship, Svein stood up with a spear in his hand. When he saw this, Earl Rognvald picked up a shield to defend himself, but Svein didn't throw the spear. The Earl realised that Svein was going to get away, so he had the shield of peace raised aloft and invited Svein to come ashore. When Svein saw the signal he told his men to row back to the island and said that he wanted nothing more than to be reconciled with Earl Rognvald.

97. SVEIN AND EARL HARALD

After that, Earl Rognvald and Svein had a long talk ashore and got on well together. As they sat talking, they sighted Earl Harald's ship sailing from Caithness to South Walls. The ship disappeared behind the island, and then Svein asked the Earl what he should do. The Earl advised him to go to Caithness at once, and the two leaders set out together, the Earl sailing to Mainland and Svein west to Stroma. This was in Lent.

Earl Harald's men spotted Svein's skiff and realised whose it was, so they swiftly changed course into the Pentland Firth and chased after them. When Svein and his companions saw

that the Earl was heading for them, they disembarked and
hid. When the Earl reached Stroma, he and his men saw the
skiff, but they did not want to go ashore as they knew there
were settlements near by.

A man called Amundi Hnefason, a friend of Earl Harald's
and uncle to Svein's step-children, set out to mediate between
them, and what he achieved was to confirm the agreement
made earlier that winter, on the same terms. Suddenly a
strong gale blew up so that both parties were forced to spend
the night on the island. Amundi so arranged things that Earl
Harald and Svein had to use the same bed, with a good many
men from either side also sleeping in the room.

After confirming the agreement, Svein sailed over to
Caithness and the Earl north to Orkney. Svein heard that the
Earl had said he regarded their settlement as only a loose
arrangement, but paid little attention, travelling south to
Argyll to spend Easter with his friend Sumarlidi. Meanwhile,
Earl Harald had gone north to Shetland and stayed there most
of the spring. After Easter, Svein travelled back north and
on the way met up with Peter Club-Foot and Blann, two
brothers of Jon Wing. Svein and his men took them captive,
stripped them of all they had, then took them ashore and
started building a gallows for them, but when everything was
ready, Svein told them to run off into the countryside, saying
that to let them off with their lives would be an even better
way to shame their brother Jon. They spent a great deal of
time out in the open and by the time they reached a farmstead, they were badly frostbitten. Svein put out again and
sailed over to Lewis in the Hebrides, where he stayed for a
while.

Jon Wing heard that Svein had captured his brothers and,
before finding out what Svein had done with them, he went to
Eynhallow and captured Olaf, the son of Svein Asleifarson and
foster-son of Kolbein Heap, taking him to Westray where
they ran into Earl Rognvald at Rapness.

'What brings you here, Olaf?' asked the Earl when he saw
him.

'Jon Wing had better answer that,' he replied.

The Earl looked at Jon.

'Why did you bring Olaf here?' he asked.

'Svein took my brothers,' answered Jon, 'and for all I know
he may have killed them.'

'Take him back at once,' said the Earl, 'and don't you dare
harm the boy, no matter what you're told has happened to

your brothers. If you do, Svein and Kolbein won't give you a moment's peace in the islands.'

98. SVEIN RETURNS

In the spring, after Easter, Svein set out from the Hebrides with a crew of sixty, making for Orkney and landing first at Rousay, where they captured a man called Hakon Karl, who had been with Earl Harald at the time Earl Erlend was killed. He was set free after paying Svein a ransom of three gold marks. On Rousay they found the longship which the Earls had taken from Svein, with two planks missing from the hull, removed on Earl Rognvald's instructions when no one would buy the ship or even take it as a gift. From there Svein sailed to Mainland where he got a friendly welcome from Earl Rognvald and stayed with him for the rest of the spring. Earl Rognvald explained that he'd had the planks taken out of the ship to stop Svein doing anything rash in the islands when he came back from the Hebrides.

At Whitsun, Earl Harald came back from Shetland and as soon as he landed in Orkney, Earl Rognvald sent messengers saying that he wanted him to make yet another settlement with Svein, so a peace-meeting was arranged, to be held on the Friday of Whit Week in St Magnus' Cathedral. Earl Rognvald carried a broad axe to the meeting and Svein accompanied him. A reconciliation was agreed on the same terms as those of the previous winter.

99. THE RECONCILIATION OF SVEIN AND EARL HARALD

At the meeting Earl Rognvald gave Earl Harald the ship that had once belonged to Svein, and to Svein he allowed whatever might be awarded him. Earl Rognvald and Svein were standing by the door of the cathedral when the sail was carried out— it had been stored in the cathedral—and an ugly-looking frown passed over Svein's face as they carried it past.

On Saturday, when Nones were over, messengers came to Svein from Earl Harald saying that the Earl wanted him to come for a talk. Svein consulted Earl Rognvald, who was not at all keen for Svein to go, saying it was hard to know what to believe. All the same, Svein decided to go, taking five men along with him.

Earl Harald was seated at the cross-dais in a small room

with Thorbjorn Clerk beside him and only a few others present. For a while they all sat drinking and then Thorbjorn went outside. Svein and his men said later that they had grave doubts about what the Earl was up to. After a while, Thorbjorn came back and gave Svein a scarlet tunic and a cloak, saying that he wasn't sure whether or not to call them a gift since they had been taken from Svein during the winter, but Svein accepted them as gifts. Then Earl Harald gave Svein the longship that had once been his, as well as half his lands and property. He invited Svein to stay with him and said that their friendship must never be broken. Svein gladly agreed to all this, went back that night to Earl Rognvald and told him what had happened between Harald and himself. This pleased Earl Rognvald, but he asked Svein to take care never to fall out with Earl Harald again.

100. THORBJORN CLERK

Shortly after this, three leading men, Svein, Thorbjorn and Einar, set off on a viking expedition, first to the Hebrides, then all the way to the Scilly Isles where they won a great victory and a massive share of plunder at Port St Mary's on St Columba's Day, after which they went back to Orkney.

After the reconciliation of Earls Rognvald and Harald with Svein Asleifarson, the two Earls spent a great deal of time together on the best of terms, with Rognvald having most say in things. On his return from the Scillies, Thorbjorn Clerk joined Earl Harald and became his counsellor.

Svein went home to Gairsay and kept a large establishment over the winter, using his share of the plunder to supplement his revenues from the islands and defray his expenses. He felt very well-disposed towards Earl Rognvald. Every summer he would go on raiding expeditions. The story goes that Thorbjorn Clerk did little to help relations between Earls Rognvald and Harald.

A man called Thorarin Bag-Nose was a friend and retainer of Earl Rognvald and stayed with him much of the time, and a man called Thorkel was a follower of Thorbjorn Clerk. The two men fell out with one another during a drinking session in Kirkwall, where Thorkel wounded Thorarin, then made his way back to Thorbjorn. Thorarin's drinking friends chased after him, but Thorbjorn and his supporters made a stand in some upper room, and there the Earls went, when they heard about it, to separate the two sides. Thorbjorn would not agree to let Earl Rognvald settle the matter and complained about how he and his friends had been chased.

After Thorarin had recovered, he killed Thorkel as he was on his way to church, then ran into the church himself, with Thorbjorn and his followers after him. When Earl Rognvald heard about this, he went to the church with a force of men and asked Thorbjorn whether he was planning to demolish it. Thorbjorn answered that it was wrong for the man sheltering inside the church to be given its protection, but Rognvald said that no damage was to be done to the church and Thorbjorn was driven away by force. No settlement was reached over the killing. Thorbjorn went across to Caithness and stayed there for some time committing various crimes, raping and killing, so no love was lost between him and the people there.

Thorbjorn sailed secretly to Orkney in a skiff with thirty men, landing at Scapa Flow and walking to Kirkwall with three companions. In the evening he rushed single handed into a tavern where Thorarin was drinking and killed him on the spot, then ran off into the darkness. For this offence Earl Rognvald declared him an outlaw throughout the land. Thorbjorn went over to Caithness and stayed in hiding with his brother-in-law Hosvir, nicknamed the Strong, who was married to Thorbjorn's sister, Ragnhild, and whose son, Stefan the Counsellor, was one of Thorbjorn's companions.

Shortly after this, Thorbjorn went to stay with Malcolm, King of Scots, who thought very highly of him.

There was a man with the King of Scots called Gilla Odran, well-connected but a terrible bully, and he was the cause of so much trouble and killing in the kingdom that Malcolm grew very angry. So Gilla Odran cleared off to Orkney where the Earls took him in and made him their steward in Caithness. There was a farmer there of good family called Helgi, a friend of Earl Rognvald's, and when he and Gilla Odran fell out over the stewardship, Gilla attacked and killed him.

After the killing, Gilla Odran travelled to the west of Scotland where a chieftain called Sumarlidi the Yeoman took him in. Sumarlidi was ruling in Argyll to the west, and was married to Ragnhild, daughter of Olaf Tit-bit, King of the Hebrides. Their children, known as the Dalesmen, were King Dufgal, Rognvald and Angus.

Earl Rognvald summoned Svein Asleifarson to him before Svein set out on his viking expedition and asked him to take care of Gilla Odran if he got the chance, but Svein said he wasn't sure it could be done.

101. THE DEATH OF GILLA ODRAN

After that, Svein set out on his viking trip with five longships. When he reached the west coast of Scotland he heard that Sumarlidi the Yeoman had gone to sea and planned to do some raiding with seven ships. One of them was captained by Gilla Odran, who had sailed into the lochs looking for people who had not yet turned up.

As soon as Svein heard about Sumarlidi, he set out to fight him, and in the fierce battle that followed Sumarlidi was killed, along with a good many of his men. Then Svein discovered Gilla Odran was missing, so he set off in search of him, catching up with him at the Firth of Forth, where he killed him and fifty of his men.

After that Svein carried on with his raiding expedition and went home in the autumn as he always did, getting together shortly afterwards with Earl Rognvald who was delighted with what Svein had managed to do.

102. THORBJORN CLERK AND HIS FRIENDS

The Earls used to go over to Caithness every summer hunting red deer and reindeer in the woods there. Thorbjorn Clerk was spending his time alternately with the King of Scots and secretly with his friends to the north in Caithness. Three of his friends there he trusted in particular, his brother-in-law Hosvir, Lifolf of Thurso Dale and Hallvard Dufuson who farmed at Forsi in Calder Dale. He was very close to all three.

103. THE DEATH OF EARL ROGNVALD

Rognvald had been ruling Earl for twenty-two years from the time Earl Paul was taken captive: late in the summer, he and Earl Harald set off as usual for Caithness. When they reached Thurso, they heard a rumour that Thorbjorn Clerk was hiding up in Thurso Dale with a good many companions, waiting for a chance to attack them from there, so the Earls gathered a force and set out a hundred and twenty strong, with twenty horsemen and the rest on foot. They made their way up the valley that evening and took overnight lodgings.

As they were sitting by the fire that night, Earl Rognvald had an attack of sneezing.

'Quite a sneeze, that, kinsman,' said Earl Harald.

Next morning they set out, and throughout the day Earl Rognvald rode ahead with a man called Asolf and one of his kinsmen called Jomar. Altogether there were five of them riding ahead all the way up to Calder Dale and, as they approached the farmstead at Forsie, Hallvard, the farmer there was standing on top of a hayrick, stacking the hay that his farmhands were carrying to him. Earl Harald and his men were riding a little way behind. As soon as Hallvard recognised Earl Rognvald, he called him by name, greeting him in a loud voice and asking the news, so that he could be heard some way off. This happened close to the farmhouse, which stood on a steep slope. People wanting to get to the farmstead had to ride up a sharply rising narrow path.

Inside, Thorbjorn Clerk sat drinking. The path led right up to the gable of the house, where there was a door with a heap of loose stones blocking the entrance, and when Thorbjorn and his men heard Hallvard welcoming Earl Rognvald they grabbed their weapons, cleared away the stones from the concealed door and ran outside, Thorbjorn beyond the gable and on to the wall at the edge of the path. Just at that moment the Earl and his men reached the door and Thorbjorn swung at him, but Asolf parried the stroke with his hand, which was sliced off. Even so, the blow caught the Earl on the chin and caused a nasty wound.

'Those who owe the Earl greater favours ought to take greater care of him,' said Asolf as he took the blow.

He was eighteen years old and had just joined the Earl.

When Earl Rognvald saw Thorbjorn he tried to dismount, but his foot was caught in the stirrup, and just at that moment Stefan came up and thrust a spear at the Earl, inflicting yet another wound. Then Jomar lunged with a spear at Thorbjorn's thigh, driving it straight into the lower guts.

Thorbjorn and his men retreated behind the house, then down the steep slope on to the swampy ground below. At this, Earl Harald and his men appeared and as they ran into Thorbjorn each side recognised the other. Earl Harald's men wanted to chase after Thorbjorn, realising what he was up to, but Earl Harald held them back and said he meant to wait and see what Earl Rognvald would decide to do.

'I'm very close to Thorbjorn, as you all know,' he said, 'in kinship as well as in many other ways.'

The men with Earl Rognvald were crowding round him as he lay dying and it was some time before Earl Harald heard what had happened. By then, Thorbjorn and his men had reached the swampy ground and crossed beyond the softest part. The Earl's men kept on at Harald and, at last, they all started to rush down to the swamp in Thorbjorn's direction. He took his stand on one side of the swamp facing the Earl and his men on the other. Those men of Thorbjorn's who had been left at the farm had begun to flock to his side, until eventually there were some fifty of them. They held their ground well, for they were in a strong defensive position, the swamp being deep and wide and the ground soft on either side. The only way to harm them was by throwing spears, but Thorbjorn ordered his men to throw nothing back. When the others had run out of missiles, Harald and Thorbjorn exchanged words.

'I'm asking you to give me quarter, kinsman,' called Thorbjorn. 'I want to place everything in your hands, for you alone to judge. I'll do anything in my power to raise your reputation, but I hope you remember there was a time, kinsman, had it come to a choice between Rognvald and myself, when you'd not have killed me despite the thing I've just done. Those were the days when he kept you under his thumb and treated your opinion about as seriously as if you'd been one of his servants, while I was giving you the best of gifts and doing all I could to add to your honour. I've committed a terrible crime, for which I'll have to pay, but remember this, the realm is in your hands now, and whatever I've done to Rognvald, it's only what he had in store for me. One thing more, kinsman—I'd like to think that had matters stood differently, with Rognvald alive and myself dead, you'd have continued to show him every respect; but now you want to see me dead.'

Thorbjorn kept speaking like this at some length and very plausibly, and there were plenty with him to plead for his life, so that in due course, with so many to argue his case, Earl Harald began to think about it very seriously.

Then Magnus, the son of Havard Gunnason spoke up, the most highly honoured man in Earl Harald's retinue and the one most favoured by his kinsmen, the Earls.

'I don't presume to advise you, sir, after such a shocking business as this,' he said, 'though I could tell you what kind of rumour would get around were Thorbjorn allowed to live on after such a crime. And here's another thing—he has the nerve to say to your face, in so many words, that he's done this foul crime for the sake of you and your honour! If the Earl isn't avenged, it will be an everlasting dishonour and disgrace to you yourself and to all the Earl's kin. As I see it, Rognvald's friends will be thinking that you had plotted his murder long before any of this took place. Do you seriously believe Thorbjorn will swear you knew nothing, once the time comes for him to make his excuses, with nobody to speak in your defence? All the more so now he's told you to your face that it was for your sake he committed the crime? You couldn't find a better way of confirming it than by sparing his life now. Whether you like it or not, he'll get no mercy from me, not as long as there are right-minded people willing to take my side.'

His brothers Thorstein and Hakon said much the same, and so did Svein Hroaldsson. Then they turned away from the Earl up along the ditch looking for a place to cross. Thorbjorn saw Magnus and the others making their way along the ditch.

'They must have disagreed about their plans,' he said. 'The Earl wants to spare me and Magnus won't have it.'

Thorbjorn and his men moved away from the ditch while they talked this over and, when he realised that he wasn't going to be offered quarter, Thorbjorn jumped nine ells, right across the ditch, carrying all his weapons. His men came leaping after him, but none of them could clear the ditch, though most managed to reach the bank and scramble up.

Thorbjorn's men tried to persuade him either to join the Earl or attack Magnus and put an end to the matter between them.

'I think everyone must look out for himself,' said Thorbjorn, 'and do whatever he thinks is best. As for me, I'm going to see Earl Harald again.'

Most of his men were against it and said he ought to head for the woods and get away, but Thorbjorn wouldn't listen. His men started drifting off, each looking for a way to save himself, so in the end he was left with only eight men. When he saw that Earl Harald had crossed the ditch, he went up to him and knelt down, saying he was surrendering his head to the Earl.

'Look after yourself, Thorbjorn,' said the Earl, 'I don't care to kill you.'

While they were talking they made their way down along Forse Water, with Magnus and his men close behind, as the Earl could see.

'Look after yourself, Thorbjorn,' he said, 'I'm not fighting my own men on your account.'

And so it was that the Earl and Thorbjorn parted company.

Thorbjorn and his companions made their way to a desolate shieling called Assery. Magnus and his men were close behind and set fire to the building, but Thorbjorn's small band defended themselves bravely. All the same, when the house was burning and crumbling they came outside and at once people began to attack them wherever they were, though the fire had already weakened them. All nine companions were killed there. When they looked at Thorbjorn's wounds, they saw that his guts had fallen out through the one given him by Jomar.

Earl Harald made his own way down the valley, but Magnus and his men went back to Forsie to take care of Earl Rognvald's body, then carried it down to Thurso.

104. EARL ROGNVALD'S BURIAL

Earl Rognvald died on the fifth day after the Feast of the Assumption. Earl Harald and his men sailed in great style from Thurso to Orkney with the body, and buried it at St Magnus' Cathedral where Earl Rognvald rested until God made manifest the worthiness of the Earl with a number of wondrous miracles, whereupon, with the Pope's permission, Bishop Bjarni had his holy relics translated. On the boulder where Earl Rognvald's blood had poured when he was killed we can still see it, as lovely as if it had been newly spilt.

Earl Rognvald was deeply mourned, for he had been much loved in the isles and in many other places too. He had been a good friend to a great many people, lavish with money, moderate, loyal to his friends, a many-sided man and a fine poet. He was survived by his daughter Ingirid who married Eirik Stay-Brails, and their children were Harald the Young, Magnus Mangi, Rognvald, Ingibjorg, Elin and Ragnhild.

105. SVEIN'S LIFE-STYLE

After the death of Earl Rognvald, Earl Harald took over the islands and became their sole ruler. He was a very tall, strong man and a great leader. A women called Afreka whom he took in marriage bore him four children, Heinrek, Hakon, Helena and Margaret.

When Hakon was past his infancy, Svein Asleifarson offered to foster him, so he was brought up on Gairsay and, as soon as he was strong enough to travel with grown men, Svein began to take him on viking expeditions every summer, doing all in his power to build up Hakon's reputation.

This was how Svein used to live. Winter he would spend at

home on Gairsay, where he entertained some eighty men at his own expense. His drinking hall was so big, there was nothing in Orkney to compare with it. In the spring he had more than enough to occupy him, with a great deal of seed to sow which he saw to carefully himself. Then when that job was done, he would go off plundering in the Hebrides and in Ireland on what he called his 'spring-trip', then back home just after midsummer, where he stayed till the cornfields had been reaped and the grain was safely in. After that he would go off raiding again, and never came back till the first month of winter was ended. This he used to call his 'autumn-trip'.

106. A GOOD VIKING TRIP

Once Svein Asleifarson set out on a spring-trip taking Hakon, Earl Harald's son, along with him. They had five big ships, all fitted for rowing, and began raiding in the Hebrides. The Hebrideans were so scared of them, they hid whatever they could carry either in among the rocks or underground. Then Svein went down to the Isle of Man, but didn't get much in the way of loot there.

Next they sailed to Ireland and started plundering there. On their way south towards Dublin they came across two merchant ships en route from England loaded with a very valuable cargo of English broadcloth. Svein made for the ships and challenged them, but they offered little resistance, and Svein and his men robbed them of every penny they had. The only things they left the English were the clothes they wore and some food, and after that they rowed away. Then Svein and his shipmates went back to the Hebrides to share out the loot, sailing back home in great style. To make a great show of what they had done, they would set up the English cloth as their awnings when they were in harbour and before they sailed to Orkney they stitched it to the front of their sails, so that these seemed to be woven of the most precious fabrics. They named this expedition 'the broadcloth viking trip'. Then Svein went back to Gairsay to his farm, with all the wine and English mead he had taken from the merchant ships.

After he had been home for a short while, he invited Earl Harald to a feast, welcoming him with a magnificent banquet, at which people had plenty to say about Svein's high style of life.

'I'd like you to stop your raiding, Svein,' said the Earl. 'It's always better to be safe back home, and you know well enough that you're only able to keep yourself and your men on what you steal. Most troublemakers are fated to end up dead unless they stop of their own freewill.'

Svein looked at the Earl and there was a smile on his face.

'Fine and friendly words, my lord,' he said. 'I'll take your excellent advice, though there are people who might say you yourself are hardly the most peaceful of men.'

'I'm responsible for my own actions,' said the Earl, 'but I must say what I think.'

'I'm sure you've the very best of intentions, sir,' said Svein, 'so this is the way it's going to be: I'll give up raiding. I'm getting on in years and not up to all the hardships of war, but I'm going on one more trip in the autumn and I want it to be as glorious as my spring-trip. When that's over, I'll give up raiding.'

'Hard to tell which comes first, old fellow,' said the Earl, 'death or glory.'

And that was the end of their conversation. When the feast was over Earl Harald was seen off with fine gifts, and he and Svein parted the best of friends.

107. THE LAST VIKING TRIP

Shortly after this, Svein got ready for a viking trip with seven longships, all big ones, and Hakon, Earl Harald's son, went with him. First they made for the Hebrides but got little plunder there, so they sailed on to Ireland where they looted everywhere they could. They went as far south as Dublin and took people so much by surprise that no one knew they were there till they were in the town, where they took a great deal of plunder. The leading man in the town surrendered to Svein and agreed to pay him everything he asked for. Svein was given control of the town, appointing his own men to rule over it. The people of Dublin swore on oath to keep this agreement. In the evening Svein and his men went to their ships, but he was to return next morning to collect the ransom, take over the town and choose hostages from among the Dubliners.

Now, during the night, things happened like this. The head men of the town held a meeting to talk over the problems people there were faced with. They weren't keen to let their town fall into the clutches of the men of Orkney, least of all to the greatest trouble-maker known to them in the western lands, so they agreed that if there was any chance, they would play a trick on Svein. This is the plan they decided to adopt.

They dug deep pits, some inside the city gates, and others here and there between the houses where Svein and his men were supposed to go. They hid armed men in buildings near by, then covered the pits with branches, arranging them so that under the weight of a man they would collapse. Finally they spread straw to hide all sign of the pits, and then they waited till morning.

108. SVEIN IS KILLED IN DUBLIN

In the morning, Svein and his men got up, armed themselves and walked to town as far as the gate. The Dubliners formed a crowd so that the way to the pits was clear, and Svein and his men, suspecting nothing, fell right into them. At once the Dubliners barred the gate, and some of them went to the pits, using their weapons on Svein and his men, who had no chance to defend themselves. So it was that Svein and all those who had gone to the town with him lost their lives, there in the pits.

The story goes that Svein was the last to die, and these were his last words.

'Whether or not I'm to fall today,' he said, 'I want everyone to know that I'm the retainer of the holy Earl Rognvald, and now he's with God, it's in him I'll put my trust.'

The survivors amongst Svein's men went straight back to their ships, and there's nothing worth recording of their journey except that they got back to Orkney. That, then, is the end of Svein's story, but people say that apart from those of higher rank than himself, he was the greatest man the western world has ever seen in ancient and modern times.

After Svein's death, his sons, Olaf and Andres, divided the inheritance between them. The summer after his death they set up partition walls in the great drinking hall he had built on Gairsay. His son Andres married Frida, daughter of Kolbein Heap and sister of Bishop Bjarni of Orkney.

109. HARALD THE YOUNG

Now Earl Harald ruled in Orkney as a great leader. His second wife was Hvarflod, the daughter of Earl Malcolm of Moray, and their children were Thorfinn, David, Jon, Gunnhild, Herborga and Langlif.

After the death of Bishop William the Second, Bjarni, the son of Kolbein Heap, a great man and friend of Earl Harald, was consecrated bishop. He had plenty of kinsmen in the islands.

Eirik Stay-Brails had three sons, Harald the Young, Magnus Mangi and Rognvald. The brothers travelled east to Norway to see King Magnus Erlingsson and he gave Harald the title of earl, just as he had Harald's grandfather, Earl Rognvald the Holy. Earl Harald the Young went back west and with him Sigurd Mite, the son of Ivar Flaw who was killed with Erling Wry-Neck at Aker. Ivar's mother was the daughter of Havard Gunnason. Sigurd Mite was still quite young, a handsome man but inclined to extravagance in matters of taste. Magnus Mangi stayed behind with the King and was killed with him at Sogn.

Harald the Young and his men first put in at Shetland, then travelled from there to Caithness and south to Scotland to see William, King of Scots. Earl Harald asked William to grant him half of Caithness, the same that had been ruled by Earl Rognvald, and the King agreed. Next, Earl Harald travelled back north to Caithness to gather forces, and was joined there by his brother-in-law, Lifolf Pate. Lifolf had a good many well-born kinsmen there and was married to Ragnhild, the sister of Earl Harald the Young, as he was called to distinguish him from Earl Harald Maddadarson the Old. Lifolf was Young Harald's principal adviser, and in charge of his troops. Messengers were sent out to Orkney asking Harald the Old to surrender half the islands to Harald the Young, but when Old Harald received the message, he refused outright to divide the land he ruled, no matter what the terms. Lifolf Pate led this mission, and before he started back the Earl had a few sharp words to say to him.

After that, Harald the Old gathered his forces and assembled quite an army. Harald the Young was still with his followers in Caithness and his own force was a modest one. When he and his people heard that Harald the Old was raising an army, they sent Lifolf north again across the Pentland Firth to do some spying. He put in on the east side of South Ronaldsay and climbed a hill. There he ran into three of Harald the Old's guards, killing two of them and taking the third man along with him for questioning. Then Lifolf sighted the Earl's forces aboard a sizeable fleet of ships, most of them fairly large, so he raced back down the hill and told his men what he had learned, saying that Earl Harald the Old had so many troops it would be madness to attack him.

'This is what I would advise,' said Lifolf. 'If we go to

Thurso today, plenty of people there will join us. But if you insist on risking a fight with Harald, you won't have a chance, no matter how things turn out.'

Then Sigurd Mite had his say.

'It's very sad,' he said, 'when the Earl's own brother-in-law crosses the Pentland Firth just to discover that he's left his guts behind.'

He added that things didn't look so well if, as soon as they caught sight of Harald the Old's troops, they all lost heart.

'When the pressure's on,' said Lifolf, 'it may not be quite so obvious who has the heart, Sigurd. As I see it, should the time ever come for me to desert Harald the Young, you supermen won't find it so easy to stick with him either.'

Nothing came of the proposed trip to Thurso and a little later they saw Earl Harald's fleet sailing close to the islands, so they got themselves ready for war. Earl Harald came ashore and deployed his very much larger forces. Sigurd Mite and Lifolf led the troops of the younger Earl, commanding one wing each. Sigurd Mite was wearing a scarlet tunic and had the front hem tucked under his belt. Some of his men suggested he should do the same at the back, but he told them not to touch it.

'They won't be seeing my back today,' he said.

When they had formed up, the battle got under way, and the fighting was fierce. There were plenty of hard fighting men in the army of Harald the Old, very tough and well-equipped, the bishop's kinsmen, for instance, as well as many of the other captains. After a while, Sigurd Mite was killed, fighting bravely like a true champion. Among the others, Lifolf fought best and the Caithness people say that he cut his way three times through the enemy ranks before he was killed and died a hero's death. Once both Lifolf and Sigurd were dead, the rest of the army scattered.

Earl Harald the Young was killed near some peat-diggings, and that same night a great light could be seen where his blood had been spilt. People in Caithness think him a true saint and a church stands where he was killed. He was buried there on the headland, and as a result of his virtues, great miracles have been performed by God as a reminder that Harald wished to go to Orkney and join his kinsmen, Earl Magnus and Earl Rognvald.

After the battle, Earl Harald the Old laid the whole of Caithness under his rule, then went straight back to Orkney, boasting of his great victory.

110. TROUBLE IN CAITHNESS

William, King of Scots, heard that Harald the Young had been killed and also that Earl Harald Maddadarson, without bothering to consult him, had taken over the whole of Caithness and sent messengers to Rognvald Godrodarson, King of the Hebrides, whose mother was Ingibjorg, Earl Hakon Palsson's daughter. At that time King Rognvald was the greatest fighting man in all the western lands. For three whole years he had lived aboard longships and not spent a single night under a sooty roof. As soon as he got the message, Rognvald started gathering men all through the Hebrides and from Kintyre, to add to a strong force he had with him from Ireland. Then he travelled north and stayed for a while in Caithness, taking over the whole territory.

Earl Harald was in residence in Orkney and paid no attention to King Rognvald's movements. However, late in the winter Rognvald got ready to return to his lands in the Hebrides and appointed three stewards called Mani Olafsson, Rafn the Lawman and Hlifolf the Old to take charge in Caithness.

Shortly after King Rognvald had gone back to the Hebrides, Earl Harald sent someone over to Caithness. He told the man that he'd consider his trip well worth the trouble if he could kill one, or better still a pair, of the stewards. The messenger was ferried across the Pentland Firth and went on his way till he came to Hafn the Lawman, who asked him where he was heading for. He had little to say.

'It's plain to see that the Earl has sent you over here to Caithness,' said Rafn, 'to do some of his dirty work. But you're a kinsman of mine, so I won't stoop to killing you.'

At that they parted, and the man went on to Hlifolf, with the result that Hlifolf was killed. After that he went back to Orkney and told Earl Harald how things had gone.

111. CAITHNESS RECONQUERED

Earl Harald got ready to sail from Orkney and, when everything was in order, he steered due south to Thurso and disembarked. In the stronghold at Scrabster there was a bishop. When the men of Caithness sighted Earl Harald's troops, they could see there were so many of them, there was no point in offering any resistance; people said the Earl was in such a mood, there was no telling whether or not he would show them any mercy. Then the bishop spoke up.

'If we get on well together,' he said, 'he'll spare your lives.

So they decided to leave things to the bishop.

As the Earl's troops stormed up to the stronghold from the ships, the bishop set out to give the Earl some kind word of welcome, but what actually happened was that Earl Harald took the bishop captive and had his tongue cut out and a knife driven into his eyes, blinding him.

While he was being tortured, Bishop Jon kept praying to the holy virgin St Tredwell, and when they set him free he went over to a hillside where he asked a woman to help him. She could see the blood streaming from his face.

'Quiet, my lord,' she said, 'I'll help you gladly.'

The bishop was taken to where St Tredwell rests, and there he was restored to health both in speech and sight.

Earl Harald marched up to the stronghold and without any argument they surrendered it into his hands. He imposed severe punishments and heavy fines on all those he thought most guilty of treason against him and had all the men of Caithness swear oaths of allegiance to him whether they liked it or not. Then he took over all the property belonging to the stewards, who had now gone back to the King of Scots, and he settled in Caithness with a very large army.

112. CONCLUSION

Now we come back to the stewards. Six of them travelled south into Scotland, reached the King of Scots during Advent and gave him a precise account of what had happened in Caithness on Earl Harald's campaign. The King flew into a rage when he heard it, but promised to pay double compensation to anyone who had lost his property. On the very first day that the stewards spent with him, the King had twenty-five ells of cloth, together with one English mark, given each of them to cover immediate expenses, and they stayed with the King of Scots over Christmas, enjoying the best of hospitality.

Immediately after Christmas, the King of Scots sent word to all the chieftains in his kingdom and raised a great force from every part of the land, leading all these troops north to Caithness against Earl Harald. It was a truly massive army that the King of Scots led. He marched ahead to Ausdale near the boundary between Caithness and Sutherland, and there his camp extended from one end of the valley to the other, quite a distance.

Earl Harald was in Caithness when he heard about it and, without wasting any time, he started to gather his own forces. People say that he raised six thousand men, but even so he was far from strong enough to fight the King of Scots, so he sent messengers to sound out the possibility of a settlement. After the King of Scots had heard the message, he said there was no point in trying to agree on a settlement unless he was granted a quarter of all the revenues from Caithness. When Earl Harald was told this, he called together the farmers and other leading men for their advice, and since they saw no alternative, the men of Caithness accepted these conditions, that they were to pay the King of Scots a quarter of all they possessed — except, that is, for those who had gone to see the King earlier that winter.

Then Earl Harald went back out to Orkney, it having been agreed that he should rule over all Caithness, as indeed he had earlier, before Harald the Young took it in fief from the King of Scots.

During the war Thorfinn, Earl Harald's son, who had been taken as hostage by the King of Scots, had been blinded. After coming to terms, the King went south again to Scotland and Earl Harald was sole ruler of Orkney.

Late in the reign of Earl Harald it happened that his brother-in-law Olaf and Jon Hallkelsson raised an army in Orkney to fight King Sverrir of Norway. Their own choice of king was Sigurd, son of King Magnus Erlingsson, and a number of well-born men from Orkney joined their force, which was very powerful. People called them 'the Islandmen' and then, for a time, 'the Golden-Legs'. They lost a pitched battle against King Sverrir at Florevag, where both Jon and Olaf were killed along with their King and most of their army.

King Sverrir grew to hate Earl Harald very bitterly, blaming him for the mustering of the army; and in the end, taking Bishop Bjarni along with him, Earl Harald had to go east to Norway, where he surrendered himself to King Sverrir and asked him to give judgment and settle everything between them. King Sverrir took back from Harald the whole of Shetland, with all its taxes and revenues, and since that time the Earls of Orkney have not ruled in Shetland.

Earl Harald was five years old when he was given the title of earl. For twenty years he was joint ruler of Orkney with Earl Rognvald the Holy. Following the death of Rognvald,

Harald was Earl of Orkney for forty-eight years and died in the second year of the reign of King Ingi Bardason. After that his sons Jon and David came to power and another son, Heinrek, ruled over Ross in Scotland.

According to people who have written on the subject, the most powerful Earls of Orkney were Sigurd Eysteinsson, Thorfinn Sigurdarson and Harald Maddadarson.

The brothers Jon and David ruled the earldom jointly after their father, till David died of a sickness in the same year as Hakon Madcap in Norway, and then Earl Jon became sole ruler in Orkney.

GENEALOGY OF THE EARLS OF ORKNEY

The table below sets out the family relationships of the Earls of Orkney, from the late ninth century to 1206. With the exception of five *italicised* names, all those listed here held the title 'Earl of Orkney'.

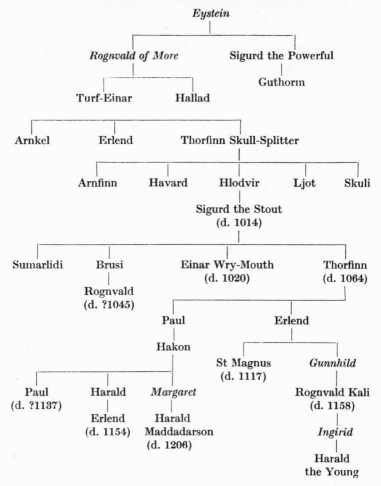

GLOSSARY OF PERSONAL NAMES

This Glossary is not a complete index of all the names in the saga: it is intended as a guide to the roles played by the major characters, to show the place of certain minor characters in relation to the events in the narrative and to place characters of historical significance in a context. Dates have been added in brackets for clarification. The numbers are those of the chapters in which the characters play a part or are mentioned.

GLOSSARY OF PLACE NAMES

The numbers refer to chapters, not pages. The Old Icelandic forms of names from the British Isles are given in square brackets.

219